TIME TRAVELS

TIME

NEXT WAVE: NEW DIRECTIONS IN WOMEN'S STUDIES

A series edited by Inderpal Grewal, Caren Kaplan,

and Robyn Wiegman

TRAVELS

Feminism, Nature, Power

ELIZABETH GROSZ

Duke University Press Durham and London 2005

©2005 Duke University Press

All rights reserved

Printed in the United States

of America on acid-free paper ∞

Designed by Amy Ruth Buchanan

Typeset in Minion by Tseng Information

Systems, Inc. Library of Congress

Cataloging-in-Publication Data and

republication acknowledgments appear

on the last printed pages of this book.

CONTENTS

ACKNOWLEDGMENTS

My thanks go to a number of institutions and individuals without whose support and prompting these essays would not have been written. The earliest of the essays were written when I worked in the Critical Theory and Cultural Studies Program at Monash University in Melbourne, Australia. The majority were written while I was employed in the Departments of Comparative Literature and English at the State University of New York at Buffalo. And the last essays, and the book as a whole, were completed when I moved to the Department of Women's and Gender Studies at Rutgers University. My great thanks to the faculty, staff, and students in these departments and universities for their patience and tolerance during the writings of these various papers. My special thanks to the organizers of various seminars and conferences for which I produced the majority of these essays. Without their invitations, and provocations, I doubt that I would have had the resources and the energy to write these for their own sake. Each was undertaken for a specific topic, purpose, or function. I hope that by modifying them and putting them together in a collection such as this, the individual inspirations for each are not lost.

I need to single out for special acknowledgment a number of individuals who read various manuscripts, provided moral support, critical comments, a shoulder to cry on, or a strong pep talk when I wanted to stop. While I can only provide a list of names here, such a list does not do justice to the depth of obligation I feel for their help. My thanks, then, to Judith Allen, Geoffrey Batchen, Sue Best, Pheng Cheah, Claire Colebrook, Drucilla Cornell, Joan Copjec, Mimi Long, Isabel Marcus, Sally Munt, Tony Nunziata, Kelly Oliver, Michael Pollak, John Rajchman, Jacqueline Reid, Jill Robbins, Gai Stern, Gail Weiss, and Carol Zemel. Your friendship and support have made an immense difference to me. My special thanks to the four anonymous readers of the manuscript for their various suggestions: the book as a whole is tighter and more cohesive because of their comments. I owe a debt that I can never repay to Nicole Fermon, whose wit and wisdom, grace and good will, buoyed and inspired me through the long period of production of this book. Without her encouragement, her suggestions and provocations, these essays would probably have remained unpublished and certainly unpolished. My gratitude to my family, to Eva Gross, Tom Gross, Irit Rosen, Tahli Fisher, Daniel and Mia Gross, as well as to Mary Gross, and Glenn, Daniel, and Luke Rosewell.

Time remains the central yet forgotten force that motivates and informs the universe, from its most cosmological principles to its most intimate living details. Cultural life in all its complications, no less than natural existence, is structured by and responds to a force that it does not control and yet marks and dates all its activities and processes. *Time Travels* brings together a series of disparate essays which focus on the implications and effects of conceiving a temporality in which the future remains virtual and beyond the control of the present. These essays are various conceptual "travels" in, explorations of, how reconsidering our concepts of time might result in new concepts of nature, culture, subjectivity, and politics: they are explorations of how far we can push the present to generate an unknown—what is new, what might not have been.[1]

Various, usually implicit, concepts of time are relevant to and underlie many of the central projects of feminist theory, theories of the law and justice, and the natural sciences and their relations to the social sciences and humanities. Questions about culture and representation, concepts of subjectivity, sexuality, and identity, as well as concepts of political struggle and transformation all make assumptions about the relevance of history, the place of the present, and the forward-moving impetus directing us to the future. But temporality is very rarely the direct object of analysis in these various discourses and projects. *Time Travels* develops a concept of a temporality not under the domination or privilege of the present, that is, a temporality directed to a future that is unattainable and unknowable in the present, and overwrites and redirects the present in an indeterminacy that also inhabits and transforms our understanding of the privilege of the present. Although they deal with a wide range of topics (from female sexuality to conceptions of power to how we understand cultural studies) and theorists (from Darwin and Nietzsche to Derrida, Irigaray, and Deleuze), they nevertheless remain focused primarily on the question of becomings: how becomings are possible, what forms they take in biological, cultural, political, and technological processes, what transformations they may effect and what implications they have for how we understand ourselves and our world.

Written over an eight-year period, these essays reflect on the question of time and its relentlessly forward movement into the future. While resisting the temptation to predict, to forecast, to extrapolate trends of the present into the future, they are all, in different ways, directed to how we can generate and welcome a future that we may not recognize, a future that may deform, inflect, or redirect our current hopes and aspirations. They welcome a concept of the future which we do not control but which may shape and form us according to its forces. These essays speculate on the becoming-art of politics; that is, they share a common interest in advocating a politics of surprise, a politics that cannot be mapped out in advance, a politics linked to invention, directed more at experimentation in ways of living than in policy and step-by-step directed change, a politics invested more in its processes than in its results.

While covering a wide variety of nineteenth- and twentieth-century thinkers, from Darwin and Nietzsche, through pragmatism and phenomenology, on to postmodern philosophy and politics, this book has attempted, wherever possible, to avoid the usual critical gestures. Rather than undertake the expected path of political and philosophical analysis, in which a thinker's position is subjected to rigorous criticism and its errors, contradictions, and points of weakness singled out or overcome, I am more concerned with seeking out positivities, crucial concepts, insights on what is of value in the texts and positions being investigated. There is not a single position or text addressed here that does not raise valuable, relevant, and perhaps even irreplaceable insights; the task is to find what relevance it might have for contexts that are yet to be developed, whose horizon is not yet elaborated. The critique of texts never actually transforms texts or even necessarily produces better, more elaborated and developed texts; nor does it commonly change the opinions of adherents to the positions and claims elaborated in these texts. Critique tends to generate defensive self-representations or gestures of counter-critique, which give the complacent reader a vague sense that one need not bother further with a position once it has been adequately criticized. It tends to function as a form of dismissal of texts, rather than as an analysis of the embeddedness of critique in that which it criticizes. I have instead tried to seize and develop what is of use in a text or position, even in acknowledging its potentially problematic claims or assumptions. No text or position is without problems, contradictions, weaknesses, points of uneasiness. I have tried to develop an affirmative method, a mode of assenting to rather than dissenting from those "primary" texts—whether of Darwin, Bergson, Merleau-Ponty, Derrida, Irigaray, or Deleuze or of feminist commentators writing on these primary figures; one can write most generously and with the most inspiration working on those texts one loves the most intensely, which have had the most direct impact on one. The rest, those one deems too problematic, can be left aside.

The various positions and texts addressed here share a respect for the force of time, its paradoxical capacity to continue endlessly and yet be capable of being squandered, wasted. To have a life of its own, time deviates, splits, divides itself—into a presence and into the perpetual fissuring of the present that its placement on the threshold of past and future entails. As Bergson recognized so astutely in *Matter and Memory*, to retain and protract itself, to stretch itself so that it can be conceived in terms of a continuity between past, present, and future, time is not divisible into three orders, but only into two. Time splits into two trajectories, one virtual, the other actual, one which makes the present pass, and the other which preserves it as past. One forms perception, the other memory; one opens onto anticipation and the unknowable future, the other onto reminiscence and the past. Time functions "simultaneously" as present and as the past of that present. The future, which has no existence in the present, is generated through the untimely reactivation of the virtuality of the past which has been unactualized in the present. Time *is* this very split, "the powerful, non-organic Life which grips the world."[2] In short, to reformulate the Bergson of *Creative Evolution*, it is we who are in time, rather than time that is in us; it is time which inhabits us, subsists or inheres within and beyond us as the milieu of the living and as the order and historicity of the universe itself. Time is the paradoxical, and perhaps unthinkable, form of interiority without itself being interior, the form of objects without being objective, the form of subjects without being subjective or psychical, the form of matter without being material. We can only approach it through its effects on objects, subjects, and matter, which tend to obscure or absorb its characteristics and its force as their own.

Time is an excess, for it can never use itself up, and yet it is the only resource we cannot protract, save up, share, or divide. It is not directly manipulable or controllable, it cannot be harnessed for profit or convenience,[3] yet it affects everything, transforms all objects, processes, events with its relentless passage. Whereas time is a continuous movement, our time, the time of the living, is finite, limited, linked to mortality, and thus irreplaceably precious. This double orientation of temporal movement—one force directed to the past, the other to the future—is a splitting of time, the generation of time's divided present, a present that is never fully present. Nature and culture, the psychical and the social, the material and the ideal, are, in part, consequences of the unique dividing and differentiating force of temporality, which is the dual force of preservation (time is preserved in and as the past) and of dissipation (the present dissipates its force in producing a future that differs from it). Culture, history, and subjectivity each exhibit this dual directionality they inherit from natural forces, from the forward push of temporality: this is culture's evolutionary inheritance from biological and chemical forces, which each different culture must harness, and deal with in its own way if it is to survive and expand.

While the essays gathered together here do not systematically explore the cultural inheritance of the force of (natural) time—this is the detailed object of investigation of a companion text, *The Nick of Time* (2004)—they do attempt to demonstrate what a focus on the reality of time might give to the ways we may reconceptualize identity, politics, culture, and sexual difference. They attempt to provide alternative methods, questions, and concepts to those that lie behind our unreflective concepts of subjectivity, identity, and the social, not so much replacing as complicating them.

If time, becomings, and the future are the primary objects of investigation in this text, there are also a number of other themes or recurring concepts that underlie and materialize and cohere in these writings on temporality, unevenly running through and threading together disparate chapters. Among these themes are:

1. The forgotten or repressed dependence of concepts of culture, desire, subjectivity, identity, and sexuality—concepts that have been the object of constructionist explanation in the humanities and social sciences—on concepts of nature, biology, and inhuman forces, which constructionism has tended to construe merely as raw materials at the very "beginning" (if there is one) of constructive processes which drop out of relevance as they are synthesized, symbolized, and transformed into cultural products. These "others," these inhuman, subhuman, and extrahuman forces—forces that structure culture, the law, representations, and all the other products of the

human—need to be understood in terms of a continuity with rather than in opposition to the human.

2. The covered-over debt that knowledges, epistemologies, methodologies—that is, various practices of knowledge-production—owe to that which conditions and incites knowledge: the real, the outside, materiality, things, forces, events, that which preexist knowledge-production, signification, or representation and constrains and limits, as well as provokes and engenders, the production of knowledges, including the natural sciences. The forgotten debt that epistemologies, images, and representations of various kinds owe to ontology, to the force of the real, to that which is larger than and beyond the control of the knowing subject, needs to be acknowledged if new kinds of knowledges and different kinds of relations to the real—beyond and within knowledges—are to be developed.

3. In restoring ontology to its rightful place at the center of knowledges and social practices, the ways in which ontology has been previously conceptualized—as static, fixed, composed of universal principles or ideals, indifferent to history, particularity, or change—require transformation and revitalization. "The real," "being," "materiality," "nature," those terms usually associated with the unchanging, must themselves be opened up to their immaterial or extramaterial virtualities or becomings, to the temporal forces of endless change, in other words, to history, biology, culture, sexuality. In this reconfigured form, ontology is no longer too broad, unchanging, or abstract to be relevant to political struggles of various kinds; instead, it is (in part, and most indirectly) what is fundamentally at stake in such struggles.

4. If temporality and the forward movement of time are crucial elements in such a reconstituted ontology, they are also relentlessly at work in all those social and political practices—feminist, antiracist, working-class, postcolonial, queer—that attempt to ameliorate existing conditions or compensate for past ones. This means that political projects, in acknowledging and welcoming an exploration of their own ontological commitments, open themselves up to a new direction or orientation, not inconsistent with various struggles for rights and equalities, but moving beyond them: an indeterminable direction, beyond planning and control in the present, that makes all plans at best provisional, open to revision, and always in the process of transformation. It opens up feminist and other political struggles to what is beyond current comprehension and control, to becoming unrecognizable, becoming other, becoming artistic.

5. Not only do forces of becoming contaminate and transform how we understand social and political struggles, they are also capable of infiltrat-

ing and transforming how we understand our own identities, agency, sexuality, and interpersonal relations. We have tended, in feminist and other political and social discourses, to understand this more intimate domain as the realm of agency, in which subjects exercise some element of freedom in their choices and decisions about how to live their lives. If we take seriously an understanding of the force of temporality and the abundance of ways in which the future exceeds our expectations, we must modify the ways we understand agency and its cognate terms. In what follows, I do not claim that agency and identity are impossible, but rather that subjectivity, sexuality, intimate social relations are in part structured not only by institutions and social networks but also by impersonal or pre-personal, subhuman, or inhuman forces, forces that may be construed as competing microagencies rather than as the conflict between singular, unified, self-knowing subjects or well-defined social groups. Subjects, groups, do not lack agency; on the contrary, they may, perhaps, have too much agency, too many agents and forces within them, to be construed as self-identical, free, untrammeled, capable of knowing or controlling themselves. This is not to claim that subjects are not free, or not agents, but that their agency is mitigated and complicated by those larger conditions that subjects do not control.

6. Sexuality, pleasure, desire need not be represented only through oppositional or binarized divisions between self and other, subject and object, heterosexual and homosexual—just as ontologies need not be understood only in terms of the divisions between matter and mind, nature and culture, the biological and the psychological, the natural and the historical. While this binary structure has long been recognized as a pervasive form of containment of the subordinated term through its negative or contradictory relation to the dominant term,[4] there are a number of strategies developed to problematize its conceptual dominance. Early feminist reversals of oppositional terms, where the dominant term is put into the subordinated position and the subordinated term in the position of dominance, were complicated and further elaborated through a more Derridean and Irigarayan understanding of the necessity, along with reversal, of revealing the dependence of the dominant term on its expulsion of the subordinate term, of showing the subordinated term as the heart or center of the dominant term. Derrida proposed a tripartite strategy for shaking up and provisionally unhinging the binary structure—reversal, displacement, and the creation of a new or third term which requires both terms—in order to provisionally enable the subordinated term an autonomy from its dominating other.[5] Derrida understood that the tenacity of the binary structure means that its terms,

even in reversed form, will tend toward oppositional or contradictory relations. A breach in this oppositional structure is only temporary, and can only sustain itself for a short time, until the oppositional forces restore it again to its oppositional structure. While Derrida's politicized understanding of this peculiar structural pairing of concepts has been immensely important in feminist and postcolonial political analyses of the binary structure, the essays that follow generally prefer to follow Deleuze's proliferation of binary terms rather than the Derridean project of reversal/displacement. My goal is to show, not that there are two terms—marked by difference—which are translated into a single (dominant) term and its negation, that is, through a structure of logical opposition or contradiction, but that the subordinate term constitutes the field, the domain, on which the dominant term differentiates itself. The subordinated term—whether it is understood as nature, the body, the real, the other, the object, intuition, indetermination, fluidity—is not a self-contained entity or unit, a concept or term, but the very terrain out of which the dominant term—culture, mind, representation, self, subject, intelligence, the determinable, the solid—emerges as a term or concept, and on which it depends. The subordinated "term" constitutes, instead of an entity or a definable term, the stratum from which the dominant term derives and which the dominant term attempts to define and contain, but which is also larger than and prior to this domination. The essays gathered here each attempt to restore to this field its place as source or ground of nourishment for these privileged terms, revealing the relations of debt and dependence that conceptually dominant terms have had to deny and cover over in their operations.

I have divided these essays into four sections, in order to draw out themes and orientations that may serve to link them to each other. Needless to say, this division is arbitrary, providing a kind of artificial rather than natural unity to the essays gathered together in each section, each of which was written for a specific occasion and a specific audience. They could have been arranged in other ways, although I have tried to select and position each essay so that similarities, common themes or arguments, are made as explicit as possible. In part I, "Nature, Culture, and the Future," I bring together three essays utilizing and developing a notion of nature no longer regarded as the polarized opposite of culture but seen as its underlying condition. Nature is understood in terms of dynamic forces, fields of transformation and upheaval, rather than as a static fixity, passive, worked over, transformed and dynamized only by culture, a view prevalent in social, political, and cultural theory. If nature, biology, and the material world are imbued with activity, with their own forces and unpredictabilities, then our concepts of the subject, culture, and the social order need to open themselves up to, rather than see themselves in opposition to, the natural order. Chapter 1, "Darwin and Feminism: Preliminary Investigations into a Possible Alliance," explores the potential relevance of Darwin's understanding of biological and cultural evolution for feminist, antiracist, and cultural theory. These discourses, and most radical political theory, have attempted to definitively separate themselves from speculations about nature, the given, that which is outside the cultural. The opening essays attempt to dispel some of the resistances to biological considerations that have dominated feminist and critical theory for three decades or more. Chapter 2, "Darwin and the Ontology of Life," furthers some of the claims developed in chapter 1 by arguing that Darwin has bequeathed the humanities and social sciences, as well as the natural sciences, a new conception of life, defined not in terms of any given characteristics, any essence or being, but in terms of an openness to history, contingency, and events. Life is a mode of self-organization that overcomes itself, diverges from itself, evolves into something different over time. The force of time is not just a contingent characteristic of the living, but is the dynamic impetus that enables life to become, to always be in the process of becoming, something other than it was. Darwinian accounts of life have transformed how we might understand not only politics, including those embodied in feminist and antiracist struggles, but also the ontologies of change that underlie them. Chapter 3, "The Nature of Culture," explores the implications of reconsidering nature as dynamic and active rather than as passive and inert for the ways in which we conceive and study the cultural order. Our understanding of the preeminent or defining characteristics of culture — whether language, representation, technology, legal and moral systems, and so on — may be enriched rather than diminished if we understand culture as a continuation and elaboration of nature rather than its overcoming, and the human as ramification, a difference of degree from the animal, rather than in opposition to it.

Part II, "Law, Justice, and the Future," brings together two essays on the ways in which legal practice indefinitely puts off or defers justice for the future to come. The legal system itself exhibits the splitting of temporality that characterizes all life: while law functions to judge and regulate behavior in the past, justice is always indefinitely postponed, deferred into an indeterminable future. Law is what we currently use to anticipate or welcome a justice to come. Chapter 4, "The Time of Violence: Derrida, Deconstruction, and Value," explores Jacques Derrida's conception of the force of law and the structures of violence that are at play in the functioning of the law. Chapter 5, "Drucilla Cornell, Identity, and the 'Evolution' of Politics," looks at the work of the feminist philosopher and legal theorist Drucilla Cornell and her understanding of the ways in which justice is an orientation directed primarily, or only, to an indeterminable future. Taken together, these two essays may serve as a brief exploration of the relevance of deconstruction for understanding the interlinkages between questions of force or violence, including the violence of social oppression, and the relentless and uncaptured movement of time always directed to an indefinitely deferred future.

If part II can be understood as an exploration of deconstructive conceptions of time and the future, part III, "Philosophy, Knowledge, and the Future," brings together four essays on Bergson's philosophy of duration, filtered through the writings of Gilles Deleuze, Maurice Merleau-Ponty, and William James. Chapter 6, "Deleuze, Bergson, and the Virtual," is a detailed analysis of Bergson's understanding of duration and its links to the question of virtuality. The virtual, in Bergson's sense, may prove to be a crucial concept in refining and elaborating our notions of change, including political and social change. Chapter 7, "Merleau-Ponty, Bergson, and the Question of Ontology," is an examination of the complex and ambivalent relations between Merleau-Ponty and his predecessor Bergson regarding the entwinement of subject with object, of consciousness with matter, of nature with culture, in what Merleau-Ponty understands as the "flesh of the world." Chapter 8, "The Thing," explores Bergson's and James's understanding of technology and the links it provides and the complications it induces in how we understand the relations between mind and matter, nature and culture, intelligence and intuition. Chapter 9, "Prosthetic Objects," examines the capacity of natural and cultural organisms to adapt extrinsic objects, things, into their bodily operations through prosthetic incorporation, an accommodation that actively transforms those bodies, bringing into the natural what is its cultural augmentation, and bequeathing to the cultural a capacity to transform natural processes and characteristics. Prostheses indicate the porous relations between the inside and the outside of the living subject, between an open-ended biology that has remarkable capacities to incorporate into its organic functions all kinds of artificial or cultural inventions and the things in the world which function otherwise through the living subject's intervention.

The fourth and final section, "Identity, Sexual Difference, and the Future," brings together four short essays on feminist theory and theories of becoming, derived from the works of Nietzsche, Foucault, Deleuze, and Irigaray. Chapter 10, "The Time of Thought," develops the claim that sexual difference, the indeterminable differences constituting the morphologies, sexualities, and positions of male and female subjects, is an irreducible difference that needs to have its impact on the future of conceptualization, to have its place in philosophy, in theory, in abstraction. Chapter 11, "The Force of Sexual Difference," is an exploration of how the concept of impersonal forces may replace the emphasis on identity so prevalent in most feminist, queer, and antiracist discourses. Chapter 12, "(Inhuman) Forces: Power, Pleasure, and Desire," examines the ways in which Foucault and Deleuze deal with the concepts of desire and pleasure, and how their work may be of relevance in feminist and queer reconceptualizations of sexuality. And chapter 13, "The Future of Female Sexuality," undertakes a detailed discussion of the work of Alfred Kinsey on female sexuality, in order to examine the ways it has both served and retarded feminist analyses by restricting female sexuality to what can be known, measured, and counted, by reducing female sexuality to what it has been rather than what it can become.

These essays may be understood as experiments in practical philosophy, philosophy harnessed to explore various social, cultural, and epistemological practices, including those that constitute feminism, from the point of view of their dynamic direction forward. Although they are readings, interpretations of, and extrapolations from, the work of some of the most abstract and difficult philosophical theorists of the twentieth century, my goal has been to use these theorists and their intriguing concepts of power, force, and difference to develop a more adequate and nuanced understanding of temporality, and above all, to explore how such a revitalized notion of temporality may help open up new fields of feminist and political conceptual and practical exploration.

CHAPTER 1

Darwin and Feminism: Preliminary

Investigations into a Possible Alliance

[Darwin has] not succeeded in explaining living beings, but in constituting them as witnesses to a history, in understanding them as recounting a history whose interest lies in the fact that one does not know a priori what history it is a question of.
— Isabelle Stengers, *Power and Invention: Situating Science*

There has traditionally been a strong resistance on the part of feminists to any recourse to the question of nature. Within feminist scholarship and politics, nature has been regarded primarily as a kind of obstacle against which we need to struggle, as that which remains inert, given, unchanging, resistant to historical, social, and cultural transformations.[1] The suspicion with which biological accounts of human and social life are treated by feminists, especially feminists not trained in the biological sciences, is to some extent understandable. "Biology" designates not only the *study* of life but also refers to the body, to organic processes or activities that are the *objects* of that study. Feminists may have had good reasons to object to the ways in which the *study*, the representations and techniques used to understand bodies and their processes and activities, have been undertaken — there is clearly much that is problematic about many of the assumptions, methods, and criteria used in some cases of biological analysis, which have been actively if unconsciously used by those with various paternalistic, patriarchal, racist, and class commitments to rationalize their various positions. But there is a certain absurdity in objecting to the notion of nature or biology itself if this is (even in part) what we are and will always be. If we *are* our biologies, then we need a complex and subtle account of that biology if it is to be able to more adequately explain the rich variability of social, cultural, and political life. It needs to be an open question: how does biology, the bodily existence of individuals (whether human or nonhuman), provide the conditions for culture and for history, those terms to which it is traditionally opposed? What are the virtualities, the potentialities, within biological existence that enable cultural, social, and historical forces to work with and actively transform that existence? How does biology—the structure and organization of living systems—facilitate and make possible cultural existence and social change?

FEMINISM AND BIOLOGY

It seems remarkable that feminists have been so reluctant to explore the theoretical structure and details of one of the most influential and profound intellectual figures of the modern era, Charles Darwin. For the last three decades or more, there has been an increasingly wider circle of male texts that have enthralled and preoccupied the work of many feminist theorists: Spinoza, Hegel, Nietzsche, Heidegger, Althusser, Lacan, Foucault, Derrida, and Deleuze are just some of the more recent and philosophically oriented additions to this ever-expanding pantheon. This makes the virtual ignorance and neglect of Darwin's work even more stark and noticeable. It is not clear why Darwin—whose enduring impact on knowledge and politics is at least as strong as that of Hegel, Marx, or Freud—has been left out of feminist readings. It is perhaps time that feminist theorists begin to address with some rigor and depth the usefulness and value of his work in rendering our conceptions of social, cultural, political, and sexual life more complex, more open to questions of materiality and biological organization, more nuanced in terms of understanding both the internal and external constraints on behavior as well as the impetus to new and creative activities.

Some feminist theorists have made tentative approaches to a theoretical analysis of Darwin's scientific contributions. The most open has been Janet Sayers, in *Biological Politics: Feminist and Anti-Feminist Perspectives* (1982). She carefully distinguishes Darwin's theory from the more pointedly politicized and self-serving readings of the social Darwinists of Darwin's own times, and their current counterparts, sociobiologists. Darwin's theory of evolution, she suggests, implies "that the species characters are not fixed but change as the effect of chance variation and of selection of those variations that prove relatively well adapted to prevailing environmental conditions" (55). She sees it as a model which signals an open-ended becoming, a mode of potentially infinite transformation, which may prove helpful in feminist struggles to transform existing social relations and their concomitant value systems. Sadly, while she notes the relative openness of Darwin's understanding of evolution, she leaves its social and political implications largely unanalyzed. There is, however, perhaps only in the last few years, an increasing unease with the rejection of biology in some more postmodern feminist concerns and the beginning of a more serious intellectual engagement with biological and scientific discourses.[2]

Other feminists, especially those working within evolutionary biology, have actively welcomed a Darwinian mode of explanation, but have commonly reduced Darwinism to a form of determinism, to a partial explanation, to be placed alongside of, or in parallel with, social and cultural accounts. This seems to be the most pervasive feminist position for those working *within* evolutionary Darwinism. Patricia Adair Gowaty, the editor of the only anthology specifically directed to exploring the relations between Darwinism and feminism, may serve here as representative of this trend. She claims that Darwinism is a discourse parallel with feminist social and political analyses. It functions in a different but contiguous conceptual space, outside the political interests of feminists. In attributing to it a *neutral*, non-infecting position vis-à-vis political, psychological, and cultural theory, she has effectively secured Darwinism against its own most radical insights (a fundamental *indetermination* seems one of the most exciting elements of Darwin's contributions to both science and politics), and has insulated feminism against any theoretical impact on, and protects feminism from being transformed by, Darwinism:

> There are multiple foci of analysis in the modern biological study of behavior (including social behavior and social organization of both human and nonhuman animals). We ask questions about neuronal causation (How do sensory signals contribute to "cause" behavior?), about hormonal causation (How do hormonal signals "cause" behavior?). How do cognitive processes "cause" behavior? How do genes cause behavior? How do emotions or feelings cause behavior? None of these levels of foci of analysis are alternative to one another, meaning that each of these levels of causation or foci of analysis might (probably) simultaneously work to "cause" the expression of this or that behavior (including sexist behavior of all kinds). (Gowaty 1997, 5)

Clearly uneasy at the notion of causation in these accounts (this explains her use of quotation marks where the word *cause* is used), Gowaty reduces both Darwinism and feminism to positions on two sides of a mutual divide. They occupy different levels or "foci"; each provides a "proximate explanation" of its own fields of endeavor, which do not come into direct contact with each other. The social is uninfected by the biological, the biological is secured from intrusion by the social. They are assumed to act simultaneously without, however, any adequate explanation of how they affect and transform each other, how they integrate together or influence each other. Gowaty's use of Darwin implies both a reduced view of feminism (feminism as the struggle for social parity) and a reduced view of science (science as the search for causal relations), as well as a commitment to the impossibility of their interaction, indeed a revelry in their neutral indifference to each other.

Sue V. Rosser outlines the way many other feminists have regarded Darwin's apparent androcentrism. She seems to endorse the common assumption that because Darwin's work is "biased," it requires a corrective lens which focuses on the active position of females rather than naturally assuming the perspective of the male as active evolutionary or sexual agent. Her position functions as an inverted Darwinism: if Darwin's theory could somehow be made more open to the position of females, it could more adequately deal with both sexes and its "bias" could be redressed. She affirms a kind of Darwinist liberal reformism:

> Many feminist scientists have critiqued Darwin's theory of sexual selection for its androcentric bias. The theory of sexual selection reflected and reinforced Victorian social norms regarding the sexes. . . . Expanding considerably on the theory first presented in the *Origin*, Darwin specified, in the *Descent of Man*, how the process functions and what roles males and females have in it. . . . According to the theory, the males who triumph over their rivals will win the more desirable females and will have the most progeny, thereby perpetuating and increasing, over numerous generations, those qualities that afforded them victory. (Rosser 1992, 57)

In short, Darwin's is a theory of "winners and losers," of those who dominate and those who have succumbed to domination or extinction, a theory that, on the face of it, seems to provide a perfect justification for the relations of phallocentric and racist domination that constituted Eurocentric, patriarchal culture in his time as much as in ours. Darwinism, it is implicitly claimed in accounts such as Rosser's, justifies—rather than providing the tools by which to problematize—relations of domination and subordination between races and sexes, as well as the domination of the human over the natural.

These claims are strikingly similar to those that surrounded Freudian psychoanalysis in the estimation of feminists openly hostile to its possible theoretical contributions three decades ago—what Freud (Darwin) says about women is phallocentric, rooted in the assumption of a natural subordination of women to men: it is sexist and biased. Each privileges the masculine and positions the feminine as its subordinated and complementary counterpart. While this is undoubtedly true, more or less, of any discourse written before the development of feminism as a theoretical and political movement, it evades the more interesting question: Without necessarily minimizing these investments in male and white privilege, do these discourses provide theoretical models, methods, questions, frameworks, or insights that nevertheless, in spite of their recognizable limitations, could be of some use in understanding and transforming the prevailing structures of (patriarchal) power and in refining and complexifying feminist analyses of and responses to these structures? Psychoanalytically oriented feminists have demonstrated, even while recognizing many of the limits of Freud's work, that it provides an account of the unconscious and of the acquisition of sexual identity that has proved crucial, if not indispensable, to the ways feminist theorists have come to understand subjectivity and desire. It seems timely to suggest that Darwin may himself prove to be as complex, ambivalent, and rewarding a figure for feminists to investigate as Freud has been. His writings may provide feminism with richer and more workable concepts of nature, the body, time, and transformation than those available to it from the discourses of cultural and political theory, history, and philosophy alone. Darwin's work may prove as rich, if not even more productive, for feminist thought as Freud's has been, in spite of its nineteenth-century conceptions of the relations between the sexes because, like Freud, Darwin opened up a new way of thinking, a new mode of interpretation, new connections and forms of explanation, indeed a new discipline, which may prove useful in highlighting and explaining the divisions and connections between nature and culture.

I will argue that Darwin's work offers a subtle and complex critique of both essentialism and teleology. It provides a dynamic and open-ended understanding of the intermingling of history and biology (indeed it is Darwin's work that most actively affirms the irreversibility of time within the natural sciences, the centrality of chance, and the accumulation of temporally sensitive characteristics) and a complex account of the movements of difference, bifurcation, and becoming that characterize all forms of life. His work develops an antihumanist—that is, a broadly mechanical or fundamentally mindless and directionless — understanding of biological dynamics which refuses to assume that the temporal movement forward can be equated with development or progress. His work affords us an understanding of the productivity, the generative surprise, that the play of repetition and pure difference — the ongoing movement of biological differences and their heritable reproduction through slight variation, which he affirms as "individual variation" — effects the becoming of species. He is perhaps the most original thinker of the link between difference and becoming, between matter and its elaboration as life, between the past and the future. Moreover, his work pays specific attention to the question of sexual difference, to which he grants prominence as a quasi-autonomous feedback loop within the larger and more overarching operations of natural selection. The status and function of sexual selection, and the intense variability, or difference, he sees both within each sex and between the two sexes, as well as within and between species and genera, occupies a central, if ambiguous, position in his work that is worthy of serious feminist investigation.

These seem to provide at least prima facie reasons why it may prove fruitful for feminists to cast their critical gaze at Darwin, not simply with the a priori aim of dismissing his work, as has been the case in many feminist responses to any kind of biological analysis, or of simply accepting it and developing scientific research projects and paradigms that function to illustrate or refine its principles, as seems to have occurred with the largely revisionist ambitions of many feminist approaches within evolutionary biology. Rather, we need to look again at his texts with the desire to see what may be of value for providing feminist theory with richer and more subtle intellectual resources to both attain its aims and to refine its goals.

DARWINIAN EVOLUTION

Although the most essential elements of Darwin's understanding of evolution are relatively straightforward and generally well known, there is a great deal of contention regarding the ways in which scientists and nonscientists have interpreted its most basic precepts. *The Origin of Species* (1996) has two aims: first, to demonstrate that contemporary species and forms of life are descended from earlier forms — if there is an "origin" of species, it is in earlier species, and their transformations; and second, to demonstrate how such an evolution, a "descent with modification," is possible, and what processes and mechanisms enable both modification and descent to produce viable new species from the mutability and transformability of existing

species. In this sense, Darwin offers an account of the *genesis of the new* from
the play of repetition and difference within the old, the generation of history,
movement, and the dynamism of evolutionary change from the impetus and
mobility of existing species.

Darwin claims that three basic and closely linked principles explain the
contrary forces at play in the evolution of species: individual variation, the
heritability of the characteristics of individual variation that lead to the proliferation of species, and natural selection. The evolution of life is possible
only through the irreversible temporality of genealogy, which requires an
abundance of variation, mechanisms of indefinite, serial, or recursive rep-
lication/reproduction, and criteria for the selection of differential fitness.
When put into dynamic interaction, these three processes provide an explanation of the dynamism, growth, and transformability of living systems,
the impulse toward a future that is unknown in, and uncontained by, the
present and its history. I will briefly outline each of these three principles.[3]

First, there is the postulate of a vast but often minute and possibly insignificant series of individual variations which may eventually lead to the
formation of different species, that is, the postulate of diversity, which Darwin calls individual variation. This is the proliferation of individuating characteristics, differences, and features that may prove more or less significant
in the successful adaptation of individuals or species to their environments.
While a large number, the majority, of variations are either irrelevant to or
positively harmful for the ongoing existence of species, there are random
variations which are or will prove to be a positive improvement relative to
the environment, whether it is fixed or changing: "No one supposes that all
the individuals of the same species are cast in the very same mould. These
individual differences are highly important for us as they afford materials for
natural selection to accumulate, in the same manner as man can accumulate
in any given direction individual differences in his domesticated production" (Darwin 1996, 39).

Second, there is an invariable tendency to superabundance, excessiveness, the generation of large numbers of individuals, in the rates of reproduction and proliferation of individuals and species. Even if they merely
reproduce their own numbers, they will eventually encounter scarcity and
thus a hostile environment. This superabundance can be understood, nega-
tively, as the struggle for existence, in which this excess drives species and
individuals to compete with each other for increasingly limited resources,
eventually eliminating the weaker and less successful in order to allow the
proliferation of the stronger and the more successful. In more positive terms,

it can be understood as the intensification of difference or variation: "There is no exception to the rule that every organic being naturally increases at so high a rate that if not destroyed, the earth would soon be covered by the progeny of a single pair" (Darwin 1996, 54).

This teaming proliferation of individuals and species suggests that the greater the proliferation of diversity, the more natural selection is able to take effect. If species reproduced themselves in ever-diminishing numbers, natural selection would be unable to weed out the less fit and provide space for the selection and profusion of the more fit.[4] The proliferation of numbers and the production of greater and greater variability does not occur untrammeled: it is restrained by a number of factors. While variation and proliferation are the very motors of the production of evolutionary change, there are nevertheless a series of limits on the type and degree of variability that any particular region or location can sustain.[5] The range and scope of diversity and variability cannot be determined in advance, but it is significant that there are inherent, if unknown, limits to tolerable, that is to say, sustainable variation: "monstrosities," teratological variations, may be regularly produced, but only those that remain both viable and reproductively successful, and only those that attain some evolutionary advantage, either directly or indirectly, help induce this proliferation.

Taken together, the two principles of individual variation and the heritability of this variation imply that if there is a struggle for existence in circumstances where resources may be harsh or scarce, then any variation, however small and apparently insignificant, may provide an individual with advantages which may differentiate and privilege it relative to other individuals. Even minute variations may provide major advantages for individuals, especially in unexpected and changing circumstances or environments. Moreover, if individual variations are inherited, whatever small advantages were bestowed on an individual may be amplified over time. It is in this capacity for individual variation that Darwin locates the origin of species and genera. Once individual variations are selected and become a force in heritable characteristics, and if there is some separation, geographical or ecological, between such individually differentiated groups, the conditions under which a new species, or several, emerge from common ancestors becomes clear: "New species are formed by new varieties arising, which have some advantage over older forms; and those forms, which are already dominant, or have some advantage over the other forms in their own country, would naturally oftenest give rise to new varieties or incipient species; for these latter must be victorious in a still higher degree in order to be preserved and to survive" (Darwin 1996, 263).

Third, and as a counterbalancing yet interrelated force to these ongoing interactions between individual variation, the struggle for existence, and the inheritance of variation is the postulate of natural selection. Natural selection functions either by inducing proliferation or by providing a hostile, or conducive, environment to select from the variety of life forms those which survive and provide reproductive continuity with succeeding generations. As its name suggests, natural selection is the process, or rather the processes (for it includes both artificial and sexual selection, discussed below) which provide selective criteria which serve to give significance and value to individual variations: "If . . . variations useful to any organic being do occur, assuredly individuals thus characterized will have the best chance of being preserved in the struggle for life; and from the strong principle of inheritance they will tend to produce offspring similarly characterized. This principle of preservation, I have called, for the sake of brevity, Natural Selection; and it leads to the improvement of each creature in relation to its organic and inorganic conditions" (Darwin 1996, 104–105).

Darwin describes natural selection as the "principle of preservation," but this preservation is quite ambiguous and multilayered. It preserves only those variations that can viably function within its parameters or conditions, and that show some marked or significant advantage over their competitors. The principle of preservation is the preservation of the fittest, of the most appropriate existences in given *and* changing circumstances, not the victorious species — the "winners" of evolutionary struggle at any particular moment — but those most open and amenable to change. Through its selective capacities, natural selection provides both a negative mechanism, which functions to eliminate much of the proliferation generated by the hyperabundance of individual variation, indirectly sorting or sifting through the variations between individuals and species, and also a more positive productivity, when it functions as the source of a pressure on those individuals and species that survive to even greater proliferation and divergence:[6] "[Natural Selection] entails extinction; and how largely extinction has acted in the world's history, geology plainly declares. Natural selection, also, leads to divergence of character: for more living beings can be supported on the same area the more they diverge in structure, habits, and constitution, of which we see proof by looking to the inhabitants of any small spot or to naturalised production" (Darwin 1996, 105).

Natural selection is rendered more intricate and complicated through the input of its two particular variations and complexifications, artificial selection and sexual selection. Artificial selection, the selective breeding of life forms through the human introduction of selection criteria, provides for Darwin a model for understanding the more general, overarching, but less visible relations of natural selection. Rather than being construed as polar opposites, as cultural and natural binaries, natural and artificial selection are regarded as two versions of the same thing, the artificial functioning according to the same principles as natural selection, but varying the criteria for selection according to the aesthetic, material, or experimental investments of human breeders. The artificial illustrates the natural because it is subjected to its forces and principles though it simplifies it and renders explicit the selective criteria utilized.

Sexual selection functions, not in opposition to or as a separate stream from natural selection, but as one of its offshoots, as one of its more specific techniques for ensuring the detailed elaboration and functioning of the criteria of survival and reproductive success. It is significant that the bulk of feminist literature on Darwinism is devoted to a discussion, usually a critique, of Darwin's account of sexual selection, with relatively little attention paid to natural selection.[7] Yet sexual selection is clearly both a sub-branch of natural selection (those beings that reproduce sexually have an evolutionary advantage over their hermaphroditic counterparts in most but not all situations by virtue of the maximum variation generated by sexual reproduction), and an additional inflection, an intricate feedback loop, further adding complexity to natural selection processes, adding other criteria (primarily, attractiveness to the opposite sex) to its operations. Sexual selection adds more aesthetic — and immediately or directly individually motivating — factors to the functioning of natural selection, and deviates natural selection through the expression of the will, or desire, or pleasure, of individuals. Sexual selection, while conforming in the long run to the principles of natural selection, nonetheless may exert a contrary force to the pure principle of successful survival, for reproductive success cannot be rendered equivalent to mere survival, though it requires it to operate.

Darwin notes that even those features of animal appearance and adornment that may in some way render the being less able to survive, more noticeable to predators, less able to protect or disguise itself than its dowdier yet fitter counterparts nevertheless have survival value. In the case of the spectacular plumage of the peacock relative to the plainness of the peahen,

Darwin's explanation is that even if its plumage and adornment make the peacock more vulnerable to attack, the more magnificent its coloring, the more bright, striking, and numerous its tail-feathers, the more attractive it is to the peahen and the more likely it is to leave numerous progeny which may inherit its sexual successes. While it is or may be disadvantaged in the stakes of natural survival, it is positively advantaged in the stakes of sexual selection.[8]

SEXUAL SELECTION AND RACIAL DIFFERENCES

It is significant that Darwin wants to link the question of sexual selection to the descent of the different races of man. Sexual selection — taste, individual choice — may have dictated that what were once slight individual variations, not yet classifiable as racial variation — variations in color, features, proclivities — would, if linked to sexual selection and repeated for a number of generations, provide criteria by which males and females choose each other as sexual and reproductive partners. Racial differences cannot be attributed directly or solely to the selective pressures imposed by environments, Darwin argues, but may be the result of a preference for particular characteristics evolved through sexual selection: "If . . . we look to the races of man, as distributed over the world, we must infer that their characteristic differences cannot be accounted for by the direct action of different conditions of life, even after exposure to them for an enormous period of time" (Darwin 1981, 1:246).

Rather than claim racial differences are the simple result of the selective capacities of extremes or particularities of environment, Darwin suggests that it may be precisely the sexual appeal or attractiveness of individual racial variations, however slight they may have been to begin with, that explains the historical variability and the genealogical emergence of racial differences. Racial differences may have been those differences that have been actively selected by individuals, and perhaps amplified through geographical dispersion and the subsequent geographical and/or cultural isolation from our racially less differentiated primordial ancestors.[9] "We have thus far been baffled in all our attempts to account for the differences between the races of man; but there remains one important agency, namely Sexual Selection, which appears to have acted as powerfully on man, as on any other animal. I do not intend to assert that sexual selection will account for all the differences between races. An unexplained residuum is left. . . . It can be shewn that the differences between the races of man, as in colour, hairyness, form of features etc. are of the nature which it might have been expected would have been acted on by sexual selection" (Darwin 1981, 1:249–250).

Sexual selection inflects, and may be productive of, racial differences in the more stark and clear-cut forms racial difference takes today, even if it is not the only contributing factor. What were once small, possibly biologically insignificant but sexually significant characteristics exert a force in the functioning of sexual attraction, and it is this sexual appeal that gives these otherwise insignificant characteristics a key role to play in inheritance and long-term survival. Darwin makes explicit that skin color and racially signifying characteristics exert a *beauty*, an aesthetic force, which has had a major impact on phenotype and long-term survival. Sexual selection exerts a powerful force on the operations of natural selection; while it may sometimes work in congruence with natural selection, where the "fittest" individuals coincide with the most sexually attractive.individuals, at other times it deviates natural selection through the detour of individual sexual preference and individual taste or discernment, even at the peril of individuals: "The best kind of evidence that the colour of skin has been modified through sexual selection is wanting in the case of mankind; for the sexes do not differ in this respect, or only slightly and doubtfully. On the other hand, we know from many facts already given that the colour of the skin is regarded by the men of all races as a highly important element in their beauty; so that it is a character which would likely be modified through selection, as has occurred in innumerable instances with the lower animals" (1996, 381).

Natural selection is the active, selective, and ever-transforming milieu of evolutionary change. It consists in what we understand as the biological context of any living being, which is comprised largely, but not entirely, of the other living beings in their various interactions with each other. It also consists in the geographical, climatological, and highly specific material context for each existent, which may be as geographically wide-ranging as continents for some species, or as small as a nest or tree for others. These conditions enable natural selection to provide ever-changing criteria by which both fitness or survival and sexual or reproductive success are measured.[10] Natural selection is not simply the passive background or context in which individual variation unfolds, a mere landscape that highlights and positions the living being; rather it is a dynamic force which sets goals, provides resources, and presents incentives for the ever-inventive functioning of species in their self-proliferation.

Between them, these three principles on the one hand provide an explanation of a series of processes and interactions that are fundamentally mindless and automatic, without plan, direction, or purpose and on the other hand are entirely unpredictable and inexplicable in causal terms. Daniel Dennett has described this as Darwin's "dangerous idea": that the "excellence of design," the apparently perfect adaptation of species to the specificities of their environment and for long-term survival, is the result of both serendipity or chance of individual variation, which produces variation or difference for its own sake, randomly, and the fundamentally blind and mindless system of selection that inadvertently yet relentlessly weeds out and diminishes the effects and operations of the less adapted, thus providing an evolutionary advantage to the more and better adapted.[11] As long as the timescale of evolutionary unfolding is long enough, the mindless automatism of natural selection and the spontaneous production and inheritance of variation have time to ensure that experiments in living, as they might be called, living in a variety of environments under a variety of conditions, produce maximal results from given and changing resources. These results then feed into the operations of natural selection to actively transform them, which in turn transforms the stakes involved in selection and which therefore work themselves out on new individuals and evolving species.

Darwin has outlined an ingenious temporal machine for the production of the new, which constrains the new only through the history that made it possible and the present which it actively transforms, but which leaves its directions, parameters, and destinations unknown and unknowable, discernible only in retrospect or artificially through analysis and reconstruction. Where variation tends to occur through small, slow accretion, that is, where variation and inheritance tend to function slowly, over a large timescale requiring many successive generations, natural selection, which generally functions with a certain regularity and predictability, may, at times, function through catastrophic leaps, major climatological, geological, or population changes, sudden and unpredictable upheavals. Its temporality is more, but not only, short-term, intensified, linked to the impact of events. It is in part the clash between the generally (but not universally) slow relentlessness of genetic variability and change and the cataclysmic or irregular time of natural selection (that is, between two durational forms, two different rhythms of becoming) that the new—both new species and new environments—is generated.

If Darwin locates chance at the center of natural selection, as that which indicates an organism's openness, its potentially mortal susceptibility to changing environments, environments hitherto unseen or not yet in existence ("fitness" designating not superiority in a given milieu or environment but rather the adaptability of the organism, in its given state, to changing environments — a notion of fitness more in keeping with Darwin's own writings than sociobiological readings of evolutionary theory, which assume a pregiven notion of fitness, will allow), then from this time on, the random, the accidental, that which befalls an individual entity, becomes an essential ingredient in the history and development of that entity and in the group in which it lives and interacts. Chance erupts at both the level of random variation and at the level of natural selection, and perhaps more interestingly, in the gap or lag that commonly exists in their interaction. At the level of individual variation, chance emerges in the processes, unknown to Darwin and still unknown today, of genetic reproduction and recombination, which produce multiplicitous, usually minute and insignificant variations in organisms. What dictates these variations is both unknown and in some sense irrelevant, at least as far as natural selection is concerned, for it works only on the viable and inherited results of such randomness. At the level of natural selection, Darwin suggests that changes in the environment and in the various pressures facing organisms within that environment are also unpredictable. But more significant than the randomness of either individual variation or the randomness of natural (or artificial) selection is the randomness of individual variation *relative to* natural selection. Furthermore, the randomness of individual variation, while in no sense causally connected to the randomness of natural selection, may actively transform the criteria by which natural selection functions.[12] In other words, evolution is a fundamentally open-ended system which pushes toward a future with no real direction, no promise of any particular result, no guarantee of progress or improvement, but with every indication of inherent proliferation and transformation.

NATURAL AND CULTURAL EVOLUTION

It is not clear that Darwin wanted to differentiate natural and cultural systems in his understanding of the differential selection of surviving variation. Evolution functions through reproduction, variation, and natural selection: as such, it should also, in principle, be able to explain the function of cultural phenomena such as languages, technologies, and social practices as readily as it can natural systems or biological species.

Darwin was fascinated by the evolutionary resemblances between species and languages. The "origin" and history of languages functions according to the same logic as biological species: proliferation, competition, natural selection, and the temporal dispersion of development are as much at the origin and history of languages as they are of species. In a sense, the matter through which such a logic operates, whether it is the matter of biology or of spoken and written languages, is of less significance than the principles of organization or emergence that govern it. And these principles are fundamentally bound up with the effectivity or use of that matter, and the weeding-out effects that this effectivity generates in its confrontation with an environment. It is thus not entirely surprising, though it seems to have evaded the reflections of some scientists working in the area, that Darwin has posited the same processes of production in natural as well as in avowedly cultural activities. His refusal to restrict the forces of evolution to biological or natural categories and activities, while deeply resented and questioned by some feminists, may prove to be part of the strength of his understanding, and its value for feminist and cultural theory. The force of his argument resides in the fact, as Dennett makes clear, that evolution, if it functions as an explanatory model at all, functions all the way up, from the lowliest species to the most elevated of cultural and intellectual activities.[13] The systematic cohesion of modes of reproduction (forms of repetition) with their resulting mutations which are imperfect or innovative copies (forms of difference) and modes of "natural" selection (systems of differentiation) produces a system, or rather, an asystematic systematicity, that is coextensive with all of life, life in its political, cultural, and even artificial as well as its natural forms.

What can feminists learn from Darwin? Of what use can Darwin's work be for feminist intellectual and political struggles? If Darwin's work provides a fundamental, indeed, canonical model for the biological sciences, is Darwin worth serious investigation for those feminists who do not work in the area of biology? These are difficult questions which require not only an openness to texts and positions that many feminists, sometimes dogmatically, have asserted are hostile to feminist interests (the discourses of nature and biology), they also require a different understanding of feminism itself. It is only if feminist theory puts itself at risk in what we might understand as its own "evolutionary" modes of self-overcoming, where it is confronted with its own limits, where it is placed in new situations and contexts, that its own explanatory power, its power to enhance both understanding and action, is tested against others, and, ideally, transformed. A more open feminist inquiry into the value and relevance of *any* discourse, not just Darwin's, involves not only feminist critique, not simply inspection for errors and points of contention, but more passively and thus dangerously, a preparedness to provisionally accept the framework and guiding principles of that discourse or position in order to access, understand, and possibly transform it, even knowing that it may remain problematic in many of its assumptions and claims. One must risk the seductive appeals of the key discourses of various disciplines and knowledges, even those that may appear hostile or antithetical to feminist concerns, in order to be able to use them rather than simply criticize them or seek to avoid them. Biological discourses are no more "dangerous," "ideological," "biased," or "misleading" than any other discourses or models; we ignore them only at the expense of our own disciplinary discourses and political models, only at the expense of our own growth and self-transformation.

I will suggest here in broad outline some of the possible ramifications that Darwin's understanding of evolution may have for the reevaluation (transvaluation?) of feminist discourses and methods.

1. Darwin's model of evolutionary unfolding provides a striking response to various theories of oppression. Oppression is the result of operations of systems of harm and injustice that privilege the bodies and activities of some at the expense of others. What Darwin's work makes clear is that what has occurred to an individual in the operations of a milieu or environment (it matters little here if it is natural or cultural) is the force or impetus that propels that individual to processes, not of remediation (remediation literally involves undoing what cannot be undone) but of self-transformation. The struggle for existence is precisely that which induces the production of ever more viable and successful strategies, strategies whose success can be measured only by the degree to which they induce transformation in the criteria by which natural selection functions.[14] This means that feminism itself must undergo continuous revision and revitalization, a thorough self-transformation of its basic presumptions, methods, and values, including its understanding of the harms and wrongs done to women. Evolution and growth, in nature as in politics, are precisely about overcoming what has happened to the individual through the history, memory, and innovation open to that individual. This is true of the survival of species as much as it is of the survival of political strategies and positions, historical events, and memories. It is only insofar as past wrongs, "injuries," are the spur to forms of self-overcoming that feminist or antiracist struggles are possible and have any hope of effectivity. Darwin makes it clear that self-overcoming is incessantly if slowly at work in the life of all species. Politics is an attempt to mobilize these possibilities of self-overcoming in individuals and groups. The logic by which this self-overcoming occurs is the same for natural as for

social forces, and social forces borrow the energy and temporality of natural systems for political modes of resistance and overcoming.

Darwin's open-ended understanding of struggle and development seems to anticipate, rather than the liberal political discourses with which it is commonly associated (e.g., John Stuart Mill), a more "postmodern" concept of emergence. Indeed, there are some remarkable convergences between Darwin's understanding of the movements of evolution and Foucault's understanding of the fundamentally bottom-up, open-ended, strategic or opportunistic dynamics of power. In Darwin, as in Foucault, there is a fundamental commitment to the intangibility of the hold of domination and its ongoing and transforming susceptibility to resistance and realignment by virtue of the very forms of distribution or patterning that power itself takes. Power generates resistance, as much as species' development generates and in turn produces natural selection, from within, as variation or difference. For Foucault, power produces resistance which transforms power which produces resistances — in a never-ending spiral of self-transformation. Resistances do not come from without but are actively generated by the forms that power itself takes, which are thereby vulnerable to the transforming effects of resistance. Neither power nor resistance has ongoing stability or a pregiven form; each is the ramifying effect of the other. In Darwin's work too there is a sense in which the domination of individuals or species is precarious and necessarily historically limited, that the very successes of dominant groups produce the conditions for the domination of other groups that differ from them and serve to transform them. In both theorists there is an understanding of the inherent productivity of the subordinated groups — precisely *not* a theory of victors who abolish the vanquished, but a theory of how transformation and change remains in principle open because of the position of the subordinated, because domination remains precariously dependent on what occurs not only "above" but also "below."[15]

2. This logic of self-overcoming, the motor of Darwinian evolution, must be recognized not only as a distribution of (geographical and geological) spacing, processes of spatial dispersion through migration and exchange, periodic isolation and relations of proximity and contact with other groups; above all, and more commonly unrecognized, it is a form of temporization, in which the pull of the future exerts a primary dispersing force. Beings are impelled forward to a future that is unknowable, and relatively uncontained by the past: they are directed into a future for which they cannot prepare and where their bodies and capacities will be open to recontextualization and reevaluation. It is only retrospection that can determine what direction

the paths of development, of evolution or transformation, have taken and it is only an indefinitely deferred future that can indicate whether the past or the present provides a negative or positive legacy for those that come. This means that history and its related practices (geology, archaeology, anthropology, psychoanalysis, medical diagnosis, etc.) are required for understanding the current, always partial and residual situation as an emergence from a train of temporal events already given, which set the terms for but in no way control, cause, or direct a future fanning out or proliferation of the present. The future follows directions latent or virtual in but not necessarily actualized by the present. Evolution represents a force of spatial and temporal dispersion, rather than linear or progressive development, movements rather than goals, processes rather than ends.

3. One of the more significant questions facing contemporary feminist theory, and indeed all political discourses, is precisely what generates change, how change is facilitated, what ingredients, processes, and forces are at work in generating the conditions for change, and how change functions in relation to the past and the present. Darwin presents in quite developed if not entirely explicit form the elements of an account of the place of futurity, the direction forward as the opening up, diversification, or bifurcation of the latencies of the present, which provide a kind of ballast for the induction of a future different but not detached from the past and present. The future emerges from the interplay of a repetition of cultural/biological factors, and the emergence of new conditions of survival: it must be connected, genealogically related, to what currently exists, but is capable of many possible variations in current existence, the exploration of its virtual tendencies as well as its actualized products. The new is the generation of a productive monstrosity, the deformation and transformation of prevailing models and norms.

4. Darwin provides feminist theory with a way of reconceptualizing the relations between the natural and the social, between the biological and the cultural, outside the dichotomous structure in which these terms are currently enmeshed. Culture cannot be seen as the overcoming of nature, as its ground or mode of mediation, the representational form that, through retrospection, produces the natural as its precondition. According to Darwinian precepts, culture is not different in kind from nature. Culture is not the completion of an inherently incomplete nature (this is to attribute to Man, to the human, and to culture the position of destination of evolution, its telos or fruition, when what Darwin makes clear is that evolution is not

directed toward any particular goal). Culture cannot be viewed as the completion of nature, its culmination or end, but can be seen as the ramifying product and effect of a nature that is ever-prodigious in its techniques of production and selection, and whose scope is capable of infinite and unexpected expansion. Nature and culture can no longer be construed as dichotomous or oppositional terms, when nature is understood as the very field on which the cultural elaborates and develops itself. Language, culture, intelligence, reason, imagination, memory — terms commonly claimed as defining characteristics of the human and the cultural — are all equally effects of the same rigorous criteria of natural selection: unless they provide some kind of advantage to survival, some strategic value to those with access to them, there is no reason why they should be uniquely human or unquestionably valuable attributes. Darwin affirms a fundamental continuity between the natural and the social, and the complicity, not just of the natural with the requirements of the social, but also of the social with the selective procedures governing the order and organization of the natural.

5. Darwin's work may add some welcome layers of complexity to understanding the interlocking and entwinement of relations of sexual and racial difference. His work makes clear how sexual selection, that is to say, relations of sexual difference, may have played a formative role in the establishment of racial differences in the terms in which we know them today, and moreover, how racial variations have fed into and acted to transform the ways in which sexual difference, subjected to the laws of heredity, is manifested. Darwin provides an ironic and indirect confirmation of the Irigarayan postulation of the irreducibility, indeed, ineliminability, of sexual difference, and its capacity to play itself out in all races and across all modes of racial difference.[16] He makes sexual difference one of the ontological characteristics of life itself, not merely a detail, a feature that will pass. Although sexual difference — the requirement of genetic material from two sexes — emerges for Darwin contingently or randomly, an ingenious "invention" of primitive life that maximizes individual variation by ensuring each generation varies from the previous one, it is now so well adapted to the generation of variation that it would be hard to imagine an invention that life might generate to compete with and supersede it. Sexual difference is an ineliminable characteristic of life because of its peculiar economy of combination, exchange, and variation, and because of its pervasive historical force and effectivity. Darwin's work indirectly demonstrates the way that racial and bodily differences are bound up with and are complicated by sexual difference and the various,

transforming criteria of sexual selection. This is not to suggest any political or logical secondariness of racial and other differences, but only their fundamental reliance on sexual difference, the ways they are fundamentally bound up with the historicity of sexual relations.

6. Darwin's work, with the centrality it attributes to random variation, to chance transformations, and to the unpredictable, has provided and will continue to provide something of a bridge between the emphasis on determinism that is so powerful in classical science and the place of indetermination that has been so central to the contemporary, postmodern, forms of the humanities. Evolution is neither free and unconstrained, nor determined and predictable in advance. It is neither commensurate with the temporality of physics and the mathematical sciences, nor is it unlimited in potential and completely free to develop in any direction. Rather, it implies a notion of overdetermination, indetermination, and a systemic openness that precludes precise determination. This is the temporality of retrospection, of reconstruction, but a reconstruction whose aim is never the faithful reproduction of the past so much as the forging of a place for the future as the new.

7. Darwin had provided a model of history that resorts neither to the telos (or a priorism of the dialectic) nor to a simple empiricism which sees history simply as the accumulation of variously connected or unconnected events. History is both fundamentally open but also regulated within quite strict parameters. There are historical, that is temporal, genealogical, constraints on what becomes a possible path of biological/cultural effectivity: it is only that which has happened, those beings in existence, now or once, that provide the germs or virtualities whose divergence produces the present and future. That which has happened, the paths of existence actualized, preempt the virtualities that other existences may have brought with them; they set different paths and trajectories than those that might have been. While time and futurity remain open-ended, the past provides a propulsion in directions, unpredictable in advance, which in retrospect have emerged from the unactualized possibilities that it yields.

While I am not suggesting that feminists now need to become adherents and followers of Darwin, as in the past it seemed imperative to embrace the discourses of Marx, or Freud, or Lacan, I am claiming that there is much of significance in Darwin's writings that may be of value for developing a more politicized, radical, and far-reaching feminist understanding of matter, nature, biology, time and becoming—objects and concepts usually considered outside the direct focus of feminist analysis. His work is not "feminist" in any sense, but as a profound and complex account of the organic be-coming of matter, of the strategies of survival and the generation of multiple modes of becomings in the face of the obstacles or problems of existence that life poses for them, it is or should be of some direct interest and value for feminists.

CHAPTER 2

Darwin and the Ontology of Life

Whatever exists, having somehow come into being, is again and again reinterpreted to new ends, taken over, transformed and redirected by some power superior to it; all events in the organic world are a subduing, a <u>becoming master</u>, and all subduing and becoming master involve fresh interpretation, an adaptation through which all previous "meaning" and "purpose" are necessarily obscured or even obliterated.
—Friedrich Nietzsche, *On the Genealogy of Morals*

While there has been a great deal of attention devoted to Darwinism, to scientific developments and elaborations within biology and its related scientific disciplines since the writings of Darwin himself, and while Darwinism has had a powerful effect on literature, on cultural and artistic representations, and on economic and political discourses particularly in the late nineteenth and early twentieth centuries, rather surprisingly, it has not had the same impact on philosophy, which has tended to address it only marginally, if at all. Only in recent years has analytic philosophy embraced Darwinian biological models as paradigms of mind (Dennett 1996); and it is even rarer to find philosophers from the Continental tradition exploring the philosophical implications of Darwin's work, though there are passing references to Darwin and Darwinism in the works of many so-called postmodern theorists, such as Foucault, Deleuze, Agamben, and Lyotard. More commonly, however, in the traditions that have impacted so heavily on feminist and critical theory—especially Lacanian psychoanalysis and Derridean deconstruction—the question of biology, nature, and even the body's materiality have been construed as impossible, unknowable, or constructed objects, the consequence of cultural and inscriptive production rather than given or directly observable. In this brief chapter, I am less concerned with the relevance of Darwinism for reconsidering subjectivity and social change—as I was in the previous chapter—than with exploring the implications of his work for our understanding of what life is, and its positioning within a larger metaphysical order, in short, its implications for reconsidering ontology. Ontology, the philosophical analysis of what exists, what is and what might be—the analysis of being and becoming—has long been subordinated to epistemological questions, questions directed to what and how we know. Yet ontology, while covered over by epistemological concerns for over a century, nevertheless continues unanalyzed, for epistemologies as well as politics and ethics inevitably make assumptions about what exists, what there is or what is in the process of becoming in order to give their arguments and claims any force or materiality. Darwin's conception of life as ceaseless becoming raises questions about being and existence that problematize and inflect both analytic and Continental conceptions of ontology and may help to revitalize what is commonly considered a moribund or redundant theoretical category, making it a relevant concern for philosophy, but also for political, cultural, and social theory.

Probably the most central philosophical concern of Darwin's own writings, one which poses a profound philosophical shift in nineteenth-century thought and whose implications have still not been drawn out and understood even today, is Darwin's new and surprising conception of life itself. This is, I believe, Darwin's gift to the humanities and social science, a concept of life as dynamic, collective, change. He has provided a unique concept, his own, to add to and complicate the history of similar concepts that have marked the histories of both biology and philosophy as disciplines. Deleuze has argued that the creation of a new concept can be marked by a proper name, which serves to locate its "origins" but does not limit its future use or value: a concept "begins," and may therefore be attributed a proper name, the name of its "inventor," but its life consists in the uses to which it is put, the different concepts that develop out of or as it.[1] Darwin has transformed this term in quite dramatic but commonly unrecognized ways, has made it his own, through elaborating it in a new way, through making new components and connections by which it is used. Life, in Darwin's writings, is transformed from a static quality into a dynamic process, being is transformed into becoming, essence is transformed into existence, the past and the present are superseded and overwritten by the future. In

Darwin's writings, life becomes definitively linked to the movement of time and the force of the unpredictable, even random, future. Life is this very openness to the dynamism of time, an active response to time's provocation to endure. In short, life is now construed, perhaps for the first time, as fundamental becoming, becoming without the definitive features of (Aristotelian) being, without a given (Platonic) form, without human direction or divine purpose. Life becomes a complex concept which, through Darwin's intervention, becomes disconnected from a given essence, form, or function and newly related to, bringing into its orbit, touching upon and sharing borders with a number of other concepts: life informs and is informed by matter, time, becoming, difference, and repetition. Life is no longer a unique quality, an essence, but a movement. Life becomes dynamized, put into interaction, made to move and interact with the forces that act and move it. Life becomes definitively entwined in both the dynamic of the natural world (its unpredictabilities and upheavals and its material and organic forces) and in the movements of elaboration and change that cultural life, life lived in large numbers, life lived among other living and nonliving becomings, requires. Tied to neither the natural nor the social spheres alone, the concept of life now serves as a bridge, a point of connection and transition between the biological and the cultural, the ways in which matter opens itself up to social transformation, and the ways in which social change works with and through biologically open, individual and collective, bodies.

Darwin develops an ontology, an account of a real, that is profoundly different from that of his predecessors and contemporaries, in which life is now construed as an open and generative force of self-organization and growing material complexity, where life grows according to a materiality, a reality, that is itself dynamic, that has features of its own which, rather than exhibiting ongoing stability or given static qualities, rather than being seen as responsive or reactive, are as readily understood in terms of the active forces of interaction that generate and sustain change. Darwin managed to make this dynamism, an imperative to irreversible change in species over time, the center of his understanding of life itself. He makes it clear, and indeed a founding presupposition, that time, along with life itself, always moves forward, becomes more rather than less complex, produces divergences rather than convergences, variations rather than resemblances. Life is a movement of temporal fanning, elaboration, and emerging complexity, always directed by the forward push of time. Descent is not the transmission of the same characteristics over time (for example, the preservation of an invariable germ-line, as Weismann suggested, or as contemporary genetics implies,[2] or the transmission of fixed and unchanging phenotypic and behavioral characteristics, as patriarchs and some sociobiologists have commonly attributed to the two sexes), but the generation of endless variation, endless openness to the accidental, the random, the unexpected. Life is that which opportunistically, in an ad hoc fashion, utilizes the contingencies of the material world to endure and extend itself, to evolve into something other than itself. The confrontation between endless, accidental variation and the more or less relentless and uncontrollable forces of natural selection is a machinery that explains the remarkable inventiveness of biological existence, and the endless generation of new species, each of which is adapted in its own ways to the necessities of survival its position in the world entails. Darwin makes temporality, the push to futurity, an irreducible element of the encounter between individual variation and natural selection, the two principles which, in interaction, produce life's rich temporal resonances, its future possibilities, its evolution beyond its past and present forms.

If Darwin creates a real that is necessarily committed to a concept of temporal becoming, he creates a science, for the first time, in which history, and thus the eruption of unexpected events, is irreducible and formative, which is focused on events, global and local. Events are always unique and unrepeatable configurations of things and processes that exert widespread, uncontainable effects on a prevailing system. They defy precise causal analysis (although they may be retrospectively reducible to causal analysis), and can only provide explanation at a certain level of generality — not precise prediction, which can calculate all the causal links constituting any event, but the articulation of broad tendencies or directions, which explain no individual in particular, but calculate species in terms of tendencies emergent from individual transformations. The movement of evolution is in principle unpredictable, in principle historical, in the sense that the nature of species in the past prefigures and provides the raw material for present and future species but in no way contains, limits, or directs them to any particular goal or destination. The sciences that study evolution — evolutionary biology and genetics, for example (and in spite of their aspirations) — become irremediably linked to the unpredictable, the nondeterministic, the movement of virtuality rather than the predictable regularity of the actual, the transmission of qualities and aptitudes rather than clearly measurable and predictable links that other sciences have tended to seek. The present and future diverge from the past: the past is not the causal element of which the present and future are given effects but an index of the resources that the future has to develop itself differently. Darwinian evolutionary theory is fundamentally retrospective, reconstructive, piecing together fragments to provide a narrative or story that is already over: given what exists now, we may be able to provide links and tracks that describe an evolutionary path, or even, in the most hypothetical forms, the evolution of all of life from its simplest origins. But given a moment in this history, it is impossible to predict what will follow, what will befall a particular trend or direction, let alone a particular individual, what will emerge from a particular encounter, how natural selection will effect individual variation, and how individual variation will respond to and transform natural selection.

As discussed in the last chapter, Darwin's model of the biological unfolding of life involves the interplay between the two independent principles: the heritability of individual variation and natural selection. Taken together, these provide, on the one hand, an explanation of a series of processes and interactions that are fundamentally mindless, automatic, and without direction, but, on the other, are also entirely unpredictable and inexplicable in causal terms or in any terms which atomize or isolate units, steps, or stages.[3] Darwin inadvertently introduces a fundamental indeterminacy, quality and intensity, into the largely Newtonian framework he aspired to transpose into the field of natural history: the impossibility of either exact prediction or even precise calculation or designation, the seeking of tendencies rather than individual causes, of principles rather than universal laws. Newtonian physics provided the model of an in principle determinable universe, governed by a relatively small number of invariable laws, in which the universe itself is regarded as a closed system. If one could somehow take a snapshot of this universe and its natural forces at any one moment, one could in principle predict the future of any element within the universe, and its configuration as a whole.

Newton posited a regular, predictable, law-abiding universe in which, if life could understand and utilize its consistencies, would find itself at home, could know, comprehend, and harness the universe and its properties for itself. While Darwin sought to model his own scientific endeavors on such an enlightened understanding of the role of science in rendering life safe, what he produced instead was a very different account. Life can be life only because the universe, at least as far as the living are concerned, is where it is never fully at home, where it can never remain stable, never definitively know itself or its universe, control itself, its world, or its future, where it must undergo change over generations, where species must transform themselves even though they do not control, understand, or foresee how. Operating at a faster or slower rate of speed than much of the universe, life is

always challenged to overcome itself, to invent new methods, regions, resources, to differ from itself, to continually create solutions to the problems
of survival its universe poses to it using the resources the universe offers to
it. Life is never stable, because it makes a difference to the universe, because
it transforms its world, creates for itself new worlds, devises concepts, practices, skills that change it in the process of changing the universe. Life is that
which does not fit in its "place," is always out of place with the natural world
though it remains part of the natural world: it is this lack of fit, this dis-
comfit, that generates biological and conceptual inventiveness. Not having a
given place in the universe — except that which it forges for itself — life is also
out of time, not simply determinable in its time and place, but is that locus
or orientation that invariably strives for a new future. Not limited by what
it was, by its form, its history, its past life can now be understood in terms
of its forces, its ability to act, to move, to survive, to make itself over into
what can survive. Darwin has introduced indeterminacy into a previously
determinable universe, and excess into a previously functional understanding of life. Life exceeds itself, its past, its context, in making itself more and
other than its history: life is that which registers and harnesses the impact
of contingency, converting contingency into history, and history into self-
overcoming, supersession, becoming-other.

Darwin introduced a new understanding of what science must be to be
adequate to the real of life itself, which has no units, no agreed upon boundaries or clear-cut objects; and to the real of time and change, which cannot be known in advance, but must be waited for, observed, opened out
before it can be known — something Newtonian physics was unable to accept. He conceptualized a machinery of natural forces — no longer gravity
or mechanics, no longer precisely predictable — that, when they operate as a
complex, as an assemblage, produce both massive variation and the beauty
and elegance of life adapted in its most intimate contours and features to its
environment. Natural selection does not just limit life, cull it, remove its unsuccessful variations: it provokes life, it incites the living to transform themselves, to differentiate themselves by what they will become. Natural selection, the living being's encounter with the unpredictability of the events that
constitute a dynamic real, provides a set of forces which set goals and provide resources and incentives for the ever-inventive functioning of species.
Natural selection entails that the material world, and the other organisms
by which a living being is surrounded and against which it measures itself,
function as provocations to the self-overcoming that is the most basic characteristic of life, this self-overcoming attesting to the irreducible investment

of life in the movement of time, its enmeshment and organization according to the ever-forward imperative of time.

What, then, does Darwin offer to metaphysics? A new understanding of life as never self-identical, life as that which never repeats itself though it varies endlessly, life as a "solution" to the problems that matter poses, the overcoming of the obstacles of material existence, life as something that cannot contain itself in its past or present but which asymptotically tends to the future. What is his contribution to ontology, to an account of the real? That life and matter are the two orientations in the universe: to the degree that matter tends to conform to the principles of closed systems, life remains in excess of systematicity, open-ended, unpredictable. Life introduces a kind of veering-off-course in the systematicity of closed Newtonian systems: it signals an irrational, excessive, or explosive investment in transformation that cannot be contained in the lawlike predictabilities of closed systems. It introduces surprise and unexpectedness into an ordered universe. But these two orientations are not originary principles regulating the whole of the universe, two equal and opposite principles: life emerges from matter, from a particular and rare configuration of unstable elements which may generate cells, membranes, organs, biological entities, that is, chemical arrangements that may under certain circumstances exhibit emergent properties and, above all, carry their past along with them into the present and the future. Life is not different in substance from matter but is a kind of opening up of matter to indeterminacy, a qualitative transformation of matter into the unexpected, the surprising, the never-seen-before and the never-able-to-be-repeated. It adds to the contained and structured material universe the openness of the virtual, the potential to be otherwise, as it transforms matter, and itself, in its self-overcoming. The impossibility of givenness, of fixity, of the eternal and the unchanging, is now attributed to the world itself. In a sense, Darwin politicized the material world itself by showing that it is an emergent or complex order that generates surprising configurations and the endlessly unexpected, by showing that it could be otherwise than its present and past forms.

What is his contribution to the humanities, whose object of general reflection is "the human"? Darwin shows that the human is both that which is in the process of necessarily transforming itself and that which can never know itself to the point of predictability. Just as the protohuman gives way to and is supplanted by the human, so too the human, the all-too-human as Nietzsche profoundly recognized, is in the process of superseding itself, becoming posthuman.[4] What such a posthumanity might be, we cannot predict. But what we can be sure of is that the human is not now, nor ever has been or will be, identical to itself, the bearer of invariant qualities or properties, which affirm its status a priori. The human, as Darwin made clear, is the result of and an elaboration on sexual difference, and thus the human, and indeed the beyond-the-human necessarily take on (at least) two forms. Moreover, what the humanities may learn from Darwin is that human products and practices—institutions, languages, knowledges—are never adequate to the real of life and matter, but are always attempts to contain them, to slow them down, to place them in a position of retrospective reconstruction in the service of life's provisional interests. Life yields more complex life; life generates inventions of matter and different rates of variation and transformation. It also yields knowledges, technologies, techniques, and practices that make it both more and less at home in the universe, that make the universe increasingly amenable to its requirements, through the labor of production, but also that make its universe more and more open to interventions that may actively transform its own qualities in unpredictable and uncontrollable ways. This lag between knowledge and life, between concepts and the real, between epistemology and ontology, is not the occasion for lament, for it makes clear that the unease that constitutes life's ongoing evolution also produces eruptions, the unexpected, which we will only comprehend after they have occurred but which change us as much as they change the world. This unease is the condition of life's ongoing capacity to astonish, to invent, to transform.

This concept of a dynamized, uncontainable, unpredictable life, a life always lived in excess of need, in variation from its past and its antecedents and beyond any containment or systematicity, while a profoundly abstract and philosophical concept developed in the rarefied context of ontological analysis, is nevertheless a central element in reconfiguring how we may understand social, political, cultural, and subjective relations, as much if not more than how we understand the natural world. Darwin's ontological provocation to philosophy is also a provocation to all those discourses involved in or indebted to philosophical concepts of identity, being, substance, materiality, culture, and so on: he bequeaths to us all a challenge to understand dynamism, movement, endless becoming as the conditions, not the limits, of life. He gives us a concept of life larger than itself, open to and directly by otherness, by forces and energies that imply newness and invention. The task ahead is to utilize such an invigorated concept of life to rethink power, politics, and struggle in new terms.

CHAPTER 3

The Nature of Culture

It is the organization of matter that, in various ways, directly shapes all aspects of human life.

—André Leroi-Gourhan, *Gesture and Speech*

In this chapter, I want to discuss how questions of biological evolution and becoming may affect the ways in which we understand and conceptualize culture, and what we consider its preeminent products, language and technology. I do not want to propose a new sociobiology, that is, a model of the cultural and the social that reduces it to the biological,[1] that explains social phenomena in terms of biological categories, as have the recent rash of texts that argue for, say, the biological or evolutionary bases of rape,[2] or war, or even the liberal or democratic state.[3] Instead of a reduction of culture to nature, as performed by sociobiological explanation, where culture is nothing but the direct and unmediated expression of a directive, even normative (genetic or instinctively given) nature, I am interested in the ways in which nature, composed of the biological and material, organic and inorganic systems that sustain life, incites and produces culture, that is, the ways in which the biological enables rather than limits and directs social and cultural life. Instead of submitting to the rigorous or binarized distinction between nature and culture that has become orthodoxy in contemporary critical, cultural, feminist, and race theory, I explore here the ways in which the natural prefigures and induces cultural variation and difference, the ways in which biology impels culture to vary itself, to undergo more or less perpetual transformation. In short, I am interested in the ways in which time, movement, change, the irresistible push to the future — as fundamental biological and material forces — affect culture and the technological developments that derive from it, and impel them to differ from themselves and to undergo more or less continuous, more or less uncontrolled, becomings — that is, the ways in which nature does not contain culture but induces it to vary itself, to evolve, to develop and transform in ways that are not predictable in advance.

It is not the natural that limits the cultural, for there is no essential characteristic that constrains cultural possibilities because the natural produces rather than inhibits; the natural is (currently) the repressed or unacknowledged condition of all cultural forms and the reason they vary from each other and from themselves. This chapter is an attempt, in other words, to redress the foreclosure, the denial, of the biological forces that press on and produce life, and thus, ironically, to overturn the repression of materiality in its most complex forms that has dominated the humanities and social sciences in their exclusive focus on cultural construction at the expense of natural production, and in the rigid divide that separates how we conceptualize the natural from how we conceptualize the cultural. It may be inaccurate to regard nature and culture as two mutually exclusive and mutually exhaustive categories, that is, as binarized or oppositional terms in which one takes on the right to define the other as its negation or deprivation; this is to regard them as contained categories, each of which has given boundaries and no space of overlap. Instead, it may prove fruitful to understand them as terms whose relation is defined by emergence. Nature is the ground, the condition or field in which culture erupts or emerges as a supervening quality not contained in nature but derived from it.

We live in the era of constructionisms of various types. Culture is usually construed primarily as artifice, fabrication, an elaborate collective product of communities and their interests; the subject is also today nearly universally regarded as a construct elaborated or produced through the linguistic and sexualizing normative structures of the family and its oedipal or behavioral imperatives. Institutions, structures, or technologies are understood as the means by which such constructions are produced, even while being seen themselves as cultural constructs. Constructionism, flourishing in the period following 1968, largely as a reaction to prevailing naturalisms that regarded the division of labor, or the division of sexes or races, as somehow justified through some natural order or givenness, viewed itself as the opposite, the other, the subordinated underside of naturalism, biologism, or essentialism, their logical or conceptual adversary. Constructionism, so it was and is believed, would enable us to consider change, upheaval, even revolution, in ways precluded by naturalism, for constructionism seemed open to individual and collective intervention; indeed it seemed a postulate necessary to constitute the very basis of any radical politics. Radicality itself seemed inherently constructionist, for what point was there in rebelling against nature, resisting what is inevitable? Culture was rendered equivalent to the changing, the historical, the unpredictable, while nature came to be understood as fixed, unchanging, limited in advance in being governed by invariable, universal, and predictive laws. Nature became the background against which the cultural elaborates itself, the contrast that distinguished variation, difference, becoming from the given, the unchanging, and the inevitable.

Nature came to be understood as timeless, unchanging raw material, somehow dynamized and rendered historical only through the activities of the cultural and the psychical orders it generates. It came to be regarded as a romantic or nostalgic anachronism. Correlatively, culture became the active force molding and reworking nature to make it amenable to individual, social, and collective use: culture tames nature, enlivening it in the process of making it function for our historically and geographically variable uses. Culture writes on and as nature, making the natural its inscriptive surface, the neutral and indifferent medium for any message. Culture scripts the natural; it writes it, divides it, manufactures it in socially useful, palatable, and expected forms. The hunt for incriminating traces of naturalism elaborated itself (especially in feminist and cultural theory) as a relentless antiessentialism, which sought out all forms of attribution of fixity, in order to position them on the natural side of a natural/cultural opposition. Essence, fixity, nature, biology, the ahistorical, predictability are identified together as resource or raw material, to be overcome or remade; what is cultural, social, political, economic, historical, or subjective—in short, what is regarded as living, and especially what is human, creative, and innovative, ethical and political—is on the other side of this divide, resisting its containment in natural categories through its immense capacity to vary itself in its cross-cultural and widely variable historical permutations. This side constitutes what is creative and productive, what makes rather than what simply is.

It is by no means surprising that radical politics, those various positions challenging the social, economic, and sexual structuring of the cultural sphere, has been tied to a resolute antinaturalism. This is a tradition that emerges largely through the pervasive and today sometimes unrecognized influence of Hegelian or dialectical models of knowledge and history: the given, that is to say nature, is that which is to be transformed and overcome or superseded through human labor, which remakes the given according to its own interests. This model of the passivity of nature and its long historical association with "femininity" seems to directly infuse Marx's own writings as well: labor is the historical movement of the transformation of a nature that gives itself up, with little resistance, to collective social endeavor, to the transformation into commodities. Politics, or cultural analysis, consists here not in the analysis of the ways in which nature is transformed, but in the analysis of the social relations that structure labor itself. Marx's conception of nature as a passivity awaiting the active and transformative, historicizing inputs of culture seems to infect the traditions of both structuralism and phenomenology that follow. Structuralism affirms the internality of social systems, their self-generated force and their logical independence from what is outside them in the creation of self-contained worlds, whether they are the kinship system (for Lévi-Strauss), linguistic systems (for Saussure), or systems of desire (for Lacan). Phenomenology affirms the productivity of consciousness in generating meaning and value from the meaninglessness of the natural order, through its difference from and superiority to the nonconscious (in, for example, Sartre's account of nausea or Beauvoir's conception of the female body). Through the pervasive influence of structuralism and phenomenology on the post-1968 revival of psychoanalytic theory (Lacan's understanding of the Real continues this tradition of conceptualizing the given, the Real, as outside symbolization, beyond representation and somehow thus outside the cultural, shaping psychic and signifying forces of the imaginary and the symbol), this view of the fabricating, productive, formgiving structure of the social and the cultural, and of nature as what must be overcome, remade, superseded appears to be nearly ubiquitous. With the exception of the ecology movement, with its eco-feminist and eco-philosophy offshoots, with which I am loath to be identified,[4] virtually all forms of contemporary political and social analysis continue this tradition of ignorance of, indeed contempt for, the natural, which today remains identified with either passivity or inertia.

The nature/culture opposition seems foundational to cultural analysis, which defines itself by excluding the natural from its considerations. If nature is not the other, the opposite, of culture but its condition, then the relations between them are much more complicated than a binary division implies. I do not want to take up the common impulse many of us have regarding binary terms—that is, to attempt to occupy a position some-where in the middle, between two binarized terms, a position that implies both terms—but instead to follow a different, less deconstructive maneuver which suggests that the subordinated term needs to be reconsidered as both the condition of the dominant term and as occupying its heart or center. Deconstruction thus involves an interplay or resonance of the terms with each other, and especially of making the subordinated term in binary pairs the irritant that undoes the dominant term's privilege. My goal here is not the undoing and redoing of binary pairs of terms but rather the greater complication of the subordinated term. I don't want to suggest that na-ture functions as the subordinated term in all those discourses that rely on a nature/culture opposition: it takes this role only in those disciplinary contexts that define themselves as outside or beyond the natural.[5] It will be my argument here that the natural is *not* the inert, passive, unchanging ele-ment against which culture elaborates itself but the matter of the cultural, that which enables and actively facilitates cultural variation and change, in-deed that which ensures that the cultural, including its subject-agents, are never self-identical, that they differ from themselves and necessarily change over time.

How we understand the nature/culture opposition depends to a large ex-tent on the ways in which we understand nature itself: to the degree that nature is regarded as inert (that is, to the extent that it is reduced to the in-organic), culture is regarded as generative, constructive, productive. But to the degree that nature is understood as dynamic, excessive, differential—that is, to the degree that it is construed as temporal, historical, and unpre-dictable (a picture that some in the biological sciences have worked hard to elaborate since the writings of Darwin himself)—culture in all its per-mutations remains indebted to its particularities and must be understood as the *gift* of nature, its increasing elaboration and complication through the efforts of life to transform itself. If we understand the relations between nature and culture as a relation of ramification and elaboration, or in the language of science, as a form of emergence or complexity, rather than one of opposition, the one, nature, providing both the means and the material for the other's elaboration, and the other, culture, providing the latest tor-sions, vectors, and forces in the operations of an ever-changing, temporally sensitive nature, cultural studies can no longer afford to ignore the inputs of the natural sciences if they are to become self-aware. An orientation to questions of materiality and of life, the objects of physics, chemistry, and biology, is not outside the scope of cultural and technological analysis, but is their limit, their implicit underside, that which the cultural always carries along with it without adequate acknowledgment.

If models of language and representation have dominated the ways in which we understand cultural life—which they have throughout the twentieth century with the dominance of structuralist and poststructuralist conceptions of the redundancy and irrelevance of the natural, the material, and what is nonstructured or outside of systems—it may be time to render such analyses more complex: for to represent culture through one of culture's own products, whether language, images, representations, or any other term, is to reduce its complexity, to flatten its multiplicity to one of its elements and to ensure that this element is itself incapable of cultural explanation, insofar as it is the resource that provides explanation for all others. We need to understand what is *outside* the cultural—indeed we need to understand, *contra* Derrida and following Deleuze,[6] that culture and representation have an outside, that they are not all-pervasive, that they are conditioned rather than conditions—in order to provide more complex and accurate models for the cultural. Models derived from the natural sciences, and particularly from a nonreductive evolutionary biology, may provide some of the more fruitful resources for understanding the complex historical nature of culture itself.[7]

If culture does not so much add activity to nature's passivity, then perhaps we may understand culture as subtractive: culture diminishes, selects, reduces nature rather than making nature over, or adding to it social relevance, significance, and the capacity for variation. Nature itself may be understood as perpetual variation, and life as the evolutionary playing out of maximal variation or difference, as Darwin's own understanding of evolutionary processes implies. If biological evolution is the generation of an immensely productive machinery for the creation of maximal difference—as I have argued in the last two chapters—then culture rather than nature is what impoverishes nature's capacity for self-variation and becoming, by tying the natural to what culture can render controllable and what it sees as desirable. Perhaps Bergson, following Darwin, is right to claim that our human activities diminish rather than augment the effects of the natural world in order that we can discriminate its features and highlight only those that interest us.[8] Culture is not the magnification of nature and its animation through human effort, but the selection of only some elements or facets of the natural, and the casting of the rest of it into shadow, a kind of diminution of the complexity and openness of the natural order. And perhaps, following

Nietzsche, also to some extent, paradoxically, a follower of Darwin,[9] we may understand that it is the natural world of forces that provides the energy and impetus for the self-overcoming of life that constitutes the very heart of radical politics.[10] In this context, Deleuze insists that, when it is a matter of forces at work, forces that are natural and cultural indistinguishably, that confront each other and play out their relations, these forces may be understood to constitute an *Outside*, that which is beyond systematicity, which is composed of forces, and which must be acknowledged as such. This outside, which is not the exterior of a subject or a culture, that is, a subject's or culture's own representation of its limit, an image or projection of an outside, is the force that disrupts, intervenes, to break down expectation and to generate invention and innovation, to enable the emergence or eruption of subjectivity or culture. The outside is the (successful or victorious) series of forces that impinge on structures, plans, expectations of the living: this outside appears to us in the form of events, natural and social, and events generate for us the problems that our inventiveness, above all our culture's ingenuity, attempts to address or resolve.[11] For Deleuze, this outside is the force that induces thinking, that shakes life from automatism, that generates culture.[12] This outside, composed of competing forces, forces in the process of their composition, can be called by a number of different names: nature, time, events. It is the force of this outside that incites culture, that at a particular historical moment induces subjectivity, and that ensures that they endlessly transform themselves.[13]

The very feature that cultural theorists single out to privilege — change, difference — is the condition of the natural order, which, from the time of Plato up until the mid-nineteenth century, has been disavowed and denied. Nature can no longer, since the intervention of Darwin, be regarded as passive, inert, unchanging, ahistorical: we need now to develop a correspondingly complex understanding of the relation between the cultural and the natural which more adequately acknowledges the dynamic force of self-differentiation or emergence that characterizes a nature conceived as evolving, as alive, as subject to upheaval and transformation, nature construed as unpredictable and open-ended, as a form of perpetual becoming.

Why is it, for example, that we happily designate the human sphere as cultural, but are reluctant to understand the animal world as cultural? Why is it that humans are said to communicate, to have language, to produce technology when it is also clear that animals communicate, evolve, transform themselves, use tools as well? Cultural studies seemed founded on the supposition of an immense, unhealable rift between the human and the rest of organic life: the human is unique, immersed in language, denaturalized through cultural and technological extension and augmentation, and thus stands outside of the natural order. But what if, as Darwin (1981) suggests, all the characteristics that we posit as uniquely human — reason, language, emotions, cultural associations, the use of tools and technologies, and so on — are simply differences of degree from the animal rather than a difference in kind? What if, instead of a rift, there is a continuity between the human and the animal? What does this imply for the study of culture? How can the study of culture acknowledge its embeddedness in nature, its immersion in an outside it cannot control but to which it must respond, without at the same time losing its nuanced capacity to read, to interpret cultural circuits and networks? How do we read culture's immersion in nature as part of cultural analysis? And equally, how do we understand the dynamism and tremendously inventive productivity of cultural life except as an exploration of the resources, the dynamic potential, of the virtuality of the natural world? Is it possible to understand culture not as the completion of nature but as the endlessly ramified and open product of nature: that is, is it possible, and productive, to understand culture as the way in which nature reflects on and articulates itself, as nature's most generous and complex self-reflection? Is culture nature's way of thinking itself, of gaining consciousness of itself, of representing itself, and of acting on itself? Instead of regarding culture as that which performatively produces nature as its "origin," as Derrida and Judith Butler imply in their understanding of performativity as iteration,[14] can we regard culture as the most elaborate invention of a nature that is continually evolving?

I want to suggest here three characteristics or features that nature, or what we might understand as the force of the outside, bestows on culture, and that each culture must somehow address, deal with, and negotiate around. These are the ways in which the outside irresistibly impinges on life to generate problems for it that require some acknowledgment, some mode of address, some form of provisional solution. First is the forward pull of temporality, its future direction, its force of development and aging on all living beings that impels an acknowledgment of human finiteness, mortality, and the temporal limits of individual effectivity, that impel, in other words, collective social (and sexual) organization to overcome the temporal limits of each individual. Second is the force of variation, the proliferation of natural differences, which propels a variety of cultural "solutions" to the problem, the provocation, of how to live in the world using the resources of the world to provide the "solutions" to the events and surprises that the world generates for living beings. Culture can be regarded as the varying innovative responses to the problems that nature poses to the living. Individual variation, geographical and historical variation, group variation generate the impetus for cultural variation through growing complexity and the eruption of unexpected emergence. Biology can be construed, as readily as culture, as the realm for the generation of nothing but pure differences, differences for their own sake, experimentation with no particular aim in mind. The third feature is the biological provocation of sexual difference, and the subsequent development of racial differences according to patterns of sexual selection, which remains one of the central challenges of all cultural interaction: the regulation of relations between the sexes and the simultaneous creation of one's own family-group-network and its increasing differentiation from other family-group-network relations (sexual, racial, and class relations).

In other words, nature bequeaths to all the forms of culture a series of problems or provocations (many more than I have suggested above), which each cultural form must address, in its own way, even if it cannot solve them: each culture must deal with, at the least, the forward drift of time; the generation of immense and uncontrolled variation or difference, exacerbated by the increasing complexity of large and growing populations; and the relations between self and other, insofar as the self is sexually, racially, geographically, and historically specific and the other is always other to and different from the self in some bodily way. These are intractable issues, forces that all cultures must, each in its own way, deal with to survive and sustain themselves, for they are forces, non-normative imperatives, of an outside that weighs on individuals and groups, in ways that they cannot control but are implicated in and are effects of. These are, in part, traces of our debt to the natural and the ongoing force of the natural, its pressure for invention from each culture.

The natural does not limit the cultural; it provokes and incites the cultural by generating problems, questions, events that must be addressed and negotiated, symbolized, or left unrepresented. Cultures distinguish themselves through the questions or problems that press most directly on them (these problems are the consequence of precise geographical, historical, and institutional contingencies), through the resources each culture (in the form of its varying natural resources and modes of technological development) gleans from its environment or context, and through the inventiveness each culture adopts to address or transform these problems or provocations so that it can gain a measure of stability and cohesiveness, a cultural "identity" directly linked to its (indirect, mediated) relations to the natural world and its elaborated relations to its own (collective) past.

Culture can be understood on such a model, not as the construction of its own principles and practices out of nothing, or merely out of cultural history alone: instead, it is the selection and harnessing of some of the forces of natural differentiation in order to cohere and give itself form and to structure its practices in highly particular, learned ways. Culture can be regarded, not as the active agency that constructs and makes but as that which reactively functions to narrow down, to slow down, to filter, to cohere and organize that which provokes and stimulates it—the unexpected force of events, the unpredictable and uncontrollable impacts of the natural world, impinging on cultural aims and intentions with their insistent resistance to understanding and containment.

Nature is the endless generation of *problems* for culture: the problem of how to live amidst the world of matter, other living beings, and other subjects is the generic problem that each culture responds to and addresses according to its own methods. It is the insistence of such intractable problems, problems that do not have solutions but generate styles of living, that prompts human, or cultural, innovation and ingenuity, self-overcoming, and the creation of the new. Cultural life does not assimilate and make over the natural order; instead, it endlessly narrows down and simplifies, but also complexifies and expands the natural. It exploits the virtuality of the natural according to the forces and materialities that the natural bequeaths to each culture. Culture can be understood as part of the ongoing evolution of the natural, the variable spirals and complications of a nature that is always already rich in potentiality to be developed in unexpected ways.

I want to end this chapter with a question, which I hope may act as its own provocation or incitement: if nature is dynamic and active, if it is not alien to culture but is the ground which makes the cultural logically and historically possible, then what would a new conception of culture, one which refuses to sever it from nature, look like? What would its intractable or irresistible forces look like? What limits and modes of creativity does the cultural have over and with the natural? What would the study of culture, cultural studies, look like if nature was regarded as framework and provocation of culture rather than its retardation? Productive and inventive answers to these questions may serve to give new life to the study of culture in the twenty-first century.

PART II.

LAW, JUSTICE, AND

THE FUTURE

CHAPTER 4

The Time of Violence:

Derrida, Deconstruction, and Value

The task of breeding an animal with the right to make promises evidently embraces and presupposes as a preparatory task that one first <u>makes</u> men to a certain degree necessary, uniform, like among like, regular, and consequently calculable. The tremendous labor . . . performed by man upon himself during the greater part of the existence of the human race, his entire <u>prehistoric</u> labor, finds in this its meaning, its great justification, notwithstanding the severity, tyranny, stupidity and idiocy involved in it: with the aid of the morality of mores and the social straightjacket, man was actually <u>made</u> calculable.

—Friedrich Nietzsche, *On the Genealogy of Morals*

Violence is clearly a contentious issue — especially in the age of uncontrollable and uncontained violent reactions, that is, in the age of state and national violences, violences enacted in the name of a region, a people, a religion, which is to say, in the age of terrorism. However, it is precisely at those moments when violence on the streets, in the air, between ethnic and religious groups, between political and cultural adversaries is at its most intense — in situations of war, rebellion, insurgency, struggle — that violence cannot be simply rejected or condemned but must be also actively harnessed and utilized by means of the very processes of rejection or condemnation. My claim is not simply that violence begets violence, which seems broadly true, but more that violence is ineliminable; it is the condition of force that must be in play even in the analysis of violence, let alone in any response to violence. The movement of troops, of occupying forces, of resistance fighters, of warring factions, whether they bring democracy and "freedom" or fascism and "ethnic cleansing," is violence enacting itself; but equally the very acts of condemnation, resistance, or defiance are acts of violence. And modes of reflecting and reporting on this recognizable violence are also forms of (commonly unrecognized) violence.

Rather than simply condemning or deploring violence, as we tend to do regarding the evils of war and suffering and the everyday horrors we believe we can ameliorate, I am interested in raising the question of violence not simply where it is most obvious and manifest — in the streets, in relations between races, classes, sexes, and political oppositions (though I hope not to avoid these issues either) — but also where is it less obvious, and rarely called by this name, in the domain of knowledges, reflection, thinking, and writing. My goal here is to explore its constitutive role in the establishment of politics, of thought, of knowledge. To the extent that we may be theorists or philosophers as opposed to activists, terrorists, or freedom fighters (though these need not be mutually exclusive categories) we play a part in the various structures of violence, whether we choose to or not, not only in our daily but also in our professional and intellectual lives. But it is rare that we have the intellectual resources by which to think the level of our investment in the very violences that constitute our relations to intellectual work and the production of knowledges. I want to use some of the rather sensitive and self-conscious resources provided by Jacques Derrida to look at the very violence of writing, of thought, and of knowing.

THE VIOLENCE OF THOUGHT

Although it has been commonplace to claim that Derrida, along with the whole of postmodernism, is a mode of depoliticization and transformation of feminist, class, and postcolonial discourses,[1] Derrida has never written on anything *other* than politics and violence, even if it is also true that he does not write *only* on politics and violence. I would argue that his are among the most intensely political texts of the late twentieth and early twenty-first centuries, though the language he uses is not one he shares with most versions of political and especially feminist theory. He is commonly accused of blurring or immobilizing politics, of refusing to provide answers or the conditions for answers to political problems, and of reducing political to theoretical problems. In this vein, Thomas McCarthy's reading of Derrida's politics may serve as representative of this position: McCarthy argues that, in the long run, Derrida produces "wholesale subversion, with no suggestion of remedies or alternatives" (McCarthy 1989–90, 157). While critical and perhaps in that sense politically useful, deconstruction in particular and postmodern theory in general remain ironic, parodic, skeptical, negative: lacking a clear plan, given goals, a set of criteria to distinguish better from worse outcomes; that is, having no clear ethical or political stand, it tends toward nihilism. Deconstructive discourse is thus construed as critical — destructive, perhaps — but never adequately constructive: able to criticize politics but never able to positively contribute to it.

I will argue, contrary to this prevailing representation of Derrida's politics as a politics of negativism, nihilism, anarchism (a position that is commonly identified with Nietzscheanism and may well be the consequence of Derrida's underlying commitment to Nietzsche), that he offers a profound if unsettling reconfiguration of political activity that centers on the question of violence. This understanding, while not directed at the violence of contemporary life, could nonetheless benefit those who wish to analyze its most concrete forms: feminists and queer activists analyzing domestic and sexual violence, political theorists analyzing nationalist and ethnic violence, leftists analyzing the violence of governments and institutions, Marxists analyzing the violence of economic privilege may feel that deconstruction is a form of intellectual mediation that deflects from their more direct and pressing activities, but until violence is understood in all its ironic complexity, it flourishes unabated. It is true, as McCarthy claims, that Derrida refuses to offer political advice, to provide solutions to the pressing, and apparently irresolvable, needs of today. But it is the very idea that we can find a solution to these questions, and to the question of violence, that is itself put under political interrogation in Derrida's writings. Derrida refuses the kinds of questions that McCarthy, Nancy Fraser, Martha Nussbaum, and others have used to define the political[2] — which does not mean he abandons or refuses politics or ethics, but that he engages in different ways and with different questions. He refuses easy answers to that which cannot be answered or solved but must nevertheless be addressed, lived with, and negotiated.[3]

The nature of the violence Derrida both articulates and mobilizes is discernible only through a careful reading of a number of texts in which he appears to be talking of other matters. The question of violence is never very far from these matters. Whenever he talks of force ("The Force of Law," 1990), of discord ("Différance," 1982), of the trace (*Of Grammatology*, 1974), of fraying ("Freud and the Scene of Writing," 1978), of dislocation ("Eating Well," 1991), as well as in texts more explicitly devoted to the question of violence ("Violence and Metaphysics," 1978, and "The Violence of the

Letter," 1974), it is with the politics of violence that Derrida deals. More-over, while accused of either political indifference or nihilism, Derrida has addressed the more manifest and concrete political issues of violence in rela-tion to race and apartheid, in his writings for Nelson Mandela (1985, 1985b), in his writings on feminist questions (1979, 1982b, 1983), in his discussions of the rhetoric of drugs (1991b, 1993), and so on — in a much more explicit and direct manner than virtually any other contemporary philosopher one can think of. That his works are seen as apolitical, as lacking a mode of political address, is surely the result of a certain freezing of politics and an attempt to constrain it to well-known or predetermined forms, forms we believe we already know (the "official" movements that attempt to represent minori-ties through some kind of representative structure, whether unions, political parties, advocacy groups, and so on) — the very forms whose naturalness or stability is contestable through deconstruction.[4]

From the very earliest conceptions of *différance* he develops an under-standing of the "worlding of the world," the marking of the earth, writing itself, as modes of cutting. *Différance* is understood as the inscriptive, dis-persing dissonance at the impossible "origin" of any self-presence. As he described it, "*Différance* is the name we might give to the 'active' moving dis-cord of different forces" (1982, 18). As an "active" moving discord of forces, that is, as a movement that precedes the opposition between active and pas-sive, *différance* is the originary tearing of that which, unknowable and un-speakable as it is, is always amenable to inscription, is never "full" enough to retain its self-presence in the face of this active movement of tearing, cutting, inscribing, or breaking apart. Which is also a bringing together, a folding or reorganizing, and the very possibility of time and becoming, of time as un-certain, open, future oriented. It is only through tearing, inscribing, which is also categorizing and sorting, that new alignments and arrangements, new organization is possible. Emergence itself is a function of violent inscription.

In *Of Grammatology*, Derrida asks the crucial question, which I want to adopt as my own: "What links writing to violence? And what must vio-lence be in order for something in it to be equivalent to the operation of the trace?" (1974, 112). Note that he does not ask the more obvious, and mani-festly Derridean, question: What must *writing* be in order for something in it to be equivalent to violence? Rather, he seeks out the modes of divergence, ambiguity, impossibility, the aporetic status of violence itself, a status that it shares with the trace, and thus with writing, inscription, or difference. This is in many senses a more interesting and complicated question, for it asks: In what ways is violence bound up with the structures of equivocation, of différance, of undecidability that so radically structure and unhinge all discourse and all representation, all modes of self-presence? If violence is no longer clearly identifiable and denounceable, if it is not readily delimited in its clearly recognizable spheres of operation, if it becomes ambiguous where the division between violence and its others can be drawn, then violence is a form, possibly the only form, that writing, *arche-writing*, or the trace can take. Derrida does not ask how violence is like writing, but rather, what is it *in* violence, what operative element in violence, is equivalent to the trace? Violence is not containable itself, a fully self-present thing, an "identity" of the trace: it is its own particularity and excessiveness over and above any conceptual schema, deconstruction notwithstanding. Derrida is inquiring into the allegiance of something in violence with writing, and indeed, with the very operations of deconstruction itself, which can be considered a writing of the violence of writing, and thus a self-consciously violent writing of writing as violence (and production, of violating production).[5]

What makes Derrida's work at once intensely political and ethical, while he remains acutely aware of the problems involved in any straightforward avowal of one's commitments to political and ethical values, is his readiness to accept that no political protocol, no rhetorical or intellectual ploy is simply innocent, motivated by reason, knowledge, or truth alone, but carries with it an inherent undecidability, an inherent iterability or repeatability that recontextualizes it and frees it from any specifiable or definitive origin or end. His politics is not the espousal of a position but rather an openness to a force, the force of difference that disperses meaning, defers a final position, and indefinitely delays its own identity. He lives up to the simultaneous necessity and impossibility of ethics, of politics, and of knowledge, the paradoxical binding of that which we must move beyond with how we move beyond it: to reject, to move beyond, to overcome is also to inhabit and to be inhabited by that which one wants to expel.

Derrida outlines his earliest linkage of violence with the structure of writing or difference, in his discussion of Lévi-Strauss in a section in *Of Grammatology* called "The Violence of Writing." There he argues that the structure of violence is itself marked by the very structure of the trace or writing: it is a three-part process in which concrete or vulgar (everyday) writing, or violence, is the reduced and constrained derivative of a more primary and constitutive arche-writing or arche-violence which is the very condition of both writing/violence and its opposite speech/peace: "In the beginning" there is an arche-writing, a primordial or constitutive violence which inscribes "the unique," the originary, the thing itself in its absolute self-proximity, into a system of differentiation, into the systems of ordering or classification that constitute language (or representation more generally). This violence is the containment and ordering of the thing, the world, to give up its thingness, its world-ness, and to submit itself to the leveling of representation, a mythical and impossible leveling that assumes a self-identity the thing itself never possessed: "To think the unique *within* the system, to inscribe it there, such is the gesture of the arche-writing: arche-violence, loss of the proper, of absolute proximity, of self-presence, in truth the loss of what has never taken place, of a self-presence which has never been given but only dreamed of and always already split, repeated, incapable of appearing to itself except in its own disappearance" (Derrida 1974, 112).

Primordial inscription, the ontological equivocation of différance, is the rendering of originary self-presence as impossible: it is the "production" of presence through the structure of the trace, the binding up of the real in writing or marking. This arche-writing, conceived as violence, inscription, or trace, brings about the system of terms, differences, through which oppositions, structures, systems, orders are made possible. Such a binding of the real in and as difference requires a second, "reparatory" or compensatory violence, the violence whose function it is to erase the traces of this primordial violence, a kind of counterviolence whose violence consists in the denial of violence. This is a malignant inscription that hides its inscriptive character, that de-materializes and de-idealizes itself, that refuses to face up to its own dependence on and enmeshment in the more primordial structure. This is a violence that describes and designates itself as the moral counter of violence. This is the violence that we sometimes name the law, right, or reason. This violence is commonly represented as a noble counterviolence, though its force and effects are no less destructive than violence in its most everyday sense.

There is, moreover, a third-order violence, one that we can understand in the more mundane and viscerally horrifying, and thus ordinary, sense of the word:

> It is on this tertiary level, that of the empirical consciousness, that the common conception of violence (the system of the moral law and of transgression) whose possibility remains yet unthought, should no doubt be situated . . . . This last violence is all the more complex in its structure because it refers at the same time to the two inferior levels of arche-violence and of law. In effect, it reveals the first nomination which was already an expropriation, but it denudes also that which since then functioned as the

proper, the so-called proper, substitute of the deferred proper, *perceived* by the *social* and *moral consciousness* as the proper, the reassuring seal of self-identity, the secret. (1974, 112)

Derrida suggests here that empirical violence, or "war in the colloquial sense" (112) rests upon, indeed is made possible by, the logically prior two senses of violence. The violence of nomination, of language or writing, is an expropriation, covered over and concealed by the violence that names itself as the space of nonviolence, the field of the law (which in its very constitution structures itself as lawful, and thus beyond or above violence, as that which justifiably judges violence, provides a tribunal on violence). Empirical violence, war, antagonisms between groups or between individuals participate in both these modes of violence (violence as inscription, violence as the containment of inscription, the containment of violence). Mundane or empirical violence reveals "by effraction" the originary violence, whose energy and form it iterates and repeats; yet it "denudes" the latent or submerged violence of the law, whose transgression it affirms, while thus affirming the very force and necessity of the law.

If Derrida refuses to locate the "mundane" violence of "evil, war, indiscretion, rape" (112) as originary, as the eruption of an unheralded violence into an otherwise benign or peaceful scene (this is how he locates Lévi-Strauss's Rousseauian resonances in *Of Grammatology*), he manages to show that everyday violence, the violence we strive to condemn in its racist, sexist, classist, and individualist terms, is itself the violent consequence of an entire order whose very foundation is inscriptive, différantial, and thus violent in itself, a kind of "pure violence." It is thus no longer clear how something like a good-faith moral condemnation of violence is possible, or at least how it remains possible without considerable self-irony. The very position from which a condemnation of (tertiary) violence is articulated is itself made possible only because the violence of the morally condemnatory position must remain unarticulated. Which is of course not to say that moral condemnation is untenable or impossible, but rather, that its own protocols are implicated in the very thing it aims to condemn. Which means that the very origins of values, ethics, morality, and law, "all things noble in culture" (as Nietzsche says) lie in the trace, that dissimulating self-presence that never existed, and whose tracks must be obliterated as they are revealed. Force, violence, writing not only "originate" but also disseminate and transform even that violence which cannot be called such: "The arche-writing is the origin of morality as of immorality. The nonethical opening of ethics. A violent opening. As in the case of the vulgar concept of writing, the ethical instance of violence must be rigorously suspended in order to repeat the genealogy of morals" (1974, 140).

VIOLENCE AND UNDECIDABILITY

Though his work strayed very far from many of his initial concerns, Derrida returned to a remarkably similar problematic in more recent works, of which a number are clearly linked to the question of violence and its founding role in the constitution of systems of ethics, morality, law, and justice (1990), in the functioning of friendship (1997), in the operation of modes of gift and hospitality (2000), in the structure of relations to the other, notions of singularity, heterogeneity, the movement of double affirmation, not to mention in his earlier preoccupations with iteration, trace, and undecidability (1988). He gives the name "violence" a number of catachrestical formulations: *force, discord, dislocation, anthropophagy* are among their more recent incarnations. These terms are not without ambivalence for him insofar as they are both "uncomfortable" and "indispensable" (1990, 929), paradoxically necessary and impossible: they must be thought, but the terms by which they are thought are complex and overdetermined and bind one to what one seeks to overcome or remove.[6]

Derrida poses the question, one of the crucial political questions of our age: "How are we to distinguish between this force of the law . . . and the violence that one always deems unjust? What difference is there between, on the one hand, the force that can be just or in any case deemed legitimate, not only as an instrument in the service of law but the practice and even the realization, the essence of *droit*, and on the other hand the violence that one always deems unjust? What is a just force or a non-violent force?" (1990, 927).

As his ostensive object of investigation, he takes Walter Benjamin's formative paper "The Critique of Violence" (1978) as his object of critical interrogation. He asks, following and problematizing Benjamin, where we can draw the dividing line between legitimized or justified force, and the forces that are either prior to, in excess of, or not obedient to law, legitimation, right, or the proper. Can there be a distinction between a constitutive and inscriptive violence and a gratuitous, excessive violence, between a founding violence and the violence of conservation, between a justifiable violence and one that is not warranted or justified, between a "just" violence and an "unjust" one? And what provides the force of justification that legitimizes one form and not another? How is it legitimated, if it functions as legitimating?

Derrida suggests, contrary to the characterization of deconstruction as apolitical, as neutral, self-preoccupied, or merely formalist and representational in its orientation, that this question of violence and its relation to the law inheres in, is, the very project of deconstruction. It is not a peripheral concern, something that deconstruction could choose to interrogate or not, but is the heart of deconstructive endeavor: the violence of writing, the violence of founding, producing, regulating, administering, judging, or knowing is a violence that both manifests and dissimulates itself. It both relies on and constitutes a space of necessary equivocation. The spaces between this manifestation and dissimulation are the very spaces that make deconstruction both necessary and impossible, the spaces that deconstruction must utilize, not to move outside the law or outside violence (to judge them from outside—which is impossible), but to locate its own investments in both law and violence.[7] Justice, law, and right are those systems, intimately bound up with writing (the law is writing par excellence, and the history of legal institutions is the history of the reading and rewriting of law), not just because the law is written, and must be to have its force, but also because law and justice (we will conflate them only for a moment) serve to order, to divide, to cut: "Justice, as law, is never exercised without a decision that *cuts*, that divides" [963]). This indeed is the very paradox of the law: that while it orders and regulates, while it binds and harmonizes, it must do so only through a cut, a hurt that is no longer, if ever, calculable as violence or a cut. Deconstruction is not the denunciation of the violence of the law but rather a mode of engagement with and participation in this violence, for it exerts its own modes of judgment, its own cuts on its deconstructive objects, including the law, ethics, morality. And it is in turn subject to other deconstructive and iterative maneuvers. That which makes the law both a part of and inherently foreign to violence is what introduces the structure of *undecidability* into the law, and thus into deconstruction itself: "The Undecidable remains caught, lodged, at least as a ghost—but an essential ghost—in every decision, in every event of decision. Its ghostliness deconstructs from within any assurance of presence, any certitude or any supposed criteriology that would assure us of the justice of a decision, in truth of the very event of a decision" (1990, 965).

The undecidable is not a thing, a substance or self-presence that inhabits any situation or judgment, decision, or action; rather it is the very openness and uncertainty, the fragility and force of judgment itself. It is the very equivocation of judgment, the limit of the law's legitimacy or intelligibility, that is the object of deconstructive interrogation. Deconstruction exploits this undecidability as its own milieu, the fertile internal ground on which it sows disseminating germs and uncertainties. It is not simply critique (as Benjamin conceives it) nor is it prophylactic: there is no "remedy" or cure (or at least no cure that isn't also *pharmakon* [1981]) for undecidability. What is marked, or unmarked, through this equivocation is always the field of violence within and through which the trace weaves its dissimulating web.

Undecidability is the hinge that renders Benjamin's clear-cut distinctions between a founding or constitutive and regulative or conserving justice, between mythic, divine, and a mortal justice, no longer tenable and on the continual verge of exchanging places and identities with each other: "The very violence of the foundation or position of law . . . must envelop the violence of conservation . . . and cannot break with it. It belongs to the structure of fundamental violence that it calls for the repetition of itself and founds what ought to be conserved, conservable, promised to heritage and tradition to be shared. . . . Thus there can be no rigorous opposition between positioning and conservation, only what I will call (and Benjamin does not name it) a *différantielle* contamination between the two, with all the paradoxes that this may lead to" (1990, 997).

It is no longer clear (if it ever was) that one can distinguish between a "good" and a "bad" violence, a violence that is necessary and one that is wanton, excessive, and capable in principle of elimination, one justified by virtue of its constructive force and the other condemned as destructive, negative. Which is not at all to say that there is no difference between forms of violence or that we must abandon the right to judge force and violence, whatever force and violence such judgments involve. Quite the contrary, it means that we must hone our intellectual resources much more carefully, making many more distinctions, subtleties, and nuances in our understanding than any binarized or dialectically structured model will allow. We must refuse the knee-jerk reactions of straightforward or outright condemnation before we understand the structure and history of that modality of violence, its modes of strategic functioning, its vulnerabilities and values.

I do not believe that Derrida abandons the moral and ethical dilemmas raised by very concrete and disturbing explosions of violence in the "real world," and indeed, much of his work is occasioned by or is an indirect response to the question: what is an academic, a writer, someone whose profession is with words and concepts, to do? His work sometimes disturbs those concerned by these concrete issues of violence (for example, LaCapra articulates a common fear that, in the abandonment of the right to provide a pure judgment about violence, violence is simply equated with justice and the right to judge, and deconstruction abandons all violences to their own devices),[8] especially because he does not attempt to provide solutions, definite responses, or unequivocal judgments. Is this the abandonment of political judgments, or simply its complexification?

What is it that undecidability changes in our conceptions of law, politics, ethics, and epistemology? Why has this concept exercised such terrifying implications for those concerned with ethical and political values? It is not the claim that political or conceptual events are *ambiguous*, and thus difficult to judge, or that they are so complex as to render judgments simplistic or irrelevant (though these may be true as well). Undecidability is another name for iteration, for différance, for the openness of destination of any articulation, any object, or any event, the propulsion of any "thing" (whether avowedly self-present or not) to a future context or scene where its current meaning, value, and status is reread, rewritten, transmuted. Undecidability is precisely the endless iterability of any articulation, the possibility of endless quotation, recontextualization, repetition in contexts yet unknown, where the most crushing defeat is made into the most complex accomplishment, and may be returned again to defeat. Undecidability dictates that the signification and effect of events or representations can never be self-present insofar as they always remain open to what befalls them, always liable to be placed elsewhere: in other words, it dictates that it is only futurity, itself endlessly extended to infinity, that gives any event its signification, force, or effect. Which has terrifying consequences for those who would like to correct situations or contexts here and now, and once and for all. What the principle of undecidability implies is that the control over either the reception or the effect of events is out of our hands, beyond a certain agentic control. This is what an openness to futurity entails: that things are never given in their finality, whatever those "things" might be. Whatever is made or found, whether it be nature or artifact, must be remade and refound endlessly to have any value: "What threatens the rigor of the distinction between the two types of violence is at bottom the paradox of iterability. Iterability requires the origin to repeat itself so as to have the value of origin, that is, to conserve itself. Right away there are police and the police legislate, not content to enforce a law that would have had no force before the police. The iterability inscribes conservation in the essential structure of foundation. This law or this general necessity is not a modern phenomenon, it has an *a priori* worth. . . . Rigorously speaking, iterability precludes the possibility of pure and general founders, initiators, lawmakers" (1990, 1007–1009).

Iterability, différance, undecidability mean that no founding violence can be contained within the moment of foundation but must endlessly repeat itself to have had any force in the first place; and that any moment of conservation must rely on the repetition of this founding violence to have any force or effect of its own, for it rides on the waves of force that différance initiates. In other words, an origin never could infect an end unless it wasn't simply an origin, and an end is always implicated in the origin that it ends. Violence and force, indeed law and right, function only in the yet-to-come, the *a-venir*. Which is the unforeseeable, the yet-to-come that diverges from the what-is-present. This is what futurity is, and the way in which the implosive effects of the to-come generate both the possibility and the undoing of force. Derrida understands the *avenir* as the domain of the new and of surprise, the very condition of iteration and context: "Paradoxically, it is because of this overflowing of the performative, because of this always excessive haste of interpretation getting ahead of itself, because of this structural urgency and precipitation of justice that the latter has no horizon of expectation (regulative or messianic). But for this very reason, it *may* have an *avenir*, a "to-come," which I rigorously distinguish from the future that can always reproduce the present. Justice remains, is yet, to come, *à venir*, it has an, it is, *à venir*, the very dimension of events irreducibly to come. It will always have it, this *à venir*, and always has" (1990, 969).

There is, in short, no way to decide in advance, through principle or by dint of position, authority, or knowledge, the standard by which to judge violence. As Drucilla Cornell argues, "there can be no projected standards by which to judge *in advance* the acceptability of violent acts" (Cornell 1992, 167). This indeed is the very heart of deconstructive reading: that the status and value of violence—given especially the role of violence in the foundation and maintenance of status and value—is only ever open to a future, and a very particular position within futurity, to decide, which itself is endlessly open to its own modes of futurity, its own disseminating flight to either oblivion (insofar as its force is spent) or its own endless production (insofar as its force remains virulent and mobilized).

THE GIFT OF THE FUTURE

What is the counter to violence? What is the other of violence? Is there another economy, another relation between terms that does not enter into, or at least deflects part of itself outside of and away from the economy of violence? If the law is no longer a barrier that divides violence from civilization, partitioning the violent, the excessive, or gratuitous as either before or outside the law, and thus subject to its judgment, and instead is understood as the space of a regulated violence that refuses to see itself as such or call itself by that name, then is there any space or time outside of or other than its economy of forces? While it is not clear that for Derrida there is a space before or free of this economy of the cut, the tearing separations of the structures of nomination, following Levinas, he seems to suggest an alternative "economy," which exceeds the very notion of economy.[9] It too, like violence, inscription, or writing, goes by many names in Derrida's writings. Among the more resonant of these is the Other, the stranger, the outsider, which he also describes, through readings of Mauss and Benveniste, in terms of the gift, hospitality, donation, generosity, or ethics. These themes are developed in *Glas* (1986), *The Post-Card* (1987), "Psyché: Invention of the Other" (1989), *Given Time I. Counterfeit Money* (1992), *The Gift of Death* (1995), *Adieu: To Emmanuel Levinas* (1999), and *Of Hospitality* (2000), among other texts.

The gift is both a part of and in some sense always beyond the economy of exchange, that economy that measures, regulates, calculates only through a kind of primary violence. The gift, and the modes of hospitality it entails, is an impossible (yet imperative) relation in which what is given cannot be what it is: the gift can only function in not being a gift. The moment an impulse to reciprocity or exchange is set up (one gift for another), the gift ceases to be a gift and becomes an object in a system of barter or exchange. To function as gift, it must be given without return, without obligation, without expectation, given "freely"; moreover, it must be taken, received without debt, without the need to return or the requirement of repayment, a pure excess, without accumulation. The gift thus cannot be anything that presents itself as gift, anything that is sent or received with a debt or the (implicit) structure of return. The gift cannot be received as such, for if it is, it is marked by debt, it is annulled as gift and reconstituted as loan: but if the gift as such cannot be given, neither can the gift be refused. For the gift is both superfluity and poison.[10] It must be given, but not in excess (for to give in excess is to reinstate the structure of reciprocity), nor in the hope of return or obligation.

The gift in this sense is outside the law, beyond calculation. But not outside of them altogether. For the gift must not only be given and received while its objectness is annulled, it must also be given *responsibly*, according to a logic of temporization, that is, according to some principle of timeliness.[11]

The gift, as Derrida says, gives time. It does not give itself, an object, the given, to be possessed or consumed: it gives temporality, delay, a timeliness without calculation. This is the very time needed for the time of judgment, the ideal of the law itself: the gift gives a possible future, a temporality in excess of the present and never contained within its horizon, the temporality of endless iteration, opening up the future:

> The gift is not a gift, the gift only gives to the extent it *gives time*. The difference between a gift and every other operation of pure and simple exchange is that the gift gives time. *There where there is gift, there is time.* What it gives, the gift, is time, but this gift of time is also a domain of time. The thing must not be restituted *immediately and right away*. There must be time, it must last, there must be waiting—without forgetting. It demands time, the thing, but it demands a delimited time, neither an instant nor an infinite time, but time determined by a term, in other words, a rhythm, a rhythm that does not befall a homogeneous time but that structures it originarily. (1992, 41)

The gift gives time not because it is placed in a structure of preexisting temporization, the rhythms and cadences of economic exchange where each loan has deadlines, due dates, the internal expectation of return; rather, it is the object, *the given* that carries with it a force, an impetus of donation, pure expenditure, of endless possibilities of variation:

> The requirement of circulatory *différance* is *inscribed in the thing itself* that is given or exchanged. Before it is a contract, an intentional gesture of individual or collective subjects, the movement of gift/countergift is a *force* (a "virtue of the thing given," says Mauss), a property immanent of the thing or in any way apprehended as such by the donors and donees. Moved by a mysterious force, the thing itself demands gift *and* restitution, it requires therefore "time," "term," "delay," "interval" of temporization, the becoming-temporalization of temporalization, the animation of a neutral and homogeneous time by the desire of the gift and the restitution. Différance which (is) nothing, is (in) the thing itself. It is (given) in the thing itself. It (is) the thing itself. It, différance, the thing (itself). It, without, anything other. Itself, nothing. (1992, 40)

The thing, like the other, is pure exteriority, with its own order, priority, time, and rhythm. Our encounters with it are in part their force or impetus upon us, and in part the force of our inscriptions of them. The problem is that it is undecidable which is which, where one crosses the other and feeds off it. The thing, whether it is the gift of language, the gift of law, the gift of life, or an object, is given as such: the gift to be received must be accepted in its singularity and specificity before it is codified, submitted to economic value, and integrated into the circuits of exchange. It gives itself up to be in some sense returned as itself.

Is it then that justice, a justice beyond the legalism and formalism of the law, moves beyond the field of violence to the structure, the non-economy, the pure excess of the gift? Does the idea or ideal of justice, a justice not given in full presence from God or derived from the Law, provide another "logic," "order," or "system" outside that of calculation, economy, derivation? Is this another way of asking: Is there, beyond violence, a way to love, that is, to give without fear of expending and to take without fear of vulnerability?

> The deconstruction of all presumption of a determinant certitude of a present justice itself operates on the basis of an "infinite justice," infinite because it is irreducible, irreducible because it is owed to the other, before any contract, because it has come, the other's coming as the singularity that is always other. This "idea of justice" seems to me to be irreducible in its affirmative character, in its domain of gift without exchange, without circulation, without recognition or gratitude, without economic circularity, without calculation and without rules, without reason and without rationality. And so we can recognize in it, indeed accuse, identify a madness. . . . And deconstruction is mad about this kind of justice. Mad about this desire for justice. This kind of justice which isn't law, is the very movement of deconstruction at work in law and the history of law, in political history and history itself, before it even presents itself as the discourse that the academy or modern culture labels "deconstructionism." (1990, 965)

The gift is not outside the economy and expenditure that is the regulated violence of the law but operates entwined with and sometimes indistinguishable from it. In this sense, law can be given and received only as gift. But beyond law, where there is "ideal justice," in the indeterminable future, the structure of the gift can function in a different way, not as other than or in a different sphere from violence. Violence gives time: it generates, proliferates, differentiates, and specializes violence to come: but equally, violence itself may follow from and be the response to an incapacity to adequately accept the gift, to receive and also to refuse it as debt.

Irigaray makes it a founding principle of her feminism that the child's, and particularly the male child's, inability to acknowledge or repay the gift of his own birth, the gift of language, bodily existence, nurturance—the gift of body and all its capacities, including conceptual—that he owes to the maternal body is this unrepayable burden of obligation that is repressed and covered over through phallic privilege and left unrepresented in patriarchal representational systems. While Levinas's understanding of an ethical relation to the other, a relation which adequately accepts and acknowledges the gifts of the other, is central to her concerns (especially in *An Ethics of Sexual Difference*), Irigaray makes it quite clear that as long as women, and especially mothers, continue to bear the weight of this structure of giving, the violence directed to women will continue.[12] While the gift of life and body cannot be received as a gift, it is converted into a debt that cannot be repaid, that cannot even be acknowledged; social, political, and cultural life bears the (violent) traces of this covering over of the gift in both the exclusion of women from active definition and direction over social, political, and cultural life (accomplished through women's "confinement" to the maternal and domestic function) and the violence of the denial of violence that marks civil society while rendering it unable to understand itself.

What violence generates, what the gift proliferates, is the time of the future, an opening of time. In the one case, violence generates other (sometimes enabling, sometimes futile) violences, violences that reinscribe the violence of founding and constituting in other terms, with other values, which are themselves infinitely capable of being reinscribed; in the other case, the gift generates the forward echo, the rhythmic pacing of a time to come in which the gift can be received as such, accepted as pure gift. Violence, force, disseminates itself into the futurity of the gift, of given time, as its mode of excessive production. It is time itself, only the future, the time to come, *avenir*, that the gift gives, that makes judgment possible (if always provisional), and that converts force into production. The what-is-to-come disseminates with its own force what the gift is. This is a double gift, a double affirmation.

CHAPTER 5

Drucilla Cornell, Identity, and

the "Evolution" of Politics

What is needful is a new <u>justice</u>! And a new watchword. And new philosophers. The moral earth, too, is round. The moral earth, too, has its antipodes. The antipodes, too, have the right to exist. There is yet another world to be discovered—and more than one. Embark, philosophers!
—Friedrich Nietzsche, *The Gay Science*

I cannot hope to do justice to Drucilla Cornell's work in its richness and breadth. Her theoretical interests are vast and encompass, among other terrains, legal studies, feminist theory, cultural and literary studies, political theory, and psychoanalysis. They range from the most abstract heights of the dialectic and the most intricate deconstructive maneuvers, to the most pressing social issues of the present: abortion, pornography, sexual harassment, homophobia, racism, violence, multiculturalism, and globalization. With great bravery and foresight, she has been almost singular in forcing social and legal theory to come to grips with the intellectual and political rigor of deconstruction, or, in her terminology, the "philosophy of the limit," and in turn, forcing deconstruction to answer to these pressing empirical questions and concerns. Instead of dealing with all of these questions—or really any of them directly—I want to look instead at an oblique strand that runs through her work, one that touches on many of these concerns without focusing on them directly.

Cornell puts the question of time and the future, if not at the center of her work, then at least at a strategically off-center position in her writings and in her vision of feminist ethics and politics, in a place where its sheen reflects on and radiates from all the questions she raises. The question of time, of past, present, and future, and their relations to identity, value, and social position, are explicit objects of speculation and reflection in all of her writings, even if they are not her major preoccupations. She is one of the very few feminist theorists to see the future neither as irrelevant nor as directly manipulable, neither as the realization of current wishes or fears (that is, as simply a projection of the present), nor as simply speculative, utopian, impossible. The future — that field to which all of ethics and politics is directed insofar as they are attempts at amelioration of the past and present — is the condition and very mode of present political, ethical, and legal action and effectivity. Cornell has done feminism an immense service by drawing attention, once again and in a radically different manner, to the dimension of time or duration, and the privilege that any politics or ethics, any position that aims to improve the present, must grant to futurity.

While the question of futurity is one of the essential ingredients of any account of politics or ethics, or for that matter any account of being, subjectivity, matter, or identity, it is remarkable how few feminists have tackled it directly. I am not thinking here of a vast series of feminist fictional works, especially works in feminist sci-fi, which predict or project a possible future: as interesting and important as these may be, they still do not raise the more philosophically and politically oriented questions about how to view the link between the present and the future, how to produce rather than imagine a future radically different from a given past and present. They produce the future as a picture or projection, an extrapolation or reversal of the present. While Cornell's work is not a detailed and sustained analysis of temporality and duration, it nonetheless contains hints and clues about a more productive way of understanding futurity and temporality than that usually assumed in feminist, literary, or philosophical theory. This orientation to the question of the yet-to-come, of what is not yet in being, has always attracted me to her work, which, for this reason, among others, is a philosophy of hope, of activity and of agency (agency, though, in a restricted sense, where it can be understood as precisely the capacity to make the future diverge from the patterns and causes of the present rather than as an inherent quality of freedom or the availability of unconstrained possibilities). Hers is a politics that envisions the capacity for transformation inherent in any ordered system, the system itself being unable to contain its own becomings and thus open to potentially endless variation.

TIME AND AGAIN

There are generally two broad ways in which time and futurity are conceived in feminist theory. I would describe the first as extrapolative: it commonly involves drawing out the implications and effects of current trends, predictions, the projected movement of present impulses. This mode is more crucial in some areas than in others (e.g., in studies of economic development, in epidemiology, in public policy and planning, and so on). It is interested in developing procedures that extrapolate from present trends, through magnification, intensification, or specialization, into the future. Most attempts to theorize or project equal rights, or to consider economic development (e.g., Iris Marion Young, Martha Nussbaum) exemplify at least elements of this tendency. The second broad trend is considerably less scientific and more imaginative in its approach. It is more closely associated with literature and the arts than with science or politics: I would describe it primarily as utopian. This involves the imaginative production of other worlds, fictional, cinematic, or cybernetic, which dramatically change certain elements of our experience and our understanding of our world. These imaginative projections are the production of what I understand to be utopian visions, visions of ideal or horrifying futures, narratives of fanciful desire.[1]

What is exciting about Cornell's work is that she thinks the question of time and futurity—or rather, the question of becoming—outside these parameters, not in ignorance of these two trends, but working beyond them and in recognition of their limitations, for ironically, neither is a way of politicizing the present by showing an alternative future, outside the orbit of the present rather than already contained within it. Her project implicitly, and at some moments explicitly, addresses the question of temporal unfolding, becoming, as its underlying logic: if the feminine is all that our culture in its patriarchal weight defines it to be, if the feminine is reduced to and identified with only a degraded and secondary version of masculinity, then feminism is ethically and politically impelled to ensure that the future does *not* resemble the past, and that the feminine "within sexual difference," a future feminine, is different from and quite other than the feminine that is defined by the masculine today as its counterpart or other. Feminist ethics and politics is inevitably propelled toward not just rectifying the wrongs done to women, but to expanding and transforming the horizons available for their self-representations, which in her own terms Cornell describes as the "imaginary domain," the domain not simply of imagination, but also the space of virtuality, of what is new and not yet actualized. This "space" of the virtual, which we need also to regard as the *time* of the "imaginary domain," the domain of what is to come, is precisely the time of wonder Irigaray speculates may come into being when it is recognized that there are (at least) two sexes, two kinds of experience, two modes of morphology, two kinds of subject.[2] This is the time of the future perfect, the future anterior, the time in which the future can look at this present as its superseded past.

Cornell raises the question of time and futurity in numerous places, from her earlier works, such as *Beyond Accommodation* (1991) and *The Philosophy of the Limit* (1992) to her more recent *The Imaginary Domain* (1995) and other co-authored works,[3] though only ever fragmentarily and indirectly. The first mention of the question of the "beyond" of the present, the excess left over in the present which enables it to generate a future unforeseen by it, occurs, not altogether surprisingly, in one of her first references to Irigaray: "The 'female blossoming that keeps open the future of sexual difference,' and at the same time allows us to judge the past as the 'silence of female history' in which our suffering was inexpressible, is dependent upon the affirmation of the specificity of the feminine as *difference* beyond the established system of gender identity (and more generally any pregiven identity). If the feminine is repudiated . . . we will be left in the masculine arena in which the old games of domination are played out. There will only be repetition, no re-evolution to the future. Irigaray is ultimately a thinker of change" (Cornell 1991, 9).

Irigaray is primarily a thinker of change: she addresses what it is to think change, to think differently, in terms that will accommodate not just otherness, but the kind of otherness that is beyond the limit, outside the definition and control of the self-same and the self-identical. This question articulates Cornell's project as much as, and in accordance with, Irigaray's, and separates them from most other feminist thinkers.[4] Cornell refers to an "unerasable trace of utopianism" (1991, 107) in all ethical and political thought, the ways in which it is crucial that thought (ethics and politics are always implicated in thought as well as, and as much as, in practice) is always a mode of *inadequation* of the real, a mode of inducing a more-than-the-real, which I understand in terms of the virtuality of the real, its latencies, its impetus to something other and more. Cornell, like Irigaray, is advocating the necessity for there to be an outside to any and every system, a locus of excess, which contains the seeds of something other or beyond the present:

> I am aware how difficult it is to understand this "unerasable" trace of utopi-
> anism. But this is why I refer to this moment . . . as endlessly "there." It is

not a chronological *moment* to be surpassed, which is why I refer to it as unerasable utopianism. Nor is it a projection of utopia: "this is what it would be like," our dream world. This trace of utopianism that cannot be wiped out can be summarized as follows. The "subject" is never just the hostage of its surroundings, because these surroundings cannot be consolidated into an unshakable reality that defines us and by so doing necessarily limits possibility to the evolution of what already "is." (1991, 107)

Cornell suggests here, as elsewhere, that the subject is always more than its social constitution, in excess of "ideology," "training," "expectation," an excess that is not just material or spatial but also necessarily temporal. She has recognized, as few others have, that this is the very condition of feminism itself: that beyond highlighting the wrongs done to women, beyond the account of women as the victims of patriarchal oppression, that very oppression also contains within it the virtual conditions of feminism and the openness of a future beyond present constraints.

In her earlier writings, Cornell attributes this position to Derrida and to deconstruction: as Derrida himself has always insisted, deconstruction, as the analysis of *difference*, is the unraveling of presence in the light of the processes of spatialization and temporization that make it possible yet which it covers over.[5] As Cornell claims, "We must look more closely at the play of *différance* as it relates to temporalization and to Derrida's unique conception of the future as the not yet of the never has been. *Différance* can be understood as the 'truth' that 'being' is presented in time, and, therefore, there can be no all-encompassing ontology of the 'here' and 'now' " (1991, 108).

The future must be understood not as the preordained, or as the constrained. In order for there to be politics and ethics now, in order for there to be history and reflection on the past, the future must be open and uncontained by the past and present, even though it is conditioned by them. This is not simply temporization, the putting of matter and events into a time line or chronology, the construction of a linear history or genealogy, but is rather the abandonment of the force of the present, whether in the givenness of the past or the self-evidence, the actuality, of the present. Which is not, as Cornell and Derrida recognize, an abandonment of responsibility but its most bitter irony: we must act in the present, with the light the past sheds on that present, but we must, by virtue of the difference that inhabits the present, cede any control of our present act to a future that we cannot foresee or understand. This is what dissemination is, the failure of definitive destination, the openness of any thing (whether it be a text, an event, a subject, a particle) to what befalls it, or more precisely, to what will have befallen it. This is the very heart of politics, and is the direct implication of Derrida's understanding of iteration, as we saw in the last chapter. It is a direct consequence of the kinds of antihumanism to which both Cornell and Derrida are committed: we must act, but have no direct control over the ramifications of our acts, which makes us, ironically, more rather than less responsible for them.

Politics requires that relations between the past, present, and future be rethought so that the conventions accumulated through the past can be re-figured, rearticulated, redone. Politics is the opening up of norms to the subversions that are already virtual within them: "Such a project demands the rethinking of the relationship between the *past*, embodied in the norma-tive conventions which are passed down through legal precedent, and the projection of *future* ideals through which the community seeks to regulate itself" (1993, 23).

Cornell understands that without some nonenvisionable future (rather than, as most political theory has it, without a definite or positive plan for improvement), the present could never be as such, and politics could not exist except as some fantasmatic consolation. She tends, in some texts, to see this in terms of the redemptive possibilities a notion of the future en-tails (this redemptive model, I believe, ties her work more closely to what I have described as a utopian feminist position, though she herself may not altogether object to this categorization):

> Once we understand the relationship between myth and allegory in ac-counts of the feminine, we can also unfold the role of the utopian, or re-demptive perspective of the "not yet." This perspective exposes our current system of gender representation as "fallen." Within feminist theory, femi-nine sexual difference has often stood in as the figure that gives body to redemptive perspectives. How should we hope to become? Where do we find the new economy of desire? . . . Ethical feminism explicitly recognizes the "should be" in representations of the feminine. . . . [E]thical feminism rests its claim for . . . intelligibility and coherence . . . not on what women "are" but on the remembrance of the "not yet." (1993, 145)

Instead of focusing only on the present, which gives us women and re-lations between the sexes only under the order of masculine domination, we need to look more carefully at the *virtuality* laden within the present, its possibilities for being otherwise, in other words, the unactualized latencies in any situation which could be, may have been, instrumental in the generation of the new or the unforeseen. This is the very condition of feminism, or any radical politics, any politics that seeks transformation, what Cornell calls the "not yet," or Irigaray might call "what will have been."

WHAT'S EVOLUTION GOT TO DO WITH IT?

Cornell is one of a few feminists to be actively interested in the philosophy of temporality and in the issues of active becoming it raises. But her understanding of futurity and becoming are closely tied to, and in many ways symptomatic of, a series of other issues she deals with, or attempts to avoid, which mitigate and problematize not only her understanding of futurity but also her conceptions of politics and ethics. I am thinking here primarily of Cornell's resistance to questions of biology, nature, and matter in favor of questions of culture, subjectivity, and desire. She very carefully observes the more conventional dividing lines feminists have drawn between oppositional categories, taking them to the "limit," perhaps, but always accepting that there is in fact a line of demarcation. In particular, the oppositions between nature and culture, and the body and the psyche, still remain aligned in her work. She carefully avoids discussion of the biological, the natural, and the real as if they in some way detract from or mitigate the cultural and political issues at hand.

There are numerous places where Cornell states that her interest is specifically *not* about biology, anatomy, or body parts, not about matter, nature, or the real. She focuses, for example, on sex "not as biological body parts, but as sexuality" (1992, 5). She argues that Lacan's work is crucial precisely because it is not the result of biology or the real but in divergence from it: "Lacan helps us to understand why this recognition [of castration] is not the result of biology but of the symbolic order" (1992, 137). Lacan is the psychoanalyst of choice because he distinguishes the penis from the phallus, the biological from the symbolic. Indeed, the politics of feminism itself, she wants to believe, is not or should not be directed to biological questions but only to questions of the symbolic, which to some extent at least means *representations* of biology rather than biology itself: "I am using flesh as a metaphor, not as a literal description of the body. . . . Flesh is the metaphor of psychicality that can never be fully articulated. There is no body that is just there" (1992, 145).

In this relegation of biology, matter, and the real to a never possible, ever

receding background upon which "originary" writing takes place, Cornell
joins Judith Butler and an entire tradition of "postmodern," "constructivist,"
or "performative" feminism in devaluing matter, or in transforming it from
noun ("matter") to verb ("mattering") and in the process desubstantializ-
ing it. For Cornell, as for Butler, the body itself dissolves, the real always
displaces itself by being written on, and matter disappears in the process of
mattering, of being valued: "To [find a way to resymbolize feminine sexual
difference], we first need an account of how bodies come to matter. As Judith
Butler shows us, the word 'matter' has a double meaning. Bodies matter,
that is, they materialize and take on reality while also carrying an implicit
normative assessment. Bodies matter, in other words, through a process by
which they come to have both symbolic and ethical significance" (1995, 34).

Following Butler here, Cornell claims a double meaning for matter:
materializing and mattering (i.e., having value). But ironically, both elide
matter itself. To understand matter as "materializing" implies a process of
putting into materiality that elides or denies that matter is itself what enables
materialization (one cannot materialize what is always already material);
and matter itself is what enables those valuations that are designated as mattering (mattering is a process of privileging one mode of materiality over
another). What slips out, what disappears, is stuff, the real, biology, nature,
matter, which are thus relegated either to Kantian noumena or to Lacanian
passivity.[6] Butler is concerned with the important question of value: what
counts as a body, as a subject, as a being; what is included (what "matters")
in social categories or what is excluded, abjected, as intolerable (or "does not
matter"). But these issues of value and valuation, of mattering, are in fact
never independent or capable of effectivity except insofar as they are lived
through bodies, in biologies, in and as the real. The process of mattering
cannot be cut off from what matter it is. Cornell follows Butler in claiming
that it is the counting, the mattering, of bodies, of anatomies, and of sexual
differences that is at stake in feminism, without acknowledging that the very
mark of being counted, of mattering, can be accomplished only through
matter, in this case, biological or organic matter. Matter is both presupposed
by and inexplicable for the kinds of culturally and psychically—i.e., sym-
bolically—oriented feminist projects undertaken by Cornell and Butler and
the entire field of feminist social constructionism.[7] My claim, by contrast, is
that if becoming, difference, and iteration are what make the self-identity
of the subject and of culture impossible, so too, they immensely complicate
and render self-identity problematic in the arena of nature, and materiality,

as well. The biological, the natural, and the material remain active and crucial political ingredients precisely because they too, and not culture alone, are continually subjected to transformation, to becoming, to unfolding over time. Moreover, ethics would itself dictate that the natural be owed the debt of culture's emergence, insofar as it is precisely the open-ended incompletion of nature itself that induces the cultural as its complexification and supplement. This is not the end or the supersession of the natural but its ever-transforming self-representation. In this sense, culture is the self-image of nature; nature is not, as cultural theory argues, the fantasmatic projection of culture.

It is this refusal to accord the natural, the biological, or the anatomical any role, even that of raw material, in understandings of the cultural, the symbolic, and the subjective that lies behind Cornell's insistent, if sometimes haphazard, division of a culturally conceived futurity, understood as "transformation" from a naturally bound and thus inherently limited futurity, that of "evolution." Although this distinction is made only in passing, it is made frequently enough (although with frustrating brevity) to allow us to believe that it is an ongoing commitment in her work. I believe that it is symptomatic of a common, near pervasive feminist refusal to attribute becoming to the domain of the natural that ties us firmly back into an unproductive natural/cultural opposition that is particularly crucial for feminist theory to challenge.

For example, Cornell begins *Transformations* (1993) by suggesting a crucial "difference that makes a difference," a difference between "transformation" and "change reduced to evolution." She understands transformation as the capacity of a system to "so alter itself that it no longer confirms its identity, but disconfirms it, and through its iterability, generates new meanings which can be further pursued and enhanced by the sociosymbolic practice of the political contestants within its milieu" (1993, 2), in other words, the capacity of a system to be contested in the future, to be different from what it is now. This is sharply contrasted with "change reduced to evolution" (1993, 2). She articulates this claim in *The Philosophy of the Limit*: "The deconstructibility of law is . . . exactly what allows for the possibility of transformation, not just the evolution of the legal system" (1992, 166). It is clear that the one side of this opposite — transformation — is privileged at the expense of the other — evolution. Not only does transformation become a methodological label for all of Cornell's work, it becomes the very title of one of her books: transformation is to culture what evolution is to nature. Or rather, with more complexity, transformation is an open-endedness of the future while evolution is construed—or rather, misconstrued—as predelimited, contained, bound to the system and its confirmation.

Cornell tends to identify autogenic or self-replicating systems, systems that exhibit emergence rather than supervening order, erroneously with determined or constrained systems, systems that function within the web of the deterministic causal chains. She tends to see nature itself, though it is rarely spoken of as such, as a self-enclosed system which, while not entirely irrelevant to cultural activity, is nonetheless entirely dispensable for understanding cultural activity. Nature functions in an enclosed net of determinations which necessarily hold the future to the terms that govern the past and the present. It requires description rather than imagination; it is mired in fact rather than in possibilities. Identifying systematicity, the systematicity of natural systems perhaps, with some of the writings of Niklas Luhmann, Cornell relegates any notion of self-enclosure to an impossible quest for presence.

Yet ironically, it is precisely the self-organization of natural systems, and particularly evolutionary systems—that is, biological systems—that perhaps best exemplifies Derridean différance in terms of their refusal to be contained as systems within the parameters and constraints that dictate their "normal" regulation. Derrida himself seems to recognize this more readily than Cornell. Evolution offers precisely the openness to contingency and to futurity that Cornell seeks in the legal system. My point here is not to correct Cornell over her misunderstanding of the concept of evolution, but to make clear that unless the same generative productivity is granted to the natural and the biological as to the cultural and the symbolic, we will have no understanding of the impetus or force of the cultural itself, nor will we understand the debt and the relation of responsibility that the cultural owes to the natural, the psychical owes to the biological, the phallus owes to the penis, the subject owes to materiality. Moreover, we will not have heeded Derrida's own understanding of the inherent seepage of oppositional pairs, the co-infection of each with the other, which is as relevant for the nature/culture opposition as it is for any other oppositional forms. Unless the active, différantial force of the biological and the natural is understood, we risk precisely what Cornell warns us against when analyzing the work of Catherine MacKinnon—that is, we reduce the subject entirely to culture, entirely to writing, and in the process efface the very matter of *resistance*, the locus of change and of transformation.

THE TIME OF THE OTHER

Cornell explicitly links the question of otherness, including the relations of sexual difference, to questions of violence and temporality. Justice is tied to the call of the other and the possible honoring of the call, a call that in a sense can never be honored, can never be adequately answered but which the subject must in any case address. This is not the striving for a Kantian ideal, but the gesture toward the satisfaction of the most intimate and concrete needs that the most concrete other calls forth from us. Justice is never given in the here and now; justice never exists in full presence but is the horizon of the yet-to-be, the future. Among Cornell's most subtle insights is her understanding, not of the impossibility of the call to justice, but of its temporal suspension. Justice demands, requires what is yet-to-come.

Cornell quotes Derrida: "There is an *avenir* for justice and there is no justice except to the degree that some event is possible which, as event exceeds calculation, rules, programs, anticipations and so forth. Justice as the experience of absolute alterity is unrepresentable, but it is the chance of the event and the condition of history" (quoted in Cornell 1991, 112).

For Cornell as for Derrida, then, justice is tied to what is not yet, what has never been but what can be, and is already being generated from the present, from the impossibility of the self-presence of the present, from the simultaneously impossible and necessary *self-replication, iteration*, and *failure* of repetition that generates the new from the latencies or virtualities of the (impossibly) present. This is a key concept in refiguring politics — which has tended to be about "calculations, rules, programs, anticipations" — for it shows the element of the accidental, of chance, of the singularity of events, in short the movement of open-endedness or indetermination — "evolution." Not an evolution in Cornell's sense of constrained, systemically dictated, regulated, ordered, contained change, but precisely the unexpected, the contingent, and the random, open-ended change. The movement of dissemination, as a movement of transformation, is precisely evolutionary becoming: a species' fitness is measured not simply by its success in a given milieu, but by its openness to upheavals in milieu, its openness to the new and the surprising. Evolution is the movement *beyond* a given situation or determination, the playing out of the excess contained within but undeveloped by its present situation or determination. It is perhaps another name for deconstruction itself.

Cornell's understanding of the complex interplay between law and justice, which is itself a balancing act between convention and precedent, between the concerns of a memorialized past and the interests of a not-yet-existent future, between the established interpretations of law and its most extreme innovations, poses precisely this movement of the opening out of being to becoming that Darwin and Bergson understood as evolution. She argues that law cannot be, and never has been, invested in simply applying technical rules in mechanical fashion, and even if it could do so (which seems hardly possible given the ever increasing subtlety of what counts as crime) this would not be justice: "Law . . . cannot be reduced to a self-generated and self-validating set of *cognitive* norms. Interpretation always takes us beyond a mere appeal to the status quo" (1992, 102). Cornell insists that justice is the call to remember and honor a past by making it open into a future that the past alone cannot call forth:

> The Good, as it is interpreted as the yet unrealized potential of the *nomos*, is never simply the mere repetition of conventional norms, because there can be no mere repetition. In this sense, the Good . . . cannot be conceived as the truth of a self-enclosed system which perpetuates itself. The dissemination of convention as a self-enclosed legal system does not leave us with a fundamental lack, but with an opening. . . . As a result, when we appeal "back" to what has been established, we must *look* forward to what "might be."
>
> Thus the deconstructive emphasis on the opening of the ethical self-transcendence of any system that exposes the threshold of the "beyond" of the not yet is crucial to a conception of legal interpretation that argues that the "is" of Law can never be completely separated from the elaboration of the "should be" dependent on an appeal to the Good. (1992, 110–111)

The time of the other, the time of justice, is the time of the future. Not a future that we can imagine from the standpoint of the present, but a future which is contained in but unconstrained by the present as its unactualized virtualities. The "beyond" that is such a crucial element in Cornell's work is neither redemptive nor utopian, though it contains elements of both. It is the very condition of the present, as well as the undoing of self-presence. This mode of self-undoing, of going beyond, is not just the condition of the legal system, or of cultural, political, and ethical relations more generally, but is the very condition of life itself. Life itself is precisely an incessant teaming, an ongoing movement to be more, to be other, to be beyond what is. This is precisely why the model of evolution is no mere metaphor of the social order but is its condition, and moreover, the very condition of ethics, politics, and justice: we are impelled, whether we choose it or not, to move forward, to innovate in the semblance of repetition, to generate the new.

THE FUTURE OF THE SUBJECT

In her more recent writings, Cornell has addressed the question of the fluidity of the subject and its openness to the future through the imaginative identifications available to it which may enable it to bypass the impacts of phallocentrism, racism, and the imperative to a broadly interchangeable uniformity generated by the forces of globalization. This is the focus of her jointly authored article with Sara Murphy, "Anti-Racism, Multiculturalism, and the Ethics of Identification" (2002).

The central argument of the essay, put crudely and simply, is that the politics of recognition, which the authors identify with seeking the "equal dignity of all peoples" (2002, 2) from the state and its instrumentalities, need not be tied to any authentic or given identity, but must be bestowed on strategic or provisional identities and identifications — not just to those with a clear-cut and recognizable history, language, or geography, but those whose identifications are in the process of being formed or changing, which direct themselves to the possibilities the present holds for the future. In short, their aim is to "disconnect the claim to 'authenticity' of identity from the demand for recognition" (2002, 420). Rather than tying recognition to a stable, "authorized," historically structured location or position, new, incipient "identities," authentic or self-consciously constructed, historically laden or recently acquired, also require the authorization of social recognition. This recognition, at least ideally, should not be a repressive or patronizing tolerance, nor should it be a mode of adjudication of the authenticity and validity of any particular identity; rather, it should affirm "as a demand of right to the state . . . under the rubric of freedom and the recognition of equal dignity" (2002, 422), the universal and reciprocally defining identification of the other as subject. Cornell and Murphy claim that such identities may be produced through those acts of self-cultivation and cultivation of collective imagination that constitute cultural life. These identities need not be bound up with bodily, geographical, historical, ethnic, and collective verities, with materialities of various kinds; what is as significant are the modes and specific forms of identification that the subject undertakes.

While the authors affirm the value of self-representation and self-definition in the constitution of one's social (and biological) identity, understood as a process of moving beyond pregiven identities and cultural stereotypes, producing new identities through new identifications and new cultural imaginings, they nevertheless accept that there are limits to the type and form of identification possible—at least for those in dominant positions, limits, ironically, directly connected to the social significance of biological characteristics. Although Cornell, in consistency with her earlier writings, wants to free the subject from the apparent fixity that is contained in and as its biology, she nevertheless wants to leave open the possibilities of extending biological and other material categories according to the options culturally open to distinct subjects:

> [There] is indeed an ethics, both as a practice of self-responsibility and as an encounter with how we come to articulate who we are through our identifications which take us beyond ourselves as individuals precisely because we can never be completely in control of the social and symbolic meanings of racial and ethnic categories.
>
> Therefore, there is a sense in which we can be called to identify, as we both feel called to do, as white and Anglo because these categories continue to not only represent privilege but to enforce it. To deny that we are part of the privileged group, then, is not only false; it is, more importantly to us, unethical. The fluidity of categories of race and ethnic identity in no way takes away from the social reality that ethically demands that we confront the meanings of our own identifications. (2002, 435–436)

There are "social realities" which "fluid identifications" must nevertheless acknowledge as an ethical imperative, at least insofar as these social realities constitute one as a member of a socially dominant group. So, although there are, as it were, limits to what one can affirm as one's identity ("like it or not we are white and Anglo because we are inevitably shaped by how we are seen"), there are no such limits on imaginative identifications—identifications with racialized, minoritarian cultural phenomena—even if not with minoritarian identities. We are free to "reform our identifications" within parameters, those which "we must also be ethically called upon to recognize as we try to articulate who we are" (2002, 437).[8]

Cornell and Murphy seek a certain kind of identity—no longer a fixed, pregiven or stereotyped identity, but one that the subject has a degree of freedom to reformulate, to reconceive, through imaginative identifications. There are, however, two sets of constraints, two unrecognized limits to these identifications, one coming from without and the other from within the subject. From without, the subject is constrained by the structure of recognition which requires the acknowledgment of value and worth—even dignity—

from the other, or at least the Other, the social order; and from within, the subject is constrained by the history of its own structures of identification, and its capacity to have an imaginative breadth in its relations to new identificatory objects.

Clustered together in Cornell and Murphy's argument is a complex of terms: *recognition / identification / subject-formation*. These terms have a long and illustrious history, as the authors acknowledge, which can be marked or dated within a quite powerful philosophical tradition starting with Hegel's *Phenomenology of Mind* and structuring the phenomenological reflections of Husserl and Heidegger, Kojève, the existentialists like Camus, Sartre, and de Beauvoir, through to the Hegelian inflection of psychoanalysis provided by Lacan, and on to the structuralist and poststructuralist versions of feminist, class, and minority identity discourses. The model of a subject produced through identification and recognition seems pervasive in the contemporary discourses of class, race, and gender primarily because these political traditions carry with them an often unacknowledged debt to Hegelianism.[9] Cornell and Murphy's project needs to be located within this framework in which the subject can become a subject as such only through being recognized by another (individual or collective) subject as a subject. This Hegelian "law of desire" informs and underlies most of what today is called identity politics: identity is not something inherent, given, or internally developed, a property of a self, but is bestowed by an other, and only an other, and thus can also be taken away by an other. Identity is rendered precarious, intangible, elusively under the other's control. The powers and dangers posed by this other, who can bestow or destroy the subject's self-identification, are enormous: there is no subject without another subject with whom to identify and who in turn can threaten the (psychical or physical) annihilation of the subject. Identity comes only as a result of a dual motion of the internalization, an introjection of otherness, and the projection onto the other of some fundamental similarity or identification with the subject. Two beings must encounter each other in their alienness for either to have an identity of its own. Hegel's paradox is that the autonomy and identity of the subject comes only at the cost of the subject's indebtedness to the alien other whom he presumes and makes his counterpart, an other for and of him.

In other words, Cornell and Murphy, as is common in much contemporary feminist, postcolonial, and antiracist theory, have wedded together a Hegelian understanding of the subject's identification/projection structure of recognition and a psychoanalytically modeled understanding of the subject as a creature of internalization, the introjective processes of taking in the other's representations of the subject as part of the subject's identity and the corresponding processes of projecting outward its own identificatory needs onto the other. In this indebtedness to Hegelianism, Cornell and Murphy share with Seyla Benhabib, Wendy Brown, Judith Butler, Nancy Fraser, and many—perhaps most—other feminist, queer, and antiracist theorists a fundamental reliance on the structures of recognition and identification which inscribe the other onto and as the subject, and the subject as the other's counterpart.[10]

Pervasive as this tradition of phenomenology has been—and it has been disproportionately influential in accounts of sexed and raced forms of subjectivity from de Beauvoir and Fanon onward—it has become the dominant and almost uncontested discourse of minority cultures by being brought together with a psychoanalytic understanding of the ego and ego-ideal as the media through which the subject is "interpellated," constituted, or comes to find itself.[11] This Hegelian strand of Cornell and Murphy's argument, that strand which underlies *all discourses* on identity that require the other's tacit implication in the subject's formation, needs to be counterbalanced with an alternative tradition, one with a considerably shorter history, and much less influence on contemporary politics, which can be dated from the Nietzschean rewriting of the Hegelian dialectic as the servile rationalizations of the slave and the herd, rather than as the movement of an enlightening "spirit" to its own self-fruition. Nietzsche offers an entirely alien framework to that posited by the Hegelians, Marxists, and phenomenologists: instead of identity, Nietzsche seeks out forces or wills; instead of dialectical, continuous self-modification, he favors the dramatic and untimely leap into futurity; instead of the becoming of being, he seeks the being of becoming; instead of identity, he seeks a model of action and activity.[12] This redirection of interest from the subject's internal constitution, its psychical interiority inhabited by the specter of the other, is turned inside out in a Nietzschean framework: what marks the subject as such is its capacity to act and be acted upon, to do rather than to be, to act rather than to identify. Where the Hegelian subject remains fundamentally vulnerable to the incursions of the other, to the other's attempted mastery over the subject's own self-definition, the Nietzsche subject, indifferent to the other, acts and, through acting, produces values, interpretations, modes of dealing with the world, and modes of addressing the other without succumbing or giving over power to the other. There is a growing influence of this Nietzschean conception in politics, through the efforts of his reader-theorists like Foucault, Deleuze, Kofman, Irigaray, and others, but these remain, in spite of their reputations within the humanities, still minority positions within a field that seems dominated by identity politics, the politics of identification with sociocultural categories, conceived outside and beyond bodies and forces in themselves.

What is it that subjects seek? To be recognized? Cornell and Murphy ask the crucial question—the question at the very heart of the Hegelian structure of recognition: to be recognized by whom? From whom do oppressed groups and individuals seek identity through recognition? Hegel's own answer (1969) changes and moves with the very structure of the dialectic itself: while two equal self-consciousnesses seek recognition from each other, the dialectic rapidly transforms this apparent or provisional equality into the very structure of lordship and bondage. Now it is the slave who seeks the recognition of the master, and paradoxically, the master has no adequate or equal other to provide recognition for him.[13] Through other permutations and developments of the dialectic, in the end, the subject seeks recognition for itself from the social and political order, seeks to be adequately represented and thus adequately recognized by having its place as a unique combination of categories and identifications affirmed socially and politically. Yet Cornell and Murphy are not able to entirely affirm Hegel's understanding: "Clearly, minority cultures are not always, or even mostly, addressing their demands for recognition to the majority culture—at least if we are to understand recognition as a comprehension of the minority culture's identity. That freedom that Hegel saw achieved in the Western European democracies has been, after all, often written on the backs of precisely those minority cultures now struggling for their own national identities, cultural voices and economic sustainability" (Cornell and Murphy 2002, 421).

While the authors confirm that it cannot be the "majority culture"—whether conceived as white, middle class, heterosexual, male, Eurocentric, English-speaking—that bestows identity on minoritarian cultures, they remain unclear about why it is a recognition structure that is the remedy for their minoritarian status. If it is not the majoritarian values that attribute an identity to the minority, if, indeed majoritarian interests are vested in nonrecognition and noncomprehension, an abjection or expulsion of "the minority culture's identity," then why is recognition necessary and what does it confer? Or perhaps this is another way of asking: why are identity and the struggles around identity—rather than, say, around the right to bodily activities and practices—the rallying cry for politics? Can we reconceive politics without identity (this is what Cornell and Murphy seek in their essay)? And if so, why do we still need the residual concept of recognition (as they continue to affirm)?

In place of the desire for recognition as the condition for subjective identity, we need to begin with different working assumptions, which may cover some of the same issues as those conceived by identity politics, without, however, resorting to the language and assumptions governing recognition. In place of the desire for recognition, the emptiness of a solipsistic existence, the annihilation of identity without the other, the relation of desperate dependence on the other for the stability of one's being, we could develop an account of subjectivity, identity, or agency at the mercy of forces, energies, practices that produce an altogether different understanding of both politics and identity.[14]

Subjects can be conceived as modes of action and passion, a surface catalytic of events, events which subjects don't control but participate in, which produce history and thus whatever identity subjects may have. This is precisely what evolutionary theory offers. In place of a phenomenology of identificatory subservience, as entailed by the adoption of Hegelian structures of recognition, the political struggles of subjugated peoples can be regarded as struggles for *practice*, struggles at the level of the pragmatic, struggles around the right to act, do, and make. Oppression cannot simply be resolved into failed, unsuccessful, or unaffirmed identities, identities lagging for want of recognition. A more dynamic and affirming representation is to understand identity in terms of bodily practices: one is what one does; the history of what one has done and what has been done to one constitutes one's character; and what one can or will do is that which is unpredictable and open. Identity is thus a synthesis of what one has done (and has been done to one) but also a dissipation of patterns and habits in the face of an open future. This identity has little to do with how one represents oneself and everything to do with the processes and actions one engenders and in which one partakes. What we are is determined to a large extent, not by who recognizes us, but by what we do, what we make, what we achieve or accomplish.

It is only if the subject (its identity, desire, and possibilities for becoming) is linked to some conception, not only of identification, imagination, projection, but of action, materiality, forces that direct it beyond its control, which position it as a subject with particular characteristics—morphological, genetic, developmental, given, acquired, or emergent—that we can understand the limits of the subject and its modes of transformation into something other and more. Sexual difference (the acquisition of at least two radically different types of subject position according to at least two differ-ent morphological structures) and racial difference (the acknowledgment of a multiplicity of corporeal and cultural variations) are neither constrained to the forms in which we currently know them, nor are they open to self-conscious manipulation, identification, or control by subjects. They are ma-terial, evolutionary forces through which we work but which we do not con-trol, which we cannot rise above but which nevertheless direct us toward the possibilities of change. Without an adequate acknowledgment of the ma-terial, natural, biological status of bodies (these terms being understood as vectors of change rather than as forms of fixity), we lose the resources to understand how to best harness these forces which invariably direct us to the future; we lose an understanding of our place in the world as beings open to becoming, open to activities, if not identities, of all types.

PART III.

PHILOSOPHY, KNOWLEDGE,

AND THE FUTURE

CHAPTER 6

Deleuze, Bergson, and the Virtual

Since the being proper to humankind is being one's own possibility or potentiality, then and only for this reason . . . humans have and feel a debt.

This is why ethics has no room for repentance; this is why the only ethical experience (which, as such, cannot be a task or a subjective decision) is the experience of being (one's own) potentiality—exposing, that is, in every form one's own amorphousness and in every act one's own inactuality.

—Giorgio Agamben, *The Coming Community*

Gilles Deleuze may prove to be one of the few philosophers committed to the task of thinking the new, of opening up thought and knowledge to the question of the future while nonetheless contesting and providing alternative readings, positions, goals to those of philosophical orthodoxy. His writings on Bergson and the Bergsonian understanding of the relations between matter and memory—which appear throughout his writings with compelling insistence—testify to the ongoing interest he has in the question of futurity and the productivity and re-energization of the virtual which may help provide some of the conditions under which we can access and live with a concept of the future open to the under- or unutilized potentiality of the past and present.

BERGSONISM

Although Deleuze may be known as a philosopher of space and place more than time and history (his preference for geography over history is by now a cliché), nonetheless it would be a mistake to ignore as irrelevant or minor his interests in and writings on Bergson and the concept of duration, which seem as central (if considerably more underestimated than his texts on Nietzsche and Spinoza) to all of his subsequent writings as any other of his many abiding concerns. His writings on the structures of memory and the paradoxical relations between present and past, and particularly his pre-scient conception of the virtual or virtuality, form one of Deleuze's most intriguing and least discussed philosophical lines of reflection.[1] Thought, genuinely innovative thought — philosophy at its best — involves harnessing the power that the virtual, in the domain of concepts, exerts.

Here I explore Deleuze's reading of Bergson, not only in the text specifi-cally devoted to him (*Bergsonism*, 1988), but in other scattered references to virtuality and duration from his earliest writings, reprinted in *Desert Islands and Other Texts, 1953–1974* (2004); to his more mature texts, *Cinema 1. The Movement-Image* (1986); *Cinema 2. The Time-Image* (1989), *Difference and Repetition* (1994), (with Guattari) *What Is Philosophy?* (1994), and elsewhere. Through these various formulations, his concept of the virtual will be linked with a notion of the future, and thus to the question of the ethics and politics of revolutionary or dynamic change. For the purposes of this chapter, which is more a reflection on virtual futures than a scholarly analysis of Deleuze's reading of Bergson, Bergson's texts will not be carefully distinguished from Deleuze's. Instead, they will be used together to build up some of the basic postulates for an account of duration, the future, and the role the virtual plays in their elaboration.

As Deleuze himself describes it, *Bergsonism* is part of a counter-history of philosophy that would also have to include Deleuze's readings of Hume, Kant, Spinoza, Nietzsche, Lucretius, Leibniz, and the Pre-Socratics, "who seemed to be part of the history of philosophy, but who escaped from it in one respect or other" (Deleuze and Parnet 1987, 14–15). Something in Bergson's work veers off from the accepted traditions of philosophy to cre-ate something new and unexpected. What Bergson offers is a philosophy of movement. Instead of asking how to dynamize a static Idea or put into mo-tion that which is arrested, a question that has occupied philosophy since the time of Plato, Bergson is above all a thinker of dynamic movement, action, change. This may explain why, although he has been widely read — at least in the past, if not very frequently or intensely for the last generation or so—the impact of his work has not been adequately digested. What Bergson has to offer by way of understanding difference, becoming, duration, and life has yet to be effective.[2]

There is something in Bergson's vitalism that is wayward or unpalatable. Or at least, Deleuze's reading of Bergson self-consciously aims at bringing out the monstrous and the grotesque in Bergson's work—or in the work of any other philosopher he deals with. He has described his project as a kind of anal seduction, a buggery, of key figures in the history of philosophy, and thus a buggery of the philosophical tradition (a metaphor that seems to have enticed Derrida in *Glas* [1986] and elsewhere just as strongly as Deleuze: it is significant that amorous deformation is metaphorized in terms of the paradoxical hetero/homosexualization of philosophy, that is, in terms of giving the philosopher in question—the simultaneous object of critical reading, feminization, and insemination—a bastard child through an amorous act of anal reproduction).[3]

Deleuze wants to bring out as well as produce a certain perversion of Bergson's writings, and in doing so, I believe, he brings us to the verge of a philosophy adequate to the task of thinking the new, a philosophy for the future, a philosophy beyond Platonism and thus beyond the phenomena of negation and dialectic which have dominated Western thought since Plato. He sees in Bergson's writings a departure from formal logic (which is regulated by the laws of contradiction and thus the primacy of negation) and an affirmation of the sphere of practice and the lived, in the tradition of C. S. Peirce and William James.[4] Bergson may provide some of the ingredients for a philosophy that affirms life, time, the future, and the new.

PERCEPTION AND ACTION

Deleuze focuses on a number of Bergson's key texts, primarily *Matter and Memory* (1988), *Creative Evolution* (1944), and *Creative Mind* (1992), where Bergson develops a position, unique in the history of philosophy, which unravels the hard and fast distinctions between objectivism and subjectivism, matter and consciousness, space and duration. Commonly represented as an unrequited metaphysician by a positivist and scientistic philosophical tradition dating from Bertrand Russell's earliest critiques (1912) and largely ignored in the late twentieth century, Bergson poses a peculiar and unexpected combination of experiential phenomenology, scientific pragmatism, and psychophysiological research that makes his work difficult to accurately classify, at least according to conventional philosophical categories. Deleuze's reading of Bergson, for the sake of argument here, can be divided into three central components: Bergson's understanding of matter and its relation to memory; his account of the relations between past, present, and future; and his understanding of the distinction between the virtual and the possible.

Bergson's opening statement in *Matter and Memory*, which defines matter as an aggregate or series of images, makes clear the ways in which his position must be distinguished from both philosophical idealism and materialism. His position encapsulates ingredients of both while denying the common ground on which they rely: "Matter, in our view, is an aggregate of 'images.' And by 'image' we mean a certain existence which is more than that which the idealist calls a *representation*, but less than that which the realist calls a *thing*—an existence placed half-way between the 'thing' and the 'representation' . . . the object exists in itself, and, on the other hand, the object is, in itself, pictorial, as we perceive it: the image it is, but a self-existing image" (Bergson 1988, 9–10).

Matter is a multiplicity or aggregate of images rather than that which lies behind or is mirrored in images. This is both a form of realism (insofar as the object exists in itself, independent of any observer or subject) and a mode of idealism (insofar as matter coincides with and resembles its various images). Bergson is drawn to the questions of perception and memory because they are located at the point of intersection or bifurcation of mind and matter. Perception and memory both reveal the complicity of mind with matter, each as it were, from a different direction: perception reveals that matter requires mind as its mode of utilization, while memory reveals a mind that requires events, material processes, as part of its history. As an exploration of the relations between mind and matter, duration and spatiality, Bergson provides a perplexing account of the ways in which memory links consciousness to duration and perception links action to spatialization.

Bergson defines perception and memory, our modes of access to the present and the past, in operational terms: the present is that which is acting, while the past can be understood as that which no longer acts (Bergson 1988, 68). Perception must be linked to nascent or dawning action, action-in-potential, action that is on the verge of beginning or being undertaken. Perception, being linked fundamentally to action, is actual, and is directed to an impending or immediate future. It is preparatory for and governed by the imperative to act, and harnesses memory to fill in the details of perception in order to most directly and easily facilitate action. Habit assures perception of its pragmatic grasp on objects.

Instead of memory being regarded as a faded perception, a perception that has receded into the past, as its commonplace representation dictates, it must be regarded as ideational, inactive, or purely virtual. "The past is only idea, the present is ideo-motor" (1988, 68). A present perception and a past recollection are not simply different in degree (one a faded, diminished, or muted version of the other) but different in kind. Perception is that which propels us toward the present, the real, to space, objects, matter, to the immediate or impending future; while memory is that which impels us toward consciousness, to the past, and to duration. If perception pushes us toward action and thus objects, then to that extent objects reflect my body's possible actions upon them. If memory directs me to the past and to duration, then it is linked not only to my body and its experiences but to the broad web of connections in which my body is located. The more immersed we are in memory, the less our actions can be directly invoked and prepared for; but the more directly and instrumentally we act, the less our reflection, memories, and consciousness intervene into and regulate our actions. Everyday behavior requires a mixture of perception and memory, perception stretched to its most detailed, memory contracted to its most habitual.

If matter is nothing but an aggregate of (self-subsisting) images, then in the perception of matter there is not a higher order image—the image of an image, an image (the object) ordered by another image (consciousness)—but rather, the same images oriented, in the first case, according to their own connections, their own milieu of other images; and in the second case, these images are directed toward the organizing force of a central image, the image of my moving body. The difference between matter and perception is not simply the difference between an object and a subject (which simply begs the question of what that difference consists in), but an understanding of the subject as a peculiar sort of object, linked to its body's central organizing position in framing the rest of matter, in providing it with a perspective.

My body is one material object among all the others that make up the world. What differentiates my body from other objects is, in the first instance, the way in which the image that is my body has a peculiarly privileged relation to action: "I call *matter* the aggregate of images, and *perception of matter* these same images referred to the eventual action of one particular image, my body" (Bergson 1988, 22).

My body is distinguished from other objects not because it is the privileged location of my consciousness but because it performs major changes in other objects relative to itself, because it is the central organizing site through which other images are ordered.[5] The question governing much of Bergson's writings is crucial: how do these two sets of images, the universe and the body, the inanimate and the animate, coexist? How can the same images belong to and function within these two quite different types of system, one with a center, the other without? In other words, what is the relation between mind and matter, and how do they affect each other?

Bergson sees this relation as one of occupation. Scattered throughout the system of linked images that constitute the material world are living systems, *centers of action*, zones of indetermination, points where images are capable of mobilizing action by subordinating other images to the variations and fluctuations, changes of position and perspective afforded by these centers of action. Life can be defined, through a difference in kind from matter, by the necessity of prolonging a stimulus through a reaction. Matter itself exhibits no hesitation: the stimulus achieves its reaction automatically, predictably. Yet in all forms of life there is a disconnection, a hesitation, the possibility of a different reaction to the same stimulus, a minimal freedom. The more simple the form of life, the more automatic the relation between stimulus and response. In the case of the protozoa, the organs of perception and the organs of movement are one and the same. Reaction seems like a mechanical movement. But even in the case of the protozoa there is some conception of "choice," some discretion in the simple movements of contraction or expansion that its capacities and environment offer it. Even here, there is a certain, certainly limited, "freedom." In the case of more complex forms of life, there is interposed both a delay, an uncertainty, between a perceptual reaction and a motor response[6] and an ever-widening circle of perceptual objects which in potential promise or threaten the organism—which are of "interest" to the organism.

This notion of life as both the organization of images around a central nucleus of bodily interest and activity, and as the interposition of a temporal delay between stimulus and response, distinguishes Bergson's position from any form of humanism or anthropomorphism, although it does link his work strongly to Darwinism. Mind or life are not special—or vital—substances, different in nature to matter. Rather, mind or life partake of and live in and as matter. Matter is organized differently in its inorganic and organic forms: this organization is dependent on the degree of indeterminacy, the degree of freedom, that life exhibits relative to the inertia of matter. It may be for this reason that Bergson develops one of his most striking hypotheses: the brain does not make humans more intelligent than animals; the brain is not the repository of ideas, mind, freedom, or creativity. It stores nothing, it produces nothing, and organizes nothing. Yet it is still part of the reason for the possibility of innovation, creativity, and freedom insofar as it is the means for the interposition of a delay between stimulus and response, perception and action, the explanation for a capacity for rerouting and reorganization which characterizes innovation:

> In our opinion . . . the brain is no more than a kind of central telephone exchange: its office is to allow communication or to delay it. It adds nothing to what it receives. . . . That is to say that the nervous system is in no sense an apparatus which may serve to fabricate, or even to prepare, representations. Its function is to receive stimulation, to provide motor apparatus, and to present the largest possible number of these apparatuses to a given stimulus. The more it develops, the more numerous and the more distant are the points of space which it brings into relation with ever more complex motor mechanisms. In this way the scope which it allows to our action enlarges: its growing perfection consists in nothing else. (Bergson 1988, 31)

The brain intercedes to reroute perceptual inputs and motor outputs, disconnecting them from predictable outcomes, to deviate them, at least on occasion, into unexpected consequences. It links, or does not link, movements of one kind (sensory or perceptual) with movements of another kind (motor). The brain functions, in his conception, not to produce images, or to reflect on them, but rather to put images directed from elsewhere into the context of action. The more developed the organism, the more action it is capable of, the wider in nature are the perceptual or sensory inputs and the broader the range of objects which make up the scope of the organism's action. The brain does not sort images or store them. It inserts a gap or delay between stimulus and response which enables but does not necessitate a direct connection between perception and action. The brain enables multiple, indeterminable connections between what the organism receives (through perception or affection) and how it acts, making possible a genuine freedom from predictability and making an open-ended future inevitable, as least as far as life itself is concerned. It is the capacity of the brain to disperse anticipated responses and to substitute others for them, enabling it to bring memory to bear on perception, widening the circle of perception's relevance.

It is precisely this delay or interval that lifts the organism from the immediacy of its interaction with objects to establish a distance and indeterminacy which allows perceptual images to be assessed and served in terms of their interest, that is, their utility or expedience for the subject.[7] This interval serves as a kind of principle of selection of those elements, images, or qualities that serve to link it to the interests of the living being. "By virtue of a cerebral interval, in effect, a being can retain from a material object and the actions issuing from it only those elements that interest him. So that perception is not the object *plus* something, but the object *minus* something, minus everything that does not interest us" (Deleuze 1988, 25).

The object can be understood to contain both real action, the indiscriminate action of its various features upon whatever surrounds it and comes into causal connection with it, as well as virtual action, that potential to exert specific effects on a living being of the kind which the being seeks or may interest it. This cerebral delay allows the object's indiscriminate actions on the world to be placed in suspension, and for the living being to see only particular elements of the object: "To obtain this conversion from the virtual to the actual, it would be necessary, not to throw light on the object, but on the contrary, to obscure some of its aspects, to diminish it by the greater part of itself, so that the remainder, instead of being encased in its surroundings as a *thing*, should detach itself from them as a *picture*. . . . There is nothing positive here, nothing added to the image, nothing new. The objects merely abandon something of their real action in order to manifest their virtual influence of the living being upon them" (Bergson 1988, 36–37).

The "zones of indetermination" introduced into the universe by all living forms produce a kind of sieve or filter, which diminishes the full extent of the object's real effects in the world in order to let through its virtual effects, in other words, enables objects to enter unexpected connections, to make something new.

MEMORY AND PERCEPTION

For Deleuze, what fills up this cerebral interval, these "zones of indetermination" that are indices of life, and interposes itself between perception and action to enrich and complicate both are affections, body-memories (or habit-memory), and pure recollections (duration). Through their interventions, perception becomes "enlivened," and capable of being linked to nascent actions.

Bergson speaks of two different kinds of memory, one bound up with bodily habits and thus essentially forward-looking insofar as it aims at and resides in the production of an action, however habitual. This habit-memory is about the achievement of habitual goals or aims. It has a kind of "natural" place in the cerebral interval between perception and action, for it is the most action-oriented, the most present- and future-seeking of memories, from the inert past. Bergson distinguishes this habit-memory from recollection or memory proper, which for him is always spontaneous, tied to a highly particular place, date, and situation, unrepeatable and unique, perfect in itself and thus incapable of developing. If habit-memory is future-oriented, memory proper is always and only directed to the past. Where habit memory interposes a body-schema between sensation and action, memory proper is directed toward an idea. If the cerebral delay could be indefinitely postponed, Bergson suggests, these memory images, precise, concrete images from the past, would serve to fill the breach. This, of course, is precisely what occurs in the case of sleep, which severs the impetus of the perception from the requirement of action, and can thus more readily tolerate the interposition of memory images. As he implies, perception always inclines us to the future; it is only in the delay or rift between perception and its future in action that this orientation to the past, and the free circulation of undirected memory, is possible. Movement and action drives the memory image away; repose and a disconnection from the pressures of action enable memory images to flood consciousness.

The act of recognition is the point at which memory proper and action are at their closest. To recognize something, however one understands the term, involves the correlation of a current perception (or perceptual object) with a memory that resembles it. But recognition is not simply the correlation of a present perception with its resembling memory, for recognition would be guaranteed to occur whenever there were memory images, and would be abolished whenever they were missing (an explanation which cannot take account of the phenomena of psychic blindness, aphasia, and apraxia). Recollection and thus recognition occur when a memory image which resembles a current perception is carried along with the perception by being extended into action. Memory can thus function in conjunction with or as an adjunct to perceptual innervations extending out to impending actions. Insofar as memory images can insert themselves successfully, it is difficult if not impossible to distinguish the (current) perceptual component from the memory images which augment and enrich it.

If memory can be carried along the path to action, it is significant that for Bergson we can also pass in the reverse direction, from movements to memory, a movement which is needed to "complete" perception of the object, which has been stripped of manifold connections in reality to serve as a point of interest for perception and action. Perception can never be free of memory, and is thus never completely embedded in the present but always straddles elements of the past. This movement from the multiple circles of memory must occur if a productive circuit between perception and memory, where each qualifies the other, is to occur, that is, if there is to be the possibility of a reflective perception or a directed recollection.

Bergson thinks of this circuit in terms of a return movement from the object to recollection, in increasingly concentrated or dilated circles. He thinks of memory as fundamentally elastic: it is capable of existing in a more or less contracted or dilated state. The whole of memory is contained within each circuit in increasing degrees of concentration. These different circuits cluster and are formed concentrically around images connected by resemblance to the object, which exist in more and more dilated form as they are further removed in immediacy from the object of present perception. As the circuits or networks widen, the memory becomes deeper and more detailed, more removed from action, and more filled with content and context; the memory images become richer and conform in their detail more to the object's perceptual image.[8] To move from one circuit to the next cannot be accomplished directly, for each time one must return to the present to be able to leap once again into the medium of the past. If in the case of mechanical recollection, the past, in the form of habit-memory, moves toward actions; in the case of attention, the past is not just directed toward action, but is expanded and grows richer, confirming and filling in the skeletal, perceptual image.

PAST AND PRESENT

The present is that which acts and lives, which functions to anticipate an immediate future in action. The present is a form of impending action. The past is that which no longer acts, although in a sense it lives a shadowy and fleeting existence; it still is, it is real. Its reality is virtual, for it exerts its influence indirectly, only through its capacity to link to and thus to inform the present. The past remains accessible in the form of recollections, either as motor mechanisms in the form of habit-memory, or more accurately, in the form of image memories. These memories are the condition of perception in the same way that the past, for Bergson, is a condition of the present. Whereas the past in itself is powerless, if it can link up to a present perception, it has a chance to be mobilized in the course of another perception's impulse to action. In this sense, the present is not purely in itself, self-contained; it straddles both past and present, requiring the past as its precondition, while being oriented toward the immediate future. Perception

[margin note: NB. live in its Shadow.]

is a measure of our virtual action upon things. The present, as that which is oriented to both perception and action, is the threshold of their interaction, and thus the site of duration. The present consists in the consciousness I have of my body. Memory, the past, has no special link with or proximity to my body.

The past cannot be identified with the memory images that serve to represent or make it actual for or useful to us; rather, it is the seed which can actualize itself in a memory. Memory is the present's mode of access to the past. The past is preserved in time, while the memory image, one of its elements, can be selected according to present interests. Just as perception leads me to objects where they are, outside of myself and in space, and just as I perceive affection where it arises, in my body (Bergson 1988, 57), so too, I recall or remember only by placing myself in the realm of the past, where memory subsides or subsists. Memory, the past, is thus, paradoxically, not *in us*, just as perception is not *in us*. Perception takes us outside ourselves, to where objects are (in space); memory takes us to where the past is (in duration).[9]

Bergson problematizes a whole series of assumptions regarding our conceptions of the present and the past. We tend to believe that when the present is somehow exhausted or depleted of its current force it somehow slips into the past, where it is stored in the form of memories. It is then replaced by another present. Against this presumption, Bergson suggests that a new present could never replace the old one if the latter did not pass while it is still present. In place of the more usual claim of the succession of the past by the present, this leads to his postulate of the *simultaneity* of past and present. The past is contemporaneous with the present it has been. They exist, they "occur" at the same time. The past and present are created simultaneously. Every present splits into a dual-sided actual and virtual, one of which has effects, the other of which joins and adds to the past. The present thus directs itself to two series, two orientations at once: to action, in space; and to memory, in duration. The past could never exist if it did not coexist with the present of which it is the past.

Bergson argues that the past would be inaccessible to us altogether if we could gain access to it only through the present and its passing. The only access we have to the past is through a leap into virtuality, through a move into the past itself, seeing that the past is outside us and that we are in it. The past exists, but in a state of latency or virtuality. We must place ourselves in it if we are to have recollections, memory images: and this we do in two movements or phases. First, we place ourselves into the past in general (which can only occur through a certain detachment from the immediacy of the present) and then we place ourselves in a particular region of the past. Bergson conceives of the past in terms of a series of planes or segments, each one representing the whole of the past in more or less contracted form. The present can be understood on such a model as an infinitely contracted moment of the past, the point where the past intersects most directly with the body. It is for this reason that the present is able to pass.

Memories drawn from various strata may be clustered around idiosyncratic points, points of intensity, "shining points of memory," as Bergson describes them, which are multiplied to the extent that memory is dilated (Bergson 1988, 171). Depending on the recollection we are seeking, we must jump in at a particular segment; in order to move on to another, we must do so through another leap (Deleuze 1989, 99). For Deleuze, this provides a model for Bergson's understanding of our relations to other systems of images as well (and hence Bergson's suitability to Deleuze's analysis of cinema).

It is only through a similar structure that we can detach ourselves from the present to understand linguistic utterances or make conceptual linkages. The structure of the time-image also contains that of the language-image and the thought-image. It is only by throwing ourselves into language as a whole, into the domain of sense in general, that we can understand any utterance, and it is only by leaping into a realm of ideas that we can understand problems.[10] In all three cases, this leap involves landing in different concentrations of the past, language, or thought, which nonetheless contain the whole within them in different degrees of relaxation or dilation.

Along with the simultaneity or coexistence of each moment of the present with the entirety of the past, there are other implications in Bergson's paradoxical account. Each moment carries a virtual past with it: each present must, as it were, pass through the whole of the past. This is what is meant by the past in general: the past does not come after the present has ceased to be, nor does the present become, or somehow move into, the past. Rather, it is the past which is the condition of the present; it is only through its preexistence that the present can come to be. Bergson does not want to deny that succession takes place—of course, one present (and past) replaces another; but such real or actual succession can take place only because of a virtual coexistence of the past and the present, the virtual coexistence of all of the past at each moment of the present, and at each level or segment of the past. This means that there must be a relation of repetition between each segment, whereby each segment or degree of contraction/dilation is a virtual repetition of the others, not identical, certainly, but a version. The degrees of contraction or dilation which differentiate segments constitute modes of repetition in difference.[11]

THE ACTUAL AND THE VIRTUAL

The concept of virtuality has been with us a remarkably long time. It is a coherent and functional idea already in Plato's writings, where both Ideas and simulacra exist in some state of virtuality, before and in excess of their materializations. Instead of too closely identifying it with the invention of new technologies, a new world to be opened up with the advances in computing—as is the current obsession with cyberculture and "virtual" reality— we must realize that since there has been writing, writing in the Derridean sense of trace—that is, for as long as there has been culture itself—there has been some idea of the virtual. The text we read may be in real space, but insofar as it is comprehensible to us, it also exists in a state of virtuality. We did not have to wait for the computer screen or the cinematic projector to enter virtual space. We live in its shadow more or less continually, if Bergson's understanding of memory and the past make sense.

Bergson claims that a distinction between subjective and objective (or, what amounts to the same thing, duration and spatiality) can be formulated in terms of the distinction between the virtual and the actual. Objects, space, the world of the inert are entirely actual; they contain no elements of the virtual. While matter may well exceed the images that we have of it, while there is more in matter than in our images of it insofar as it is the ongoing occasion for the generation of images, the images that our perception gives us of it are nonetheless of the same kind as our images. That is, because matter has no virtuality, no hidden latency, it is assimilable to the images we have of it, even if it is not reducible to our image alone:

> There is in matter something more than, but not something different from, that which is actually given. Undoubtedly, conscious perception does not compass the whole of matter, since it consists, in as far as it is conscious, in the separation or "discernment," of that which, in matter, interests our various needs. But between this perception of matter and matter itself there is but a difference of degree and not of kind, pure perception standing toward matter in the relation of the part to the whole. This amounts to saying that matter cannot exercise powers of any kind other than those which

we perceive. It has no mysterious virtue; it can conceal none. (Bergson 1988, 71)

If everything about matter is real, if it has no virtuality, this means that the object's medium is spatial. The object, while it exists in duration, while it is subject to change, does not reveal more of itself in time: it is "no more than what it presents to us at any given moment." By contrast, what duration, memory, consciousness bring to the world is the possibility of an unfolding—a narrative—a hesitation. Not everything is presented all at once. This is what life (duration, memory, consciousness) brings to the world: the new, the movement of the actualization of the virtual, the existence of duration: "Thus the living being essentially has duration; it has duration precisely because it is continuously elaborating what is new and because there is no elaboration without searching, no searching without groping. Time is this very hesitation" (Bergson 1992, 93).

If matter can be placed on the side of the actual and the real, and if mind, life, or duration are to be placed on the side of the virtual, we need to be more clear about how Bergson distinguishes the two oppositions, between the virtual and the actual, and the possible and the real, and about how Deleuze wants to use this Bergsonian distinction, for on it hangs Deleuze's idea of the future.

In the conceptual pairs virtual/actual and possible/real, the possible can never be real but may be actual; the virtual precludes the actual, but it must be considered real.[12] Possibilities may be realized (in the future), while virtualities are real (in the past) and may be actualized in the present and future. Like Bergson, who rejects the possible/real couple in favor of the virtual/actual pair, Deleuze argues that there is a closure in the process of realization which the process of actualization overcomes. The movement of becoming, for him, must be understood as a process of actualization rather than realization, just as the movement of evolution, for Bergson, at least in *Creative Evolution*, must be seen as an unpredictable leap forward. The passage from virtual to actual occurs only on the field of duration.

The process of realization is governed by two principles—resemblance and limitation: the real exists in a relation of resemblance to the possible. Indeed, the real is an exact image of the possible, with the addition of the category of existence or reality. Conceptually, in other words, the real and the possible are identical (since, as Kant argued, existence is not a quality or attribute). Moreover, the process of realization involves the limitation, the narrowing down of possibilities, so that some are rejected and others

NB.

Time is a creative force

selected for real existence. The field of the possible is wider than that of the real. Deleuze suggests that implicit in this pairing is a preformism: the real is already preformed in the possible insofar as the real resembles the possible. The possible passes into the real through limitation, the culling of other possibilities; through this resemblance and limitation, the real comes to be seen as given rather than made.[13]

Thus the possible is both more than but also less than the real. It is more in the sense that the real selects from a number of possibles, limiting their ramifying effects; but it is less in the sense that it is the real minus existence. Realization is a process in which creativity, production is no longer conceivable and thus cannot provide an appropriate model for understanding the innovation and invention that marks evolutionary change. Making the possible real is simply giving it existence without adding to or modifying its conception. But, as Deleuze asks, does the possible produce the real, or does the real in fact project itself backward to produce the possible? The processes of resemblance and limitation that constitute realization are, according to Bergson, subject to the philosophical illusion which consists in the belief that there is *less* in the idea of the empty than the full; and less in the concept of disorder than order, whereas in fact the ideas of nothing and disorder are *more* complicated than those of existence and order:

> I find the same illusion in the case in point. Underlying the doctrines which disregard the radical novelty of each moment of evolution there are many misunderstandings, many errors. But there is especially the idea that the possible is *less* than the real, and that, for this reason, the possibility of things precedes their existence. They would thus be capable of representation beforehand; they could be thought of before being realized. But it is the reverse that is true. . . . [W]e find that there is more and not less in the possibility of each of the successive states than in their reality. For the possible is only the real with the addition of an act of mind which throws its image back into the past, once it has been enacted. But that is what our intellectual habits prevent us from seeing. (Bergson 1992, 99–100)

The real creates an image of itself, which, by projecting itself back into the past, gives it the status of the always-having-been-possible. The possible is ideally preexistent, an existence that precedes materialization. The possible, instead of being a reverse projection of the real, might be better understood in terms of the virtual, which has reality without being actual: in Proust's formulation, which Deleuze compulsively repeats in all his writings on virtuality, the virtual must be conceived as "Real without being actual, ideal without being abstract."[14] To reduce the possible to a preexistent phantom-like real is to curtail the possibility of thinking the new, of thinking an open future, a future not bound to the present, just as the present is itself a production of the past:

> As reality is created as something unforeseeable and new, its image is reflected behind it into the indefinite past; thus it finds that it has from all time been possible, but it is at this precise moment that it begins to have been always possible, and that is why I said that its possibility, which does not precede its reality, will have to precede it once the reality has appeared. The possible is therefore the mirage of the present in the past; and as we know the future will finally constitute a present and the mirage effect is continually being produced, we are convinced that the image of tomorrow is already contained in our actual present, which will be the past of tomorrow, although we did not manage to grasp it. (Bergson 1992, 101)

In elaborating this notion of the virtual in *Difference and Repetition*, Deleuze refines and complicates the concept. He claims that the virtual must be distinguished from the possible on three counts: First, in talking of the possible rather than the virtual, the status of existence is what is in question. Existence, the acquisition of reality by the possible, can only be understood as both an inexplicable eruption and a system of all or nothing—either it "has" existence, in which case it is real, or it "lacks" existence, in which case it is merely possible. But if this is true, then it is hard to see what the difference is between the existent and the nonexistent, for the nonexistent is a possibility and has all the characteristics of the existent. Existence is generally understood as the occurring in space and time, in a definite situation or context. But with this understanding of the possible, the real seems absolutely indifferent to its context of emergence. By contrast, it is only the reality of the virtual that produces existence in its specific context, in a space and time of emergence. The actual is contingently produced from the virtual. Second, if the possible is thought in place of the virtual, difference can only be understood as restriction, the difference between the possible and the real, a difference of degree not kind. The possible refers to a notion of identity which the virtual renders problematic, the self-identity of the image, which remains the same whether possible or real. Third, while the possible produces the real by virtue of resemblance, the virtual never resembles the real that it actualizes. It is in this sense that actualization is a process of creation that resists both a logic of identity and a logic of resemblance to substitute a movement of differentiation, divergence, and innovation (Deleuze 1994, 211–212).

The possible must be in excess of this restrictive understanding, for it makes both a reality which corresponds to it possible, and also makes possible the projecting back of the present reality into a modality of the past.[15] A different, more positive sense is required to add the dimension of creativity and productivity to this otherwise smooth, seamless transition from the possible to the real.

The process of actualization is a process of genuine creativity and innovation, the production of singularity or individuation. Where the possible/real relation is regulated by resemblance and limitation, the virtual/actual relation is governed by the two principles of difference and creation. For the virtual to become actual, it must create the conditions for actualization: the actual in no way resembles the virtual. Rather, the actual is produced through a mode of differentiation from the virtual, a mode of divergence from it which is productive. The process of actualization involves the creation of heterogeneous terms. The lines of actualization are divergent, creating the varieties that constitute creative evolution. This is a movement of the emanation of a multiplicity from a virtual unity, the creation of divergent paths of development in different series and directions.[16]

The movement from a virtual unity to an actual multiplicity requires that there is a certain leap, this time a leap of innovation or creativity, the surprise that the virtual leaves within the actual. The movement of realization seems like the concretization of a preexistent plan or the realization of a program; by contrast, the movement of actualization is the opening up of the virtual to what befalls it. This indeed is what life, the *élan vital*, is of necessity—a movement of differentiation of virtualities in the light of the contingencies which impact it. *NB.*

If there is a movement of differentiation from a virtual unity, the unity of the past as a whole contracted in different degrees in the process of actualization, Deleuze (unlike Bergson at this point) suggests that there is also a complementary movement from the actual multiplicity to the virtual underlying it: "The real is not only that which is cut out according to natural articulations or differences in kind; it is also that which intersects again along paths converging toward the same ideal or virtual point" (Deleuze 1988, 29). This point of convergence, reconfiguring the movements of divergence and differentiation that made a process of actualization of the virtual occur, is the point at which memory is reinserted into perception, the point at which the actual object (re)meets its virtual counterpart.[17]

Insofar as time, history, change, the future need to be reviewed in the light of this Bergsonian disordering of linear or predictable temporality, perhaps the open-endedness of the concept of the virtual may prove central in reinvigorating the concept of an open future by refusing to tie it to the realization of possibilities (the following of a plan) and linking it to the unpredictable, uncertain actualization of virtualities.

UPHEAVALS PAST AND YET TO COME

Bergson's understanding of duration provides us with an understanding of the ways in which the future, as much as the present and past, is bound up with the movement and impetus of life. While duration entails the coexistence of the present with the past, it also implies the continual elaboration of the new, the openness of things (including life) to what befalls them. This is what time *is* if it is anything at all: not simply mechanical repetition, the causal effects of objects on objects, but the indeterminate, the unfolding and the emergence of the new: "Time is something. Therefore it acts. [T]ime is what hinders everything from being given at once. It retards, or rather it is retardation. It must, therefore, be elaboration. Would it not then be a vehicle of creation and of choice? Would not the existence of time prove that there is indetermination in things? Would not time be that indetermination itself?" (Bergson 1992, 93).

The future is the ongoing promise of both the continuity and discontinuity of duration. What endures, what is fundamentally immersed in time is not what remains unchanging or the same over time, a Platonic essence, but what diverges and transforms itself with the passage of time. Although there is a fundamental continuity between the past and the present—the present being the culmination of the past, its latest layering—there is a discontinuity between the present and the future, for the future is not contained in (and thus preempted by) the present but erupts unexpectedly from it. Duration is the movement of divergence or differentiation between what was and what will be, a movement from one mode of virtuality (the past) to another (the future). Duration infects not only all of life, which carries the past along with its present; it also affects the universe as a whole. Not only does all of life proceed by differentiation, the material universe as a totality also functions through history, through deviation and surprise.

What Bergson, and through a productive buggery of him, Deleuze, manage to show is that life, duration, and thus history (whether of species or of individuals and groups) are never either a matter of unfolding an already worked out blueprint or simply the gradual accretion of qualities which progress stage by stage or piecemeal over time. Duration proceeds not through the accumulation of information and the growing acquisition of knowledge, but through division, bifurcation, dissociation—by difference, through sudden and unpredictable change, change which overtakes us with its surprise. Duration differs from itself while matter retains self-identity. It is the insertion of duration into matter that produces movement; it is the confrontation of duration with matter as its obstacle that produces innovation and change, evolution and development. Differentiation is thus both external (in the encounter with matter *qua* obstacle) and internal to duration as its energetic force or impetus. Differentiation renders history as the discursive representation of the past for the interests of the future problematic. This is not to make study of the past impossible or unedifying. It is simply to complicate the ways in which history may be harnessed to understand change in terms of what is known, already contained, and understood. The force of difference, the force of virtuality ensures the future the innovative power of a leap.

While Bergson's work has functioned as one of the last flourishings of the tradition of metaphysical thought, a tradition commonly understood as outside of and before the more contemporary concerns with social, cultural, sexual, and political life, his concern with bigger, more abstract, and at times unanswerable questions of life, matter, and duration are nevertheless remarkably timely reminders that the social, cultural, sexual, and political questions—questions of identity, subjectivity, desire, and power that have occupied much of feminist thought for decades—require a bigger and more abstract framework to contextualize them and link them to forces beyond the control of subjects and social groups, forces such groups may utilize but not control.

CHAPTER 7

Merleau-Ponty, Bergson, and

the Question of Ontology

The relation of the philosopher to being is not the frontal relation of the spectator; it is a kind of complicity, an oblique and clandestine relation.
— Merleau-Ponty, *Signs*

I intend to deal here with Merleau-Ponty's relevance to feminist theory somewhat indirectly, largely because I believe that feminist theory, like philosophical theory more generally, must and does always address problems, questions, that rarely admit solutions or have adequate answers. The question or problem is more significant in many ways than the answer or solution, for unless the question is well-formulated, unless the problem provokes us in the right kind of way its answers or solutions make no difference, or they confirm what we already know or feel sure about. Feminist theory addresses, among other things, the problem of how to live in a culture in which the status of women is subordinated to that of men and in which all forms of representation, knowledge, and discourse are generated from the interests and perspectives of only one sex. Feminist theory has commonly mis-taken its task simply as the amelioration — the "solution" — of this status, without adequately asking the related questions of what constitutes improvement, in what and whose terms improvement is to be understood. Rather than solving problems, the task of philosophy, including feminist philosophy, should be to address them adequately, to understand what they implicate us in, to see the pressing events by which the real provokes or generates necessary or pressing questions whose solution is never given, and which would, in any case, not eliminate the question but complicate and elaborate it. At its best, feminist theory, like philosophy, attempts to address the real, the force of events, through the production of questions, concepts, and practices that engage the real without necessarily circumscribing or directly controlling it. These feminist texts are attempts to address the real in terms more inventive and provocative than found in other discourses, both in order to see what underlies other discourses and what is left out of other discourses, but also to transform those discourses and thus to address the real in concrete, complex, inclusive, and varied ways, to enable a multiplicity of perspectives and positions to be relevant to understanding and representing the real.

ONTOLOGIES OF BECOMING

So instead of the more pressing feminist questions directed to political, legal, and ethical concerns, to guaranteeing a specific mode and direction of change, I want to step back to take up a position of greater distance and abstraction, a position where the solution has no place, but where the question as such must be raised: to ontology and thus, ultimately, to metaphysics, that undecidable arena where feminism is required to turn, in spite of itself, in reformulating the questions of subjectivity, intersubjectivity, identity, the body, and materiality that are so central to the long-term development of its political and intellectual projects. I need here to turn away from feminism, at least to turn away from it directly, in order to be able to see it more indirectly and thus less instrumentally. We need a sketch of how to understand what we are thrown into, find ourselves enmeshed in, the given we cannot simply bracket out or ignore. This is not the task of every feminist project, or even most of them. But without some reflection on the most general and abstract conditions of corporeality and materiality, and the forces that weigh on our bodies and their products, we do not have the perspective—the distance—required to see what has commonly remained invisible or unseen in our everyday, even our feminist, habits and assumptions.

We must return, as Merleau-Ponty did, to the question of "wild being," to the question of the substance of the world, to the relations between mind and matter, the living and the natural, and the centrality of perception to conceptualizing their interface, a concern which occupied all of his work, and became the focus of his enigmatic final writings, but which have evaded much feminist conceptualization over the last three decades.[1] The question of the substance of the world, the nature of materiality, the composition of the body, the ingredients of subjectivity, and their relations to the material universe are as worthy of feminist investigation as pragmatic questions of institutional and social change: unless they are addressed in some ways, in some texts, feminism is unable to see any conceptual horizon beyond what the present offers. Without broader and different concepts of the real, the ontological, and the relation between the problem and solutions, feminist theory is unable to invent or develop its own cosmologies, its own ontologies and epistemologies, and ultimately to regenerate or revitalize its political practices.

These questions of mind, matter, things — the provocation of the world, the entwinement of the thing with the subject and the subject with the thing, the ways in which subjects are or can be differentiated from each other, and their different perspectives on and interests in the world — in short, the questions surrounding how we conceive ontological difference — are twentieth-century reformulations of metaphysics, the ways the contemporary forms of philosophy have reconceptualized the intractable metaphysical problems of classical philosophy into the most fundamental if implicit questions of experience, its frame and horizon. I want to explore without defensiveness the metaphysics of Merleau-Ponty, its disavowed relations to a philosophy of process and action developed early in the twentieth century and thus, indirectly, to explore the necessity of a return to the ontological as a question by and for feminist theory as well. As heir to a tradition of concepts developed through the history of Western thought, feminism too needs to inspect and reconsider what its ontological commitments are in order to be able to develop them more explicitly and consciously.[2]

In this highly provisional and exploratory chapter, I would like to position Merleau-Ponty's writings in a different context than that in which it is commonly placed: rather than within his own self-consciously acknowledged lineage of phenomenological thinkers, from Hegel through Husserl to Heidegger, Sartre, and de Beauvoir (and on to feminist phenomenology), I will place his work in a less understood and examined context (though well documented in his own writings): the philosophy of nature, of biology, and of movement of evolutionary theory developed since the mid-nineteenth century. In the time since the provocations of Darwin, whose work on the active dynamism of the natural world, and thus on the active thing and the active subject it generates, transformed the biological sciences (which Merleau-Ponty, more than most philosophers, addresses), the very task and image of philosophy itself has also changed. Philosophy after Darwin could no longer justifiably devote itself to the classical contemplation of unchanging forms or essences, or even Hegelian a priori historical convolutions, but convert itself into something like an attunement to the particular and its history. It is required henceforth, as Merleau-Ponty's work testifies, to take seriously the immersion of consciousness in life, and the immersion of life in time and materiality that Darwinism has left as a question, a gift, to philosophy. In particular, I would like to counterpose Merleau-Ponty's work, not with Darwin himself, though that would be an interesting project, but with the most Darwinian of philosophers, Merleau-Ponty's own predecessor (literally, in the Chair of Philosophy at the Collège de France), Henri Bergson. Instead of comparing and contrasting them, I want to look only at the ways in which Merleau-Ponty addresses Bergson's work, his complex and changing relations with Bergsonism and with Bergson's concern with an ontology of becoming.

In establishing his own phenomenology of perception, one in which perception is understood as intermediary between mind and matter, Merleau-Ponty retains a peculiar ambivalence to Bergson's writings, while remaining tantalizingly close to his position. He insists, in ways that are not entirely fair or accurate, that Bergson be positioned within the vitalist tradition, the tradition that is committed to the belief in a universal life force, a force that all forms of life share and which serves to distinguish the living from nonliving forms; this he counterposes with mechanism, though Bergson himself remains highly critical of vitalism. Bergson too had eschewed any superadded integrity, transcendent unity, or telos to organic existence and instead sought out the latent or immanent forces, impulses that lie behind not only life in its specificity but also in the world of matter considered in its interlocking totality, matter as a whole, the material world from which life emerges and against and within which it develops. There is no life force if one understands that to be a particular, invariant quality conceived external to the living being: life is emergent, developed from below, from particular organizations of matter, not a mystical force, a kind of modern "soul" that animates life from above. One suspects that in the too rapid dismissal of Bergson's key concepts — intuition, duration, intellection — and in the accusations of mysticism and a lack of interest in history that Merleau-Ponty fears in Bergson there is an anxiety of influence, which has often been noted.[3]

Merleau-Ponty devotes two papers directly to Bergson's work and its heritage for the philosophy that followed: his inaugural lecture at the Collège de France, presented in 1953 and published as a long section called "Bergson" in part 2 of *In Praise of Philosophy* (1970); and "Bergson in the Making," a lecture presented in May 1959 for the centenary of Bergson's birth, translated in *Signs* (1964). There is scarcely a text by Merleau-Ponty in which Bergson's name is not mentioned in passing: the trace of Bergson-ism is faint, though ineradicable and it returns to haunt Merleau-Ponty's writings until the end. These texts Merleau-Ponty devotes directly to Berg-son explicitly to honor him; yet there is a reluctant subtext within them, in which he attempts to establish as much distance as possible, to character-ize Bergson with little generosity in elaborating his position. In his earliest paper on Bergson, Merleau-Ponty explicitly welcomes Bergson's openness to the questions of life and the living, his refusal to tie the study of life to the protocols of the natural sciences, academic philosophy, or institutionalized religion: "If we have recalled these words of Bergson, not all of which are in his books, it is because they make us feel that there is a tension in the relation of the philosopher with other persons or with life, and that this uneasiness is essential to philosophy. We have forgotten this" (1970, 33).

Merleau-Ponty seeks to return to the freshness of things in the making (including philosophy itself), rather than things made, seeing in Bergson an opponent of the trends that followed, which he described as Bergson-ian, the continuous grasping for the new and the unthought, the disquieting and the unsettling of philosophical and scientific systems. The Bergson that Merleau-Ponty admires cannot be identified simply with either his earlier or later periods, but with the spirit and intellect that remains consistently committed throughout all his works to the refusal to accept what is given without submitting it to the exigencies of an analysis of its role in experience, in lived reality, without submitting it to intensity:

> The truth is that there are two Bergsonisms. There is that audacious one, when Bergson's philosophy fought and . . . fought well. And there is that other one after the victory, persuaded in advance about what Bergson took a long time to find, and already provided with concepts while Bergson himself created his own. When Bergsonian insights are identified with the vague cause of spiritualism or some other entity, they lose their bite; they are generalized and minimized. What is left is only a retrospective or ex-ternal Bergsonism. . . . Established Bergsonism distorts Bergson. Bergson disturbed; it reassures. Bergson was a conquest; Bergsonism defends and justifies Bergson. Bergson was in contact with things; Bergsonism is a col-lection of accepted opinions. (1964, 182–183)

In spite of his reluctant openness to Bergson himself, what marks these early papers is his refusal of Bergsonism in the derivative sense. Especially after the First World War, Bergsonism became more and more attenuated from its roots in both the history of philosophy and in the natural sciences, became more and more orthodox and dogmatic, as of course is the tendency with all discursive positions which gain a certain level of popularity or notoriety (we have witnessed it ourselves more directly with the rise and fall of various figures—Sartre, Lacan, Althusser, Foucault, Derrida, and so on). Merleau-Ponty quite justifiably remains wary of what he calls Bergsonism while embracing elements of Bergson's own writings. He aspires to a Bergsonism in the first sense, while attempting to distance himself from it in the second sense.

RESONANCES

In spite of his reluctance to be too closely identified with Bergsonism, nevertheless, in a less doctrinaire sense of the word, Merleau-Ponty can, and possibly should, be understood as Bergsonian.[4] There are a number of apparent homologies or close resemblances between their respective positions, which I will broadly indicate.

1. Like Bergson, Merleau-Ponty is committed to the primacy of perception, though unlike Bergson, for whom it is fundamentally connected to the practically oriented intellect and thus to action, for Merleau-Ponty perception is our living immersion in matter, a synthetic, additive rather than an analytic, subtractive ability. Perception synthesizes our relations with a world, projecting onto the world its status as milieu or horizon, rather than reducing and simplifying, silhouetting a world, as Bergson claims. Perception remains, for both, the active energy of labor that brings together the living and the human with the resources of the nonliving.

2. Bergson's understanding of the convergence of matter with memory in action and intuition, like Merleau-Ponty's understanding the relations of subject and object as a shared self-enfolding flesh, move toward what might be understood as a fundamental ontology of difference, in which there are not two opposed identities, mind and matter, subject and object, consciousness and world, but a relation of emergence (and thus debt) from the one to the other, a relation in which one mind, subject, consciousness emerges from and establishes itself through a relation of differentiation from the body, objects, and the world. This relation is not a reciprocity of two terms, the mutual embrace of equivalents, but a relation of debt and belonging.

3. Nature is not understood as passive inertia, Cartesian substance, fixed immanence, on which mind imposes its categories, its designs, and plans, but must be seen as a dynamic and productive set of forces in which the

constraints of determinism in the nonliving world, and the more complex constraints of biological regulation in the living world, do not clash with or complement each other but differentiate out of one another, and thus merge by degrees, from certain points of view and levels of explanation.[5] Nature is that which is both within and without us, a nonnormative order which suffuses but never fixes us, which always places us within its constraints and requirements while generating numerous options for growth, development, and use.

4. The subject is neither a free consciousness, existing independently of perception and action, nor a being immersed in mere reaction to the world but fully corporeal, a being whose corporeality extends it indefinitely out into the world, in its projects, through its virtual and real actions. This being is neither free nor determined, separable from neither other subjects nor from objects except by abstraction and analysis. These are not just subjects in the world; they are subjects for whom perception and proprioception, comportment, the configuration of the senses that constitute the human provide limits and directions within which there is immense flexibility for production and innovation, for newness. Where Merleau-Ponty posits a certain indetermination in the subject's perceptual rendering of the world, Bergson positions this indetermination only in the interval or gap between stimulus and reaction, within the nervous system and the ramifying, infinitely elaborating structures of neuronal organization. This indetermination is the site of a freedom to elaborate and invent.

5. The subject is not a subject because of a particular consciousness but rather because of a particular biological and bodily constitution. Where for Bergson it is primarily creative evolution, for Merleau-Ponty it is phylogenetic development that brings this subject into being: but for both, the subject is not a divergence from biological or bodily processes but the consequence of a particular and concrete bodily configuration, the capacities for activity in a given body. Hence neither Bergsonism nor phenomenology in Merleau-Ponty's terms retains a trace of the hostility toward the biological, the physiological, or the natural science that has marked much of metaphysics, most of phenomenology, and feminist theory. Rather, each remains avidly interested in the empirical formulations offered by scientific observation and speculation. Biological and physiological discourses provided data to be used rather than refuted, tools for speculation and conjecture that are elaborated in and as experience.

6. For both, the body-subject is the site of an inherent doubling: for Berg-

son the body is simultaneously the locus of a geometrical, spatial, material calculation and the site of consciousness with its own complexity and corporeal parameters that remain fundamentally qualitative. These are not two bodies or two locations but one, which is both fully spatial, occupying all of space, and is always and only localized and concerned with the practice of acting upon its desires and needs. In other words, it is both a vast body and a local, small one, depending on where it is focused and whether it functions through intuition or perception:

> For if our body is the matter to which our consciousness applies itself it is coextensive with our conscious, it comprises all we perceive, it reaches to the stars. But this vast body is changing continually, sometimes radically, at the slightest shift of one part of itself which is at its centre and occupies a small fraction of space. This inner and central body, relatively invariable, is ever present. It is not merely present, it is operative: it is through this body and through it alone, that we can move parts of the larger body. And, since action is what matters, since it is an understood thing that we are present where we act, the habit has grown of limiting consciousness to the small body and ignoring the vast one. . . . [T]he surface of all our actual movement, our huge inorganic body is the seat of our potential or theoretically possible actions. (Bergson 1977, 258)

The vast and small body is given its scope and constraints through degrees of contraction and dilation, relations of proximity and possible effect: the smaller body is the center of directed action, the larger body the locus of theoretical, possible, or virtual action.[6] For Merleau-Ponty too, the body is always doubled, reduplicated either in the form of a corporeal schema which re-presents its organic capacities in a psychical and signifying mapping of the body (producing a ghostly and relatively autonomous spectral representation in his earlier writings),[7] or of an enfolding, intertwining of living and nonliving bodies (the seer doubled up in the seen in his later writings): "We say there that our body is a being of two leaves, from one side a thing among other things and otherwise what sees and touches them; we say, because it is evident, that it unites these two properties within itself and its double-belongingness to the order of the 'object' and the order of the 'subject' reveals to us quite unexpected relations between the two orders. It cannot be an incomprehensible accident that the body has this double reference" (Merleau-Ponty 1968, 136).

This duplicity of the body—its simultaneous orientation to the world and its own inner states, to space and to duration, to objects and to its own psychological states—is necessary to account for its complex emergence from the world and its capacity to live in and remake the world.

7. Both Bergson and Merleau-Ponty situate the living being, in its corporeal locatedness, as both a world in itself and a small participant in the world, a being who lives in a world but relocates and resignifies a transcribed world of relevance within itself. For Bergson, it is our participation in our own individual duration, in specific movements as we live them in their unity and simplicity, that necessarily places us with the more cosmological universal duration. Each duration forms a continuity, a single, indivisible movement; and yet, there are many simultaneous durations, which implies that all durations participate in a generalized or cosmological duration, which enables them to be described as simultaneous or successive. For Merleau-Ponty too, our smallness, our concrete locatedness in our bodies directly yields for us the larger world, a greater context, out of which the living are produced. The "fundamental narcissism of all vision" as he describes it (1968, 139) entails that we find in ourselves the very substance of the world; from within our selves we have presented to us the world we live in, as our condition of living in it.[8]

COMPLEXITY

Most significantly, what Merleau-Ponty and Bergson share is an ontology of becoming, an ontology in which consciousness and life, respectively, do not find themselves in a world but make themselves subjects, and make the world into things, objects, entities through their activity, their engagement, their labor. Active becoming is an emergent property of matter itself, its virtual development beyond its given properties. It elaborates itself from and on a field of active forces as their contingent frame. Instead of a being dictated by the world, or at the mercy of other subjects (as Sartre hypothesized), both speculate that the living and the human, perceptual beings, are simultaneously dynamic sites of unpredictable productivity; and systems of coherence, both organic and conceptual unities, drawn from fields of disparity, which partially integrate and cohere what is fundamentally a mode of difference, the being's difference from itself, its inherent orientation to the future, to what it is becoming, to what does not yet exist.

Merleau-Ponty recognizes in Bergson's heritage this affinity of life with matter, the ways in which matter induces in life, in consciousness, a kind of elevation of itself to the realm of indeterminate creativity, as well as a sharing, a coexisting in time between the living and the nonliving: "We are not this pebble, but when we look at it, it awakens resonances in our perceptive apparatus; our perception appears to come from it. That is to say our perception of the pebble is a kind of promotion to (conscious) existence for itself; it is our recovery of this mute thing which, from the time it enters our life, begins to unfold its implicit being, which is revealed to itself through us. What we believe to be coincidence is coexistence" (Merleau-Ponty 1964, 17).

It is perhaps Bergson's fascination with this question, the problem and the provocation that matter and the event hold as the resource and resistance necessary for life and for thought, that most attracts Merleau-Ponty to him; and it is Bergson's apparent recourse to mysticism surrounding his understanding of intuition as a direct communion with things that repels Merleau-Ponty. But this hypothesis remains unclear, for the animus to Bergson's earlier writings, and especially *Matter and Memory*, erupts at virtually every opportunity — generally in the form of elaborate, detailed, and often gratuitous footnotes.

To briefly highlight the general thrust of Merleau-Ponty's critical remarks, I will simply indicate the tenor of charges and criticisms he levels at Bergson. Virtually all of Merleau-Ponty's claims here seem to be based on a misreading or a misunderstanding of Bergson's position. Nevertheless the criticisms he levels at Bergson are worth exploring. First, Bergson remains, in spite of the complexity of his position, a vitalist, with all the idealist and preformist resonances this term has. And the vitalism of life itself that Bergson espouses, Merleau-Ponty suggests, leaves untouched the mechanism of bodily processes. His vitalism is a form of irrational mysticism, and leaves him open to a surreptitious mechanism as well. In other words, in spite of himself, Bergson reintroduces the mind/body split: "The relation of the vital élan to that which it produces is not conceivable, it is magical. Since the physico-chemical reactions of which the organism is the seat cannot be abstracted from those of milieu, how can the act which creates an organic individual be circumscribed in this continuous whole and where should the zone of influence of the vital élan be limited? It will indeed be necessary to introduce an unintelligible break here" (Merleau-Ponty 1983, 158).

Then, in a series of closely related, perhaps even cascading objections, Merleau-Ponty claims that retaining the mind/body dualism infects Bergson's understanding of duration, which is thereby fissured into a fixed divide between a continuous, snowballing present — the experience of the body — and a permanent and fixed past — the world of mind or memory — such that this ruptures the very cohesion and continuity of duration Bergson seeks to elucidate:

Generally speaking, Bergson saw that the body and the mind communicate with each other through the medium of time, that to be a mind is to stand above time's flow and that to have a body is to have a present. The body, he says, is an instantaneous section made in the becoming of consciousness (*Matière et Mémoire*, p. 150). But the body remains for him what we have called the objective body; consciousness remains knowledge; time remains a successive "now," whether it "snowballs upon itself" or is spread as spatialized time. Bergson can therefore only compress or expand the series of "present moments"; he never reaches the unique movement whereby the three dimensions of time are constituted, and one cannot see why duration is squeezed into a present, or why consciousness becomes involved in a body and a world" (Merleau-Ponty 1962, 78–79 fn)

Merleau-Ponty's third claim targets Bergson's direct equation of the epistemological with the ontological, collapsing our knowledge of a thing with its being. This slippage between what I know and what there is conflates the subject with the object. This conflation is the consequence of Bergson's problematic understanding of intuition as the coincidence of the subject with the fullness or plenitude of the object, indeed, in Merleau-Ponty's terms, the reflection of the object in the subject:

> The core of philosophy is no longer an autonomous transcendental subjectivity, to be found everywhere and nowhere: it lies in the perpetual beginning of reflection, at the point where individual life has to reflect on itself. Reflection is truly reflection only if it is not carried out inside itself, only if it knows itself as reflection-on-an-unreflected-experience, and consequently as a change in structure of our experience. We earlier attacked Bergsonian intuitionism and introspection for seeking to know by coinciding. . . . Bergson's mistake consists in believing that the thinking subject can become fused with the object thought about, and that knowledge can swell and be incorporated into being. The mistake of reflective philosophies is to believe that the thinking subject can absorb into its thinking or appropriate without remainder the object of its thought, that our being can be brought down to our knowledge. (Merleau-Ponty 1962, 62)

The fourth claim addresses Bergson's concept of duration. Although Bergson's understanding of duration did in effect revolutionize the way in which time could be philosophically conceptualized, his conception nevertheless, in spite of its claims to a fundamental fluidity (Bergson describes it as a liquid conception of time) is an arresting and freezing of time, the rendering of either a complete merging of past, present, and future or their absolute isolation from each other:

> The consciousness of my gesture, if it is truly a state of undivided consciousness, is no longer consciousness of movement at all, but an incommunicable quality which can tell us nothing about movement. . . . If, in virtue of the principle of continuity, the past still belongs to the present and the present already to the past, there is no longer any past or present. If consciousness snowballs upon itself, it is, like the snowball or everything else, wholly in the present. If the phases of movement gradually merge into one another, nothing is anywhere in motion. The unity of time, space and movement cannot come about through any coalescence, and cannot be understood either by any real operation. If consciousness is multiplicity, who is to gather together this multiplicity in order to experience it as such, and if consciousness is fusion, how shall it come to know the multiplicity of moments which it fuses together?" (1962, 276 fn)

Each of these claims, if it is accurate, constitutes a devastating criticism, which, taken together, would be enough to convince the average reader to believe Merleau-Ponty had repudiated the value of Bergsonism. But nothing is further from the truth. The more critical of Bergson he explicitly becomes, the more Merleau-Ponty (unconsciously?) seems to absorb a more accurate Bergsonism, and the more his own writings become Bergsonian. What is striking about his last writings, gathered together in *The Visible and the Invisible* (1968) is the remarkable convergence of his conception of the flesh of the world with the Bergsonian understanding of the becoming of being.

THE FLESH OF THE WORLD

Merleau-Ponty's final and posthumously published collection *The Visible and the Invisible*, as is well known, presents a breathtaking departure from the more structural and structured writings he had previously published. In the paper "The Intertwining—the Chiasm," as well as in the detailed working notes published in that collection, he turns to a new ontology and a new conception of the relations between mind and matter, subject and object, consciousness and the world. While this vision remains both highly suggestive and largely underdeveloped, it harkens back more to the writings of Bergson than it does to the tradition of phenomenology.

Whereas in his earlier works Merleau-Ponty stresses the fundamental interimplication of the subject in the object and the object in the subject and the necessary integration of the visual in the tactile and vice versa,[9] in his last text, he explores the interrelations of the inside and the outside, the subject and object, one sense and another, in a common flesh — which he describes as the "crisscrossing" of the seer and the visible, of the toucher and the touched, the indeterminacy of the "boundaries" of each of the senses, their inherent transposability, their refusal to submit to the exigencies of clear-cut separation or logical identity.[10] What is described as flesh is the shimmering of the world's difference from itself, and thus the subject's difference from itself.[11] "The flesh" is the term Merleau-Ponty uses to designate being, not as plenitude, self-identity, or substance, but as divergence (*écart*), noncoincidence, or difference. For him, the notion of flesh is no longer associated with a privileged (animate) category, but is being's most elementary ontological level. Flesh is being as reversibility, its capacity to fold in on itself, its dual orientation inward onto psychical states and outward to the world.

It is possible to indicate the Bergsonism of Merleau-Ponty's last work, his gesturing toward a conception of the cosmological world in which there is a univocity of being, a single flesh which includes, as its two surfaces or planes, the world of inert objects (matter) and the world of living beings (consciousness). No longer are the subject and the object two separate, other-affirming, self-identical entities; no longer does consciousness bestow signification on the world of the in-itself: the in-itself and the for-itself are melded into a single, self-enfolded flesh, a single substance with a conscious reverse and a material obverse: "There is here no problem with the *alter ego* because it is not *I* who sees, not *he* who sees, because an anonymous visibility inhabits both of us, a vision in general, in virtue of that primordial property that belongs to the flesh, being here and now, of radiating everywhere and forever, being an individual, of being also a dimension and a universal" (1968, 142).

Merleau-Ponty suggests a notion of flesh as a designation of the world's capacity to turn in on itself, to cycle itself through the living and the non-living as modes of their mutual entwinement and necessary interlinkage.[12] The flesh of the world does not just clothe all — subjects, objects, and their relations — with its touch; it doubles back on itself, it reduplicates itself as the invisible underside of the visible, the push, in Bergsonian terms, of the virtual on the actual, the clothing of all materiality with an inner lining of ideality, of potentiality to transmute itself, through a virtual reversibility, into the substance of beings and things:

> Once we have entered into this strange domain [of the flesh], one does not see how there could be any question of *leaving* it. If there is an animation

of the body; if vision and the body are tangled up in one another; if . . . the surface of the visible, is doubled over its whole extension with an invisible reserve; and if finally, in our flesh as in the flesh of things, the actual empirical, ontic visible, by a sort of folding back, invagination, or padding, exhibits a visibility, a possibility that is not the shadow of the actual but is its principle, that is not the proper contribution of a "thought" but is its condition — then the immediate and dualist distinction between the visible and the invisible, between extension and thought, [is] impugned, not that extension be thought and thought be extension, but because they are the obverse and the reverse of one another, and the one forever behind the other." (1968, 152)

Merleau-Ponty presents a vision, a conceptualization, of the malleability of substance, its hitherto unconsidered complexity, its capacity to redouble itself, to invaginate itself, without actually detailing it. He presents a picture of a vast, dynamic universe which provides itself with a mode of reflection in the form of the perceptual agents that are both part of it and are capable of provisionally seeing it from a point of view, framing it, acting within and with it. It is only this fundamental belonging together of consciousness and knowledge to the complexity of the world that enables consciousness to know, to have language, to represent and reflect as well as to act. Flesh brings to the world the capacity to turn the world back on itself, to induce its reflexivity, to fold over itself, to introduce that fold in flesh in which subjectivity is positioned as a perceiving, perspectival frame. The flesh is composed of "leaves" of the body and "leaves" of the world: it is the chiasm linking and separating the one from the other, the "pure difference" whose play generates subjects and things, and their belonging together. Things solicit the flesh just as the flesh beckons to and is an object for things. Perception is the flesh's reversibility, the flesh touching, seeing, perceiving itself, one fold (provisionally) catching the other in its own self-embrace.

It is of some significance that in his final notes Merleau-Ponty explicitly refers to Bergson's account of a universal movement toward complexity, a movement in which no object is capable of anything but a pragmatic separation from the rest of being, and in which the subject has no sovereignty or control but functions as an element or factor. It seems clear from these published fragments that he intended to further elaborate this understanding of a wild being in part through a return to, and hopefully a reevaluation of, Bergson's most central precepts regarding memory, the past, perception, things, and subjectivity:

I said: the openness to the world such as we rediscover it in ourselves and the perception we divine within life (a perception that at the same time is spontaneous being [thing] and being-self ["subject"] — Bergson once explicitly said . . . that there is a consciousness that is at the same time spontaneous and reflected) intertwine, encroach upon, or cling to one another.

Make clear what that means.

That evokes, beyond the "point of view of the object" and the "point of view of the subject," a common nucleus which is the "winding," being as a winding (what I called "modulation of the being in the world"). It is necessary to make understood how that . . . is a perception "being formed in things." This is still only an approximate expression, in the subject-object language (Wahl, Bergson) of what there is to be said. That is, that the things have us, and that it is not we who have the things. That the being that has been cannot stop having been. The "Memory of the World." That language has us and it is not we who have language. That it is being that speaks within us and not we who speak of being. (1968, 193–194)

Is the flesh of the world Merleau-Ponty's mode of reformulating what Bergson understands as creative evolution? Is Merleau-Ponty more Bergsonian than he would like? Or has he reviewed his earlier opinion of Bergson's writings and seen them in a more positive light? "In reality, life is a movement, materiality is the inverse movement, and each of these two movements is simple, the matter which forms a world being an undivided flux, and undivided also the life that runs through it, cutting out in it living beings all along its track. Of these two currents the second runs counter to the first, but the first obtains, all the same, something from the second. There results between them a *modus vivendi*, which is organization" (Bergson 1944, 249–250).

The striking resonances between this shimmering of being that constitutes a world-becoming in Bergson and which constitutes flesh in Merleau-Ponty point to an opening up of Merleau-Ponty to metaphysical questions, those questions linked to the limits of subjectivity and the limits of materiality, so powerfully posed by Bergson.

ONTOLOGIES OF THE QUESTION

I began this chapter by claiming that the ontological is that real which provokes, incites and induces, a real that is one of the objects of political struggle but has never been adequately addressed in ontological terms. The ontological has been reduced, bit by bit, to the epistemological, to the representational, and to the reflective, but it remains an abiding, indeed an intractable commitment that politics, ethics, aesthetics—the realm of the intersubjective and the collective more generally—must make in spite of themselves.[13] The crucial questions of subjectivity and intersubjectivity to which feminist theory has addressed itself have an unacknowledged underside: the subjective, the intersubjective, the human must be positioned in a context in which the subhuman, the extrahuman, and the nonhuman play a formative but not a determining role, in which the human in its diverse forms and corporealities emerges from and functions within natural, technological, and social orders in which it finds itself placed as event and advent rather than as agent.

What Merleau-Ponty grasped toward, throughout his writings, was a way of understanding our relation to the world, not as one of merger or oneness, or of control and mastery, but a relation of belonging to and of not quite fitting, a never-easy kinship, a given tension that makes our relations to the world hungry, avid, desiring, needy, that makes us need a world as well as desire to make one, that makes us riven through with the very nature, materiality, worldliness that our conception of ourselves as pure consciousness, as a for-itself, daily belies.

What has this to do with feminist theory? Why are these obscure, abstract, and nonpractical questions—questions without instrumental value—of any relevance to feminist or other political concerns? Because they are irreducible questions, because we make assumptions about the real, about nature (our own and the world's), about matter whenever we act: all our actions presuppose a world, worlds, in which those actions are both viable and capable of signification and effectivity. As Bergson makes clear, and Merleau-Ponty affirms, it is the resistance of the world to the immediacy of human wishes, its capacity to make us wait, that makes us produce and invent, that makes us human, conscious beings. It is because we cannot but be beings who deal with and through matter, objects, things that we invent, imagine, and use the world to live in. It is the adversity of matter itself, just as it is adversity of political and social kinds, that precisely generates problems, and frames the inventions that act as its temporary solutions. The task facing feminist theory, in this moment of its maturing, is to provide the formulation of those kinds of questions that will generate inventiveness, new models, frameworks, tools for new activities: "The truth is that in philosophy and even elsewhere it is a question of *finding* the problem and consequently of *positing* it, even more than of solving it . . . stating the problem is not uncovering, it is inventing. Discovery, or uncovering, has to do with what already exists actually or virtually; it was therefore certain to happen sooner or later. Invention gives being to what did not exist; it might never have happened. Already in mathematics and still more in metaphysics, the effort of invention consists most often in raising the problem, in creating the terms in which it will be stated" (Bergson 1992, 58–59).

Bergson may well have stated the most succinct formula for politics in articulating his metaphysics: politics, as much as life itself, is that which "gives being to what did not exist." This too is the task of feminist politics and feminist knowledges: to give being to that which may become, to explore openly that which we do not yet know, to expand on that which we might come to know and on our ways of knowing. This expansion of feminist theory—beyond feminism's common focus on dealing with empirical women as its objects and beyond its analysis of (the repression or expression of) femininity and its representations within the patriarchal order to raise new questions about materiality, cosmology, the natural order, about how we know and what are the limits, costs, and underside of our knowledge— is necessary in order to develop new ideals, new forms of representation, new types of knowledge, and new epistemological criteria. Merleau-Ponty and Bergson, while being unable to account for or elaborate new concepts of woman or the feminine, may nevertheless prove indispensable in helping to formulate how we might know differently, how we might challenge and replace binarized models (of subject and object, self and object, consciousness and matter, nature and culture) with concepts of difference. Thus we may consider what the objects of our representational and epistemological practices might be if they were undertaken with this concept of difference, the difference in being that is becoming, the difference in subjectivity that is biological open-endedness, this difference in the world that is life, were a guiding principle. A feminism of difference, no longer restricted to sexual difference but based upon it, may find its intellectual predecessors in the wayward writings of those (male) philosophers whose own openness to difference has given hints of how far sexual difference can go: to the furthest reaches of the cosmos, and into every kind of knowledge.

Philosophy should be an effort to go beyond the human state.
—Henri Bergson, *The Creative Mind*

The thing goes by many names. Indeed the very label, "the thing," is only a recent incarnation of a series of terms which have an illustrious philosophical lineage: the object, matter, substance, the world, noumena, reality, appearance, and so on. In the period of modern philosophy, from Descartes through Kant to Hegel, the thing became that against which we measured ourselves and our limits, the mirror of what we are not. But instead of outlining *this* history, paying homage to the great thinkers of the thing, and particularly to the scientists who devoted their intellectual labors to unraveling its properties and deciphering the laws regulating its relations, I am seeking an altogether different lineage, in which the thing, the object, or materiality is not conceived as the other, the binary double, of the subject, the self, embodiment, or consciousness, but is the resource for the subject's being and enduring. Instead of turning to Descartes or his hero Newton to understand things and the laws governing them, we must instead begin with Darwin, and with his understanding of the thing—the dynamism of the active world of natural selection—as that which provides the obstacle, the question, the means by which life itself grows, develops, undergoes evolution and change, becomes other than what it once was. The thing is the provocation of the nonliving, the half-living, or that which has no life, to the living, to the potential of and for life.

THINGS

The thing in itself is not, as Kant suggested, noumenal, that which lies behind appearances and which can never appear as such, that which we cannot know or perceive. Rather, if we follow Darwin, the thing is the real which we both find and make. The thing has a history: it is not simply a passive inertia against which we measure our own activity. It has a "life" of its own, characteristics of its own, which we must incorporate into our activities in order to be effective, rather than simply understanding, regulating, and neutralizing it from the outside. We need to accommodate things more than they accommodate us. Life is the growing accommodation of matter, the adaptation of the needs of life to the exigencies of matter. It is matter, the thing, that produces life; sustains and provides life with its biological organization and orientation; and requires life to overcome itself, to evolve, to become more. We find the thing in the world as our resource for making things, and in the process we leave our trace on things, we fabricate things out of what we find. The thing is the resource, in other words, for both subjects and technology.

As the pragmatists understood, the thing is a question, provocation, incitement, or enigma.[1] The thing, matter already configured, generates invention, the assessment of means and ends, and thus enables practice. The thing poses questions to us, questions about our needs and desires, questions above all of action: the thing is our provocation to action, and is itself the result of our action. But more significantly, while the thing functions as fundamental provocation, as that which, in the virtuality of the past and the immediacy of the present cannot be ignored, it also functions as a *promise*, as that which, in the future, in retrospect, yields a destination or effect, another thing. The thing is the precondition of the living and the human, their means of survival, and the consequence or product of life and its practical needs. The thing is the point of intersection of space and time, the locus of the temporal narrowing and spatial localization that constitutes specificity or singularity. Things are the localization of materiality, the capacity of material organization to yield to parts, microsystems, units, or entities. They express the capacity of material organization to divide itself, to be divided from without, so that they may become of use for the living.

SPACE AND TIME

The thing emerges out of and as substance. It is the coming-into-existence of a prior substance or thing, in a new time, creating beneath its processes of production a new space and a coherent entity. The thing and the space it inscribes and produces are inaugurated at the same moment, the moment that movement is arrested, frozen, or dissected to reveal its momentary aspects, the moment that the thing and the space that surrounds it are differentiated conceptually or perceptually. The moment that movement must be reflected upon, analyzed, it yields objects and their states, distinct, localized, mappable, repeatable in principle, objects and states capable of measurement and containment. The depositing of a mappable trajectory by movement, its capacity to be divided and to be seen statically, are the mutual conditions of the thing and of space. The thing is positioned or located in space only because time is implicated, only because the thing is the dramatic slowing down of the movements, the atomic and molecular vibrations and forces, that frame, contextualize, and merge with and alongside of other things.

The thing is the transmutation, the conversion of two into one: the conversion of the previous thing, plus the energy invested in the process of its production as a different thing, a unity or a one. The making of the thing, the thing in the process of its production as a thing, is that immeasurable process that the thing must belie and disavow to be a thing. Both James and Bergson agree that, in a certain sense, although the world exists independent of us, although there is a real which remains even when the human disappears, things as such do not exist in the real. The thing is a certain carving out of the real, the (artificial or arbitrary) division of the real into entities, bounded and contained systems, nominal or usable units, that exist within the real only as open systems.

The thing is what we make of the world rather than simply what we find in the world, the way we are able to manage and regulate it according to our needs and purposes. It is an outlined imposition we make on specific regions of the world so that these regions become comprehensible and facilitate our purposes and projects, even while limiting and localizing them. Things are our way of dealing with a world in which we are enmeshed rather than over which we have dominion. The thing is the compromise between the world as it is in its teaming and interminable multiplicity—a flux as James calls it, an undivided continuum in Lacan's conceptualization, or waves of interpenetrating vibrations, in Bergson's understanding—and the world as we need it to be or would like it to be—open, amenable to intention and purpose, flexible, pliable, manipulable, passive, a compromise between mind and matter, the point of their crossing one into the other. It is our way of dealing with the plethora of sensations, vibrations, movements, and intensities that constitute both our world and ourselves, a practical exigency, indeed perhaps only one mode, not a necessary condition, of our acting in the world. Just as Kant imposed space and time as a priori intuitions, which we have no choice but to invoke and utilize, so too we must regard objects, distinguished from other objects and from a background, as necessary if limited conditions under which we act in the world.[2] As Bergson makes clear in his conversions of Kantianism into an ontology of becoming, time is not *in* us, for we are in time, it is our limit and our condition for action. Space, time, and things are conceptually connected: space and time are understood to frame and contextualize the thing, they serve as its background, and they are, as it were, deposited by or inhere in things and processes: "Cosmic space and cosmic time, so far from being the intuitions that Kant said they were, are constructions as patently artificial as any that science can show. The great majority of the human race never use these notions, but live in the plural times and spaces" (James 1970, 118).

Bergson elaborates and develops James's position: the world as it is in its swarming complexity cannot be an object of intelligence, for it is the function of intelligence to facilitate action, practice — distancing himself, along with James, from the Kantian concept of a temporality and spatiality internal to the order of reason. The possibility of action entails that objects and their relations must remain as simplified as possible, as coagulated, unified, and massive as they can be so their contours or outlines, their surfaces most readily promote indeterminate action. We cannot but reduce this multiplicity to the order of things and states if we are to act upon and with them in any way, and if we are to live among things and use them for our purposes. Our intellectual and perceptual faculties function most ably when dealing with solids, with states, with things, though we find ourselves at home most readily, unconsciously or intuitively, with processes and movements, modes of variation, or flux:

> Reality is mobile. There do not exist *things* made, but only things in the making, not *states* that remain fixed, but only states in process of change. Rest is never anything but apparent, or rather, relative. . . . *All reality is, therefore, tendency, if we agree to call tendency a nascent change of direction.*
>
> Our mind, which seeks solid bases of operation, has as its principal function, in the ordinary course of life, to imagine *states* and *things.* Now

and then it takes quasi-instantaneous views of the undivided mobility of the real. It thus obtains *sensations* and *ideas*. By that means it substitutes fixed points which mark a direction of change and tendency. This substitution is necessary to common sense, to language, to practical life, and even . . . to positive science. *Our intelligence, when it follows its natural inclination, proceeds by solid perceptions on the one hand, and by stable conceptions on the other.* (Bergson 1992, 223; emphasis in the original)

We stabilize masses, particles large and small, out of vibrations, waves, intensities, so we can act upon and within them, rendering the mobile and the multiple provisionally unified and singular, framing the real through things as objects for us. We actively produce, make, objects in the world and in doing so we make the world amenable to our actions, but also render ourselves vulnerable to their reactions. This active making is part of our engagement in the world, the directive force of our perceptual and motor relations within the world. Our perception carves up the world, and divides it into things. These things themselves are divisible, amenable to calculation and further subdivision. They are the result of a subtraction: perception, intellectual cognition, and action reduce and refine the object, highlighting and isolating that which in it is of interest or of potential relevance to our future action. The object is that cutting of the world that enables me to see how it meets my needs and interests: "The objects which surround my body reflect its possible action upon them" (Bergson 1988, 21).

> The separation between a thing and its environment cannot be absolutely definite and clear-cut; there is a passage by insensible gradations from the one to the other: the close solidarity which binds all the objects of the material universe, the perpetuality of their reciprocal actions and reactions, is sufficient to prove that they have not the precise limits which we attribute to them. Our perception outlines, so to speak, the form of their nucleus; it terminates them at the point where our possible action upon them ceases, where, consequently, they cease to interest our needs. Such is the primary and the most apparent operation of the perceiving mind: it marks out divisions in the continuity of the extended, simply following the suggestions of our requirements and the needs of practical life. (1988, 209–210)

This cutting of the world, this whittling down of the plethora of the world's interpenetrating qualities—those "pervading concrete extensity, *modifications, perturbations,* changes of *tension* or of *energy* and nothing else" (1988, 201)—into objects amenable to our action is fundamentally a *constructive* process: we make or fabricate the world of objects as an activity we undertake by living with and assimilating objects. We make objects in order to live in the world. Or, in another, Nietzschean sense, we must live in the world artistically, not as *homo sapiens* but as *homo faber*:

> Let us start, then, from action, and lay down that the intellect aims, first of all, at constructing. This fabrication is exercised exclusively on inert matter, in this sense, that even if it makes use of organized material, it treats it as inert, without troubling about the life which animated it. And of inert matter itself, fabrication deals only with the solid; the rest escapes by its very fluidity. If, therefore, the tendency of the intellect is to fabricate, we may expect to find that whatever is fluid in the real will escape it in part, and whatever is life in the living will escape it altogether. *Our intelligence, as it leaves the hands of nature, has for its chief object the unorganized solid.* (Bergson 1944, 153)

We cannot help but view the world in terms of solids, as things. But we leave behind something untapped of the fluidity of the world, the movements, vibrations, transformations that occur below the threshold of perception and calculation and outside the relevance of our practical concerns. Bergson suggests that we have other access to this rich profusion of vibrations that underlie the solidity of things.[3] He describes these nonintellectual, or extraintellectual impulses as instincts and intuitions, and while they are no more able to perceive the plethora of vibrations and processes that constitute the real, they are able to discern the interconnections rather than the separations between things, to develop another perspective or interest in the division and production of the real. Intuition is our nonpragmatic, noneffective, nonexpedient, noninstrumental relation to the world, the capacity we have to live in the world in excess of our needs, and in excess of the self-presentation or immanence of materiality, to collapse ourselves, as things, back into the world. Our "artisticness," as Nietzsche puts it, our creativity, in Bergsonian terms, consists in nothing else than the continuous experimentation with the world of things to produce new things from the fluidity or flux which eludes everyday need, or use-value.

TECHNOLOGY AND THE EXPERIMENTAL

Technology, as material invention, is clearly one of the realm of "things" produced by and as the result of the provocation of things-as-the-world. While things produce and are what is produced by the activities of life, things themselves are the object and project not only of the living but also of the technological. Technology is metaproduction: the production of things to produce things, a second-order production. Technology is in a sense the inevitable result of the encounter between life and matter, life and things, the consequence of the living's capacity to utilize the nonliving (and the living) *prosthetically*. There has been technology for as long as there has been the human: the primates' capacity for the use of found objects prefigures both the human and the technological. From the moment in which the human appears as such, it appears alongside of both artifacts and technologies, *poesis* and *techné*, which are the human's modes of evolutionary fitness, the compensations for its relative bodily vulnerability. According to Bergson, it is the propensity of instinct (in animals) and intelligence (in higher primates and man) to direct themselves to things, and thus to the making of things; and for Bergson, it is the status and nature of the instruments to which life is directed that distinguish the instincts from intelligence, yet connect them in a developmental continuum, with intelligence functioning as an elaboration and deviation of instinct.

> Instinct perfected is a faculty of using and even of constructing organizing instruments; intelligence perfected the faculty of making and using unorganized instruments.
>
> The advantages and drawbacks of these two modes of activity are obvious. Instinct finds the appropriate instrument at hand: this instrument, which makes and repairs itself, which presents, like all the works of nature, an infinite complexity of detail combined with a marvelous simplicity of function, does at once, when required, what it is called upon to do, without difficulty and with a perfection that is often wonderful. In return, it retains an almost invariable structure, since a modification of it involves a modification of the species. . . . The instrument constructed intelligently, on the contrary, is an imperfect instrument. It costs an effort. It is generally troublesome to handle. But, as it is made of unorganized matter, it can take any form whatsoever, serve any purpose, free the living being from every new difficulty that arises and bestow on it an unlimited number of powers. Whilst it is inferior to the natural instrument for the satisfaction of immediate wants, its advantage over it is greater, the less urgent the need. Above all, it reacts on the nature of the being that constructs it; for in calling on him to exercise a new function, it confers on him, so to speak, a richer organization, being an artificial organ by which the natural organism is extended. For every need that it satisfies, it creates a new need; and

so, instead of closing, like instinct, the round of action within which the animal tends to move automatically, it lays open to activity an unlimited field into which it is driven further and further, and made more and more free. (1944, 140–141)

Bergson suggests that instinct finds a kind of technology ready at hand in the body and its organs, in found objects whose use is instinctively dictated, and in the differential dispersal of instinctual capacities in highly stratified social animals, as many insects are. Intelligence, on the other hand, invents, makes technology, but also diverts natural objects into technological products through their unexpected and innovative use.

Animals invent. They have instruments, which include their own body parts, as well as external objects. Humans produce technologies, and especially instruments that are detached and different from their own bodies, instruments which the body must learn to accommodate, instruments which transform both the thingness of things, and the body itself:

> Invention becomes complete when it is materialized in a manufactured instrument. Towards that achievement the intelligence of animals tends as towards an ideal. . . . As regards human intelligence, it has not been sufficiently noted that mechanical invention has been from the first its essential feature, that even today our social life gravitates around the manufacture and use of artificial instruments, that the inventions which strew the road of progress have also traced its direction. . . . In short, *intelligence, considered in what seems to be its original feature, is the faculty of manufacturing artificial objects, especially tools to make tools, and of indefinitely varying the manufacture.* (Bergson 1944, 138–139; emphasis in the original)

Technologies involve the invention of things that make things, second-order things. It is not that technologies mediate between the human and the natural — for that is to construe technology as somehow outside either the natural or the human (which today is precisely its misrepresented place) instead of seeing it as the indefinite extension of both the human and the natural and their point of overlap, the point of the conversion of the one into the other, the tendency of nature to culture, and the cleaving of culture to the stuff of nature. Rather, the technological is the cultural construction of the thing that controls and regulates other things, the correlate of the natural thing.

As Bergson acknowledges, technological invention, while clumsy and cumbersome relative to the instrumentality our bodies provide us, does not succumb to a preexistent function. While technology is in a sense made by us and for our purposes, it also performs a transformation on us: it increasingly facilitates not so much better action, but wider possibilities of acting, more action. (It is certainly not clear that the human, with technology, is any better prepared for the task of survival than the insect with its instinctual attunements to its environment.) Technology is the great aid to action, for it facilitates, requires, and generates intelligence, which in turn radically multiplies our possibilities of action, our instrumental and practical relation with the world: "The essential function of intelligence is . . . to see the way out of a difficulty in any circumstances whatever, to find what is most suitable, what answers best the question asked. Hence it bears essentially on the relations between a given situation and the means of utilizing it" (1944, 150–151).

In an extraordinary passage, Bergson claims that the intellect transforms matter into things, which render them as prostheses, artificial organs, and in a surprising reversal, at the same time, it humanizes or *orders* nature, appends itself as a kind of prosthesis to inorganic matter itself, to function as its rational supplement, its conscious rendering. Matter and life become reflections, through the ordering the intellect makes of the world. Things become the measure of life's action upon them, things become "standing reserve," life itself becomes extended through things:

> All the elementary forces of the intellect tend to transform matter into an instrument of action, that is, in the etymological sense of the word, into an *organ*. Life, not content with producing organisms, would fain give them as an appendage inorganic matter itself, converted into an immense organ by the industry of the living being. Such is the initial task it assigns to intelligence. That is why the intellect always behaves as if it were fascinated by the contemplation of inert matter. It is life looking outward, adopting the ways of unorganized nature in principle, in order to direct them in fact. (1944, 161)

Inorganic matter, transformed into an immense organ, a prosthesis, is perhaps the primordial or elementary definition of architecture itself, which is, in a sense, both the first prosthesis — the first instrumental use of intelligence to meld the world into things, and through a certain primitive technicity, to produce those things that may alleviate even as they produce the needs of the living — and the first art form, the most primitive and elementary form of framing, which may, following Deleuze and Guattari (in *What*

Is Philosophy?), be understood as a primary deterritorialization of the earth and its intensities, a primitive and provisional creation of a plane of consistency from the chaos of the natural forces of the earth. The inorganic becomes the mirror for the possible action of the living, the armature and architecture necessary for the survival and evolution of the living. Making, acting, functioning in the world, making oneself as one makes things—all these processes rely on and produce things as the correlate of intellect, and leave behind the multiple, ramifying interconnections of the real out of which they were drawn and of which they are simplifications and schematizations.

MAKING

What is left out in this process of making/reflecting is all that is in matter, all that is outside the thing and outside technology: the flux of the real (Bergson 1944, 250), duration, vibration, radiance, contractions and dilations, the multiplicity of the real, all that is not contained by the thing or by intellectual categories. What is left out of the world of things is the pure difference out of which they are cut. The uncontained, the outside of matter, of things, that which is not pragmatically available for use, is the object of different actions than that of intelligence and the technological. This outside, though, is not noumenal, outside all possible experience, but phenomenal, contained within it. It is simply that which is beyond the calculable, the framed, or contained. It is the outside that the arts, the sciences, and philosophy each require but cannot claim as their own, and which contaminates each with the concerns of the others. Bergson understands this outside in a number of ways: as the real in its totality, as mobility, as movement, flux, duration, the virtual, the continuity which places the human within and as the material. It is the making of things, and that from which things are made, rather than the things themselves that are now in question. It is this which the rigorous process of intuition draws us toward, not things themselves so much as the teaming, suffuse network within which things are formed and outlined.

This teaming flux of the real, "that continuity of becoming which is reality itself" (1988, 139), the integration and unification of the most minute relations of matter so that they exist only by touching and interpenetrating, the flow and mutual investment of material relations into each other must be symbolized, reduced to states, things, and numeration in order to facilitate practical action. This is not an error that we commit, a fault to be unlearned, but a condition of our continuing survival in the world. We could not function within this teaming multiplicity without some ability to skeletalize it, to diagram or simplify it. Yet this reduction and division occurs only at a cost, which is the failure or inability of our scientific, representational, and linguistic systems to acknowledge the in-between of things, the plural interconnections that cannot be utilized or contained within and by things but which makes them possible. Things are solids, more and more minute in their constitution, as physics itself elaborates more and more minute fundamental particles. "Our intelligence is the prolongation of our senses. Before we speculate we must live, and life demands that we make use of matter, either with our organs, which are natural tools, or with tools, properly so-called, which are artificial organs. Long before there was a philosophy and a science, the role of intelligence was already that of manufacturing instruments and guiding the actions of our body on surrounding bodies. Science has pushed this labor of intelligence much further, but has not changed its direction. It aims above all at making us masters of matter" (Bergson 1944, 43).

While the intellect masters what we need from the world for our purposes, it is fundamentally incapable of understanding what in the world, in objects and in us, is fluid, innumerable, outside calculation.[4] The limit of the intellect is the limit of the technical and the technological. The intellect functions to dissect, divide, atomize: contemporary binarization and digitalization are simply the current versions of this tendency to the clear-cut, the unambiguous, the oppositional or binary impulses of the intellect, which are bound by the impetus to (eventual or possible) actions. The technological, including and especially contemporary digital technologies, carries within it both the intellectual impulse to the division of relations into solids and entities, objects or things, ones and zeros, and the living impulse to render the world practically amenable. Digitization translates, retranscribes, and circumscribes the fluidity and flux by decomposing the analogue or the continuous into elements, packages, or units, represented by the binary code, and then recomposing them through addition: analysis then synthesis. But these activities of recomposition lose something in the process. The sweep and spontaneity of the curve, represented only through the aid of smaller and smaller grids, or the musical performance represented only through the discrete elements of the score, represent a diminution of the fullness of the real performance; the analogue continuum is broken down and simplified in digitization.[5] What is lost in the process of digitization, in the scientific push to analysis or decomposition, is precisely the continuity, the force that binds together the real as complexity and entwinement:

> Suppose our eyes [were] made [so] that they cannot help seeing in the work of the master [painter] a mosaic effect. Or suppose our intellect so made that it cannot explain the appearance of the figure on the canvas except as a work of mosaic. We should then be able to speak simply of a collection of little squares. . . . [I]n neither case should we have got at the real process, for there are no squares brought together. It is the picture, i.e. the simple act, projected on the canvas, which, by the mere fact of entering our perception, is *de*composed before our eyes into thousands and thousands of little squares which present, as *re*composed, a wonderful arrangement. (Bergson 1944, 90)

This is a prescient image of digitization: the recomposition of the whole through its decomposition into pixel-like units, the one serving as the representation of the other. The curve, the continuous stroke, the single movement of an arm is certainly able to be decomposed into as many stops, straight lines, or breaks as one chooses, but the reconstitution of these stops in a continuity always falls short of the cohesion and singularity of movement: "A very small element of a curve is very near being a straight line. And the smaller it is, the nearer. In the limit, it may be termed a part of the curve or a part of the straight line, as you please, for in each of its points a curve coincides with its tangent" (1944, 32).

Something of the curve or movement is lost when it is recomposed of its linear elements or grids, when the parts are added together — the simplicity and unity, the nondecomposable quality disappears to be replaced by immense complexity, that is, the duration of the movement disappears into its reconfiguration as measurable and mappable space, object, or movement. Yet that which disappears in the schematization and rendering of matter, as pragmatically available through scientific and technological elaboration, is precisely what can reemerge through the use of scientific information and technological invention for artistic creation, in its nonexpedient, nonpragmatic immersion in the qualities, processes, and intensities that the sciences and their technological achievements leave out.

The thing and the body are correlates: both are artificial or conventional, pragmatic conceptions, cuttings, disconnections, that create a unity, continuity, and cohesion out of the plethora of interconnections that constitute the world. They mirror each other: the stability of one, the thing, is the guarantee of the stability and ongoing existence or viability of the other, the body. The thing is "made" for the body, made as manipulable for the body's needs. And the body is conceived on the model of the thing, equally knowable and manipulable by another body. This chain of connections is mutually confirming. The thing is the life of the body, and the body is that which unexpectedly occurs to things. Technology is that which ensures and continually refines the ongoing negotiations between bodies and things, the deepening investment of the one, the body, in the other, the thing.

Technology is not the supersession of the thing, but its ever more entrenched functioning. The thing pervades technology, which is its extension, as well as extends the human into the material. The task before us is not so much to make things, and resolve relations into things, more and more minutely framed and microscopically understood; rather, it may be to liberate matter from the constraint, the practicality, the utility of the thing, to orient technology not so much to knowing and mediating as to experience and the rich indeterminacy of duration, to a making without definitive end or goal. Instead of understanding the thing and the technologies it induces through intellect, perhaps we can also develop an acquaintance with things through intuition, that Bergsonian internal, intimate apprehension of the unique particularity of things, their constitutive interconnections, and the time within which things exist.[6] Perhaps it is art itself, all of the arts, that provide the social and individual impetus for the production and absorption of intensities, durations, flux, and vibration, the place where intuition, instead of constraining itself to language, can experiment in expression.

The issue is not, of course, to abandon or even necessarily to criticize the sciences, technologies, or our preoccupation with the pragmatics of the thing, but rather, with Bergson, to understand both their limits and their residues, with what they have been so far incapable of dealing. Perception, intellection, the thing, and the technologies they spawn proceed along the lines of practical action, and these require a certain primacy in day-to-day life. But they leave something out, the untapped, nonpractical, nonuseful, nonhuman, or extrahuman continuity that is the object of intuition, of empirical attunement without means or ends.

One of the questions ahead of us now is this: what are the conditions of digitization and binarization? Can we produce technologies of other kinds? Is technology inherently simplification and reduction of the real? What in us is being extended and prosthetically rendered in technological development? Can other vectors be extended instead? What might a technology of processes, of intuition, rather than things and practices, look like? What might technologies that revel in their artistic capabilities rather than in their harnessable consequences look like? And what might it be like to invent machines, things, objects, not for what we can do with them, but for the ways in which they transform us, beyond even our own control?

CHAPTER 9

Prosthetic Objects

The thing is a pole of the body and vice versa. Body and thing are extensions of each other. They are mutual implications: co-thoughts of two-headed perception. The two-headed perception is the world.
— Brian Massumi, *Parables of the Virtual*

In the previous chapter, I discussed the broad relations between human technological production and our relations of provisional and purposive action within the material world through our technological harnessing of aspects or elements of the world that we congeal into objects. In this chapter, I am interested in exploring a narrower subsection of our relations of the material forces and qualities of the world, those relations of incorporation that characterize prosthetic objects, parts of the material world that we are capable of accommodating into the living practices (and experiences) of the body. I explore what a body is such that it is capable of expanding itself to include within its most intimate operations external, inert objects, prosthetic extensions, organs artificially or culturally acquired rather than organically evolved.

I have been fascinated for many years with the body's capacity for prosthetic extension, its capacity to link with objects in ways never conceived before, to incorporate objects into its bodily operations, to become social and historical in the most fundamental sense.[1] It was Darwin's insight that no living body, human or nonhuman, exists outside of at least two distinct organizational networks, one related to individual variation and the other to natural selection. The one regulates the internal (organic or biological) formation of the individual and coordinates and structures its bodily morphology and the processes that make up its development, growth, aging, and decay. Bergson understands these processes as the positive and productive forces of creative evolution, the internal impetus in all forms of life to make it expand itself and become more and other than its past. Individual variation, which we now understand as a being's genetic particularity and the expression of that genetic particularity in a physiological singularity, finds its culmination in an individual living entity. The other network of forces, natural selection, regulates its relations with what is outside its body, structuring its connections with others of the same type or species, with others of different types or species, and above all, with its changing material and spatio-temporal environment. A living body is this duality — not mind and body, as Western philosophy has conjectured since its modern emergence in Cartesianism — but a single surface or plane, as Merleau-Ponty has suggested, that is capable of being folded, twisted, or inverted, which may be seen to contain one side and another, or rather, an inside and an outside, two overlapping and superimposable ever-changing networks or strata, *separated* by a relatively porous sac, an epidermal clothing or biological architecture, yet *linked* by practice, action, or movement, through ingestion, incorporation, and action.

· What is the nature of this "inside," the biological forces of the body, that has its own passions and actions, its own orientations and drives, its own activities and processes, that requires an outside to provoke its internal structuring? And what is this outside, an outside of events, acts, relations, both benign and catastrophic, that affects and transforms, that structures and completes the inside? Prosthetic incorporation is not a rare or isolated phenomenon but seems pervasive in all cultural life, whether considered in human or, more broadly, in animal or insect form. What must a body, a "subject," be to make, inhabit, and transform its social and natural environment? What is this "external" environment, context, surrounding that excites and transforms the bodies, individual and collective, that inhabit it? And what might their relations become in the future?

Human bodies, and many animal and insect bodies, are fundamentally prosthetic. How we understand the status and ontological implications of these wide-ranging and sometimes unrecognized prostheses dictates how we understand the relations between the inside and the outside of the body and how we understand the complex relations between nature and culture.[2] Living bodies tend toward prostheses: they acquire and utilize supplementary objects through a kind of incorporation that enables them to function as if they were bodily organs. Many living creatures use tools, ornaments, appliances to augment their bodily capacities and to enhance their sexual attractiveness. Primates commonly use sticks, stones, and other found objects to accomplish various tasks; birds and insects use seeds, feathers, various shiny objects, sticks, and so forth to adorn themselves, to attract mates, or to build or decorate their nests. Are their bodies lacking something, which they need to replace with artificial or substitute organs, with extrabodily augmentations?[3] Do prostheses function because the body lacks something, which it uses an external or extrinsic object to replace? Are prostheses an attempt to substitute for and augment the body's organic inabilities? Are prostheses to be conceived on a model of practical reason, as substitute organs, organs which duplicate or approximate and replace missing or impaired limbs and organs (artificial legs, glasses, contact lenses, cochlear implants, wheelchairs, dental fillings, etc., let alone the increasingly elaborate forms of contemporary cosmetic augmentation that occur under the epidermal surface) and enable the body to function according to its preestablished patterns or norms of performance and action? On such an understanding, prostheses are organized by utility, adaptation, or need: the body and its functions are seen in terms of pregiven performance capacities, pregiven possibilities of movement and action, and prostheses restore these functions and practices to a newly reconstituted yet partly artificial organic totality. The prosthesis restores the body's given configuration, enabling the completion of movements and activities that would otherwise be impaired.

Or conversely, should prostheses be understood more in terms of aesthetic reorganization and proliferation, the consequence of an inventiveness that functions beyond and perhaps in defiance of pragmatic need? (This seems to be the rationale for much cosmetic transformation: the "client" does not need collagen, silicone, botox, and so on, but desires them to make him- or herself "better," "younger," "sexier.") Are prosthetic bodies excessive, capable of more and different activities than their given limbs and organs allow? In its etymological sense, a prosthesis "adds to," is supplementary of, an already existing and functional body. But prostheses may also be regarded, not as a confirmation of a pregiven range of possible actions, but as an opening up of actions that may not have been possible before, the creation of new bodily behaviors, qualities, or abilities rather than the replacement of or substitute for missing or impaired organs. Rather than understanding prosthetic incorporation as the completion or finalization of an existing body image and the body's associated and expected practices, that is, instead of regarding the prosthetic as the corporeal completion of a plan already given, an ideal or norm, it can be understood in terms of the unexpected and unplanned-for emergence of new properties and abilities. In the language of Bergson and Deleuze, the prosthetic may no longer be able to be construed as a possible capable of realization;[4] instead, prostheses may actualize virtualities that the natural body may not in itself be able to access or realize, inducing a mutual metamorphosis, transforming both the body supplemented and the object that supplements it. To narrow these questions down just a little: are architecture, makeup, clothing, food, and art natural extensions of the living body through an accommodation of external objects? Or are they a form of denaturalization, an enculturation, part of an endless and ongoing socialization, and thus a transformation of human or living form? At stake in these questions is a clearer understanding of the relations between nature and culture: is culture (the prosthetic) an addition to nature (the given biological body in its specificity)? Is it the transformation of nature? Or is it the undermining and replacement of nature?

Freud and Freudian-based psychoanalytic theory understood man's relations to objects as a relation of extension: through the acquisition of clothing, armor, housing, tools, and technologies, man extends and fortifies his relatively fragile and precarious reach over the world of objects, not only amplifying his bodily capacities but, above all, extending and cathecting the ego's libidinal reach: in making himself more than himself, man aggrandizes his capabilities, makes himself master of more than he can directly touch. According to Freud, "man" approaches the status of "prosthetic god," developing a fantasy of omnipotence, of a body which extends itself well beyond its physical, geographical, and temporal immediacy. When the body incorporates a host of instrumental supplements, enhances its range and reach in the world, the ego (or at least its ideal) is magnified and aspires to a megalomania worthy of gods: "With every tool [man] is perfecting his own organs, whether motor or sensory, or is removing the limits to their functioning. Motor power places gigantic forces at his disposal, which, like his muscles, he can employ in any direction; thanks to ship and aircraft neither water nor air can hinder his movements. . . . Man has, as it were, become a kind of prosthetic God. When he puts on all his auxiliary organs he is truly magnificent, but these organs have not grown onto him and they still give him much trouble at times" (Freud 1929, 90–92).

For Freud, man's capacity for prosthetic extension enhances and extends his own bodily reach. His instruments enable man to become more than he is; culture augments and magnifies nature, enabling man at least the fantasy of attaining a future in which his bodily form poses no obstacle to his aspirations, indeed in which his body is now construed as perfectible instrument, able to be replaced, bit by bit, with artificial substitutes. This Freudian prosthesis enables him the illusion of a control over himself, his objects, and his desires that belies his fundamental dependence on and identification through the specificities of his bodily form. He transforms his nature, and not without some discomfort or some feedback in relation to the body thus augmented. Man's nature, for Freud, is both extended and denaturalized through its prosthetic magnification: his prosthetic organs do not grow "naturally" but artificially, and change the body they supplement in ways that perhaps the subject cannot know or control. Man transforms the world according to his interests, and in the process he transforms himself in ways that he may not be able to acknowledge. He denaturalizes himself in making himself other: the boundary between natural and artificial organs is in danger of blurring. And in the process, the world which enriches him through the harnessing of its material resources becomes the domain or territory of the subject, becomes colonized as his, even though he is no longer at home in it.

Bergson too affirms the fundamentally prosthetic nature, not of the ego, as Freud suggests, nor of the subject, but of one agency or orientation in subjectivity, intelligence, in its close and continuing tie with material invention, with the unexpected use of what is found. Intelligence is fundamentally prosthetic: it constitutes itself as such through its ability to take on and make matter its own. Invention in fact accelerates the rate of change beyond its biological speed, for external tools, invented and used for specific purposes, are incorporated and transformed at an exponentially increasing rate, faster and much more directed and focused than bio-evolutionary change itself. We change and develop tools and instruments much more rapidly than we are able to change and develop our bodily forms. Bergson carefully distinguishes between tools that are part of the body itself, tools which for him are to be understood in terms of instincts (instinct is not a pre-formed behavioral pattern but the tendency to use the body in particular ways, according to its possibilities of movement)[5] and tools which are external to the body, which need to be invented, acquired, and culturally inherited, and which require learning or training to use. These are the tools fashioned by intelligence, which tends to the practical facilitation or control of selected elements of an environment. Both instinct and intelligence are evolutionary heirs, the products of two lines of divergence in evolutionary forms, the line that culminates in insects (instinct) and the line that culminates in vertebrates (intelligence). This change in material environment is precisely the invention and intervention of the customary, the social, and the historical into the biological, something for which the biological prepares itself through the elaboration and development of intelligence.

Instinct, and the insect line, finds its tools and instruments already given in the various capacities for movement and action given by its bodily morphology. Its tools are given, and not capable of modification, but are uniquely suited through natural selection to their objects and have provided immense evolutionary success with relatively little modification over long periods of time. On the other hand, such tools are rigid, unalterable. They come into play even at times when they imperil the insect (when, for example, the moth is irresistibly drawn to a flame): they lack discernment of other objects than those with which they have co-evolved (Bergson 1944, 140).

By contrast, in the case of intelligence—the vertebrate line—tools that are manufactured are far from perfect and require considerable effort to accommodate them. They are perfectible, insofar as they are always capable of being superseded without necessarily ensuring major morphological upheavals in species; and they are readily replaceable with a more ingenious design and more adept adaptations of matter:

> The instrument constructed intelligently . . . is an imperfect instrument. It costs an effort. It is generally troublesome to handle. But, as a mode of unorganized matter, it can take any form whatsoever, serve any purpose, free the living being from every new difficulty that arises and bestow on it an unlimited number of powers. Whilst it is inferior to the natural instrument for the satisfaction of immediate wants, its advantage over it is the greater, the less urgent the need. Above all, it reacts on the nature of the being that constructs it; for in calling on him to exercise a new function, it confers on him, so to speak, a richer organization, being an artificial organ by which the natural organism is extended. For every need that it satisfies, it creates a new need; and so, instead of closing, like instinct, the round of action within which the animal tends to move automatically, it lays open to activity an unlimited field into which it is driven further and further, and made more and more free. (Bergson 1944, 140–141)

Bergson's understanding of the prosthetic orientation of life is perhaps more complex and intriguing than Freud's, although it resembles it in some ways. For Freud, man expands himself and his narcissistic reach over the world by incorporating external objects into the orbit of his bodily control, subordinated to the body image already given by the natural—that is, the unadorned and unaugmented—body. These external objects are rendered objects *for man*, who becomes magnified in the process. These objects, however, become reduced: they become, no longer wood, plastic, minerals, but a leg, an arm, spectacles—that which is now only measured by its relevance for and relation to man. Man masters these objects in making them function for him, even though he loses a certain mastery of himself and his bodily skills. For Bergson, *life* expands itself by generating new capacities in *both* the living being *and* in the prosthetic object. The object is always, for him, reduced by its perception by and usefulness for an observer, its multiple facets simplified and narrowed to those qualities that life can extract from it. But equally, objects, in being extricated from the multiplicity of connections they exert in the material world, are given new qualities, new capacities, a virtuality that they lack in their given form. Intelligence endows objects with virtuality while "stealing" from them all the qualities that are considered useful or relevant. The living being and the objects now rendered prosthetic transform each other, and each undergoes a not entirely determinable becoming through their interaction. The living transform nonliving objects, and these objects in turn transform the parameters and possibilities of life. The artificial leg, even as a replacement for a natural limb, can function only through a body-phantom whose very existence becomes evident through some bodily trauma or amputation. The phantom functions virtually, and is actualized in the body's activities and movements. Yet the artificial limb induces other actualizations, and produces different potentialities, virtualities than the organic limb might have had. It "feels" different from the organic limb, and its spectral properties deviate it from the function of the organic limb. It can, for example, generate sensations of passage, as if it had passed right through solid objects. The artificial limb is both a replacement of a lack and the production of an excess, just as the body itself is the ongoing activity of making ever greater connections with objects in wider and wider networks.

Must we restrict prosthetic extension to inorganic or inert matter? Can other living beings, cultural institutions, social practices also be construed as prosthetic? Is a virus prosthetic to its host? Are slave ants prostheses for their ant masters? Is language a human prosthesis? Does architecture or art complete the beings who inhabit or make it, much as the colony or nest completes and overrides the needs of its inhabitants, the ants, wasps, or bees?[6] These questions make it clear that the division between an inside and an outside, an object and a prosthesis, a natural organ and an artificial organ, a body and what augments it is not as clear-cut as it may seem and the boundaries more porous and productive than the mere addition or supplementation of an external object implies.

To take architecture as one significant example of prosthetic augmentation—Deleuze and Guattari see architecture as the first production, the first form of art, in human evolution[7]—is architecture the practical completion of man's need for shelter, for interpersonal connections and other social and biological needs? Or is architecture one of the elements directing a becoming other than what the human is? Clearly there are two kinds—at least two kinds—of architecture, just as there are two types of prosthesis: one which accommodates existing needs, which fits into the body's current and recognized needs and desires; and another which introduces new aesthetic and practical possibilities not yet available, still awaiting prosthetic incorporation, yet to be incorporated into human need—the first in accordance with the actual and the already existing and the second welcoming and making space for that which cannot yet be imagined or lived. Are architecture, clothing, food, our use of the materials and objects around us for our practical needs that which extends us and enables us to protect, conserve, and develop what we have? Or are they also capable of transforming us into what we cannot yet know? This ambiguity—for prostheses both augment and generate, they both confirm an already existing bodily organization and generate new bodily capacities—is the very ambiguity of the material world for living consciousness: as both resource and limit, the material world is the ongoing source and condition for life, the surface on which life elaborates itself and that against which it distinguishes and changes itself. It remains ambiguous, as the interplay between Freud's and Bergson's understanding makes clear, whether it is the nonliving, the inhuman which functions as prosthetic for living beings, or whether, on the contrary, living beings are the prosthetic augmentations of inert matter, matter's most elaborate invention and self-reflection.

PART IV.

IDENTITY, SEXUAL DIFFERENCE,

AND THE FUTURE

CHAPTER 10

The Time of Thought

The entire apparatus of knowledge is an apparatus for abstraction and simplification—directed not at knowledge but at taking possession of things: with "end" and "means" one takes possession of the process (one invents a process that can be grasped); with "concepts," however, of the "things" that constitute the process.
—Friedrich Nietzsche, *The Will to Power*

I am interested here in the question of how to engender and stimulate not only new political practices but, above all, new thought, new modes of conceptualization, new theories and models adequate to the complexity and hitherto unrepresented qualities and characteristics of women, the feminine, and sexual difference. Of course each discipline and conceptual practice evolves, changes, is fraught with the particularities of its history and social context: each discipline has come to accommodate—or foreclose—feminist questions and insights. My question here is not free of such disciplinary constraints, for it is a largely philosophical question, or a question directly largely toward philosophy: how can new models of thought, new intellectual practices come into being? What modes of connection with and disconnection from prevailing conceptual models will enable the elaboration of new paradigms, new methods, new questions?

This question is linked to a cluster of others, in particular to: (1) the question of the future, how to think the future, live the future, produce a future that is different from the present and that can be joyously welcomed instead of feared (which is the preeminent question of politics); (2) a not unlinked question of how thought itself, how modes of thinking, philosophizing, theorizing, conceptualizing can be transformed to think the new, to be more able and adequate to think unpredictable futures (the question of the boldness and novelty of discourses, the risks they take, the new forms that can emerge);[1] and (3) how it is that feminist discourses, those concerned with the questions of sexual difference, with how differences of all kinds may articulate themselves, can participate in, be engineers of, the movement toward the future, the future of thought.

While philosophy as a discipline has had an exemplary history of excluding women as its proponents and practitioners,[2] and of eliding the identification of many of its central terms with masculine and feminine associations,[3] and while feminists of earlier generations have commonly identified philosophy as resolutely patriarchal and phallocentric, these two interests, fields, have always intersected even if not always directly or obviously. I have tried to entwine these two interests with each other, bringing philosophical frameworks, methods, and assumptions to bear on feminist writings and in turn trying to make philosophy a little more answerable regarding the place of women and femininity in philosophical and social history. These two interests and fields are not unrelated: the traditional goals of philosophy (to understand being, knowing, thinking) are intimately bound up with what we value and struggle for, in other words, with ethics and politics, including the ethics and politics bound up with living in and as sexed bodies. How we develop and negotiate ethical and political issues is intimately conjoined with how we understand existence and knowledge. I will look here at the future of thought, the virtualities latent in the present which may ramify and develop themselves productively and in ways that address some of the key concerns of feminist theory—the future of sexual difference and its relevance to the future of thought. Feminist theory needs now to address the possibilities for reconceptualizing what thinking is, how it relates to the world of practice, and how it may productively serve the political interests of feminism and its related struggles (class, race, sexuality, religion, etc.).

FUTURES

In addressing this question of the future of thought, it is not possible to leap out of our own time and into the reality of the future-made-present. At best, what we have access to are the most complex and cutting-edge discourses and practices (political, scientific, and artistic), those that seek out a future, those that take risks, that welcome innovation and transformation. Although these may not prove to be indices to predicting the future of thought, they do provide lines of flight, directions of movement that are *virtual in the present*, laden with potentialities, and that thus have some impetus or force in engendering a future that is different from what we have now. These current sites of transformation are our most direct means of welcoming the future and participating in it, producing it, ourselves: of being inspired by the bravest, the riskiest, and boldest innovations that inform our present and using them as a kind of bridge to a future that we cannot know or control but are ineluctably drawn toward as it opens out in front of us.

Each person is of course free to see in any discourse—whether it constitutes the acknowledged cutting edge of present disciplines (as does, for example, the work of Deleuze or Irigaray in the discipline of philosophy) or whether it is a forgotten or misunderstood text of the past (as, for example, the recent revivals of interest in the writings of Nietzsche and Bergson suggest)—a passage of thought that anticipates the future—either its future or our own. That, indeed, is the wonder of history itself—that it can revivify any particular figure in the present or the past as a mode of access to or anticipation of a future yet to come. In this chapter, I want to look, briefly, at some of the resonances of Deleuze's work on the question of thought, and to link this question to that of sexual difference, particularly as it is represented in the work of Irigaray. In attempting to establish some link or movement between them, I do not want to tame either, or to reductively explain one in the terms or language of the other. Rather, I want to see how these two very strong and original discourses, which gaze reflectively back on the history of Western philosophy in order to explore their most hidden and surprising virtualities, may disturb each other, may generate lines of divergence or difference which may help open up new modes of thought. Between these two discourses and sets of interests, we can chart some possible or even desirable futures for that region of overlap or commonness that philosophy and feminist theory share, their common if unrecognized interests in ontology and epistemology and their fundamental connections to and investments in ethics and politics.

DELEUZE AND THOUGHT

Is there a way to think about thought other than those ways in which it has structured itself as syllogism, as argument, as persuasion, as "theory" before and beyond practice? Is it possible to develop an understanding of thought that refuses to see thought as passivity, reflection, contemplation, or representation, and instead stresses its activity, how and what it performs, how it is a force that exists alongside of and in concert with other kinds of forces that are not conceptual?[4] Can we deromanticize the construction of knowledges and discourses to see them as labor, production, doing? Is thinking a mode of acting? These questions, it seems, require a new way of understanding both epistemology and ontology, and thus new ways of being able to pose the ethical and political questions that are the boundaries or horizon of contemporary philosophy and feminist theory and the site of their interaction.

Deleuze refuses to engage with or understand theory as a unified and systematic ordering of concepts, theory as a structuring of argument.[5] Indeed, from his earliest and most conventionally philosophical writings, he has raised the question of the force of concepts, the impetus or push that they play both within philosophical systems (such as Spinoza's and Kant's) and within broader social relations. And from his more recent writings, especially those where he deals with the work of Foucault (Deleuze 1988b), he develops an understanding of theory as a relay within a web of other (nontheoretical) practices. He is interested in the components or ingredients of theory or knowledge, its "atoms" or elements, concepts. He seems less concerned about the systematicity of systems of knowledge than with their matter, the "stuff" with which they work. He is less interested in understanding theory as a system or a structure, than as a collection of heterogeneous elements, atoms, whose molecular forms are of more interest than their molar alignments. His understanding is refreshingly pragmatic, and linked in some ways to the work of Dewey, James, Peirce, and the philosophical pragmatists, who are more concerned with the operational effects of discourses than with their signification or their reference. He is above all interested in what theory enables us to do, to make, more than, or beyond, what it says. Discourses are not just the repositories of truths, of concepts and knowledges; they are also, and most significantly, modes of action, practices we perform to facilitate or enable other practices, ways of attempting to deal with and transform the real.

Knowledges, theories are composed of *concepts*, and concepts themselves are always and only occasioned by *problems*. Concepts are, for Deleuze, never unitary or singular: "clear and simple ideas" are a philosophical fabrication. They are always composite, a multiplicity, a mixture of disparate elements which function to produce effects, other concepts, other actions and practices: "There are no simple concepts. Every concept has components and is defined by them. It therefore has a combination [*chiffre*]. It is a multiplicity, though not every multiplicity is conceptual. There is no concept with only one component" (Deleuze and Guattari 1994, 15).

Concepts are always at least doubled, for every concept not only requires a delimitation to give it some "identity," however historically provisional; it also requires a ground, a mode of connection with the world, whether it is through contemplation, reflection, judgment, or through incitement, experiment, and enactment. These provisionally totalized fragments, a "fragmentary whole" (Deleuze and Guattari 1994, 16) are both historically connected to those concepts which preceded them and enabled them to develop, as well as unique, historically locatable, often nameable entities (Platonic ideas, Cartesian mind, Spinozist substance). They are connected to the resolution of problems or questions, for it is problems or questions which occasion concepts, and concepts are developed as a mode of addressing questions: "All concepts are connected to problems without which they would have no meaning and which can themselves only be isolated or understood as their solution emerges" (Deleuze and Guattari 1994, 16).

Concepts are points of multiplicity, connections of components, which share "zones of proximity," borders, with other concepts, marked by irregular contours, an improper or imperfect fit. This is why, although they attain a certain cohesion, they cannot align to form systems. It is propositions, statements, claims that form systems through their orderly arrangement, their commitments to uniformity and cohesion. Propositions function in a relation of representation, of correspondence, and qualify for claims of truth and validity. Arguments can only be made using propositions. If propositions form systems, then concepts emerge from and link to *events*.[6] Events are always specific, historically particular emergences, "hecceities," which do not form systems but induce intensities, do not cohere to form patterns but function as modes of affection, and as speeds of variation. Events are nonrecurrent, singular, unrepeatable, and uncontainable; they generate, through their unique unpredictability, problems for the living. Events are affective impingements of an outside, of forces on living subjects, whether human or otherwise. They occasion responses rather than statements: "Concepts are centers of vibrations, each in itself and every one in relation to all the others. This is why they all resonate rather than cohere or correspond with each other. There is no reason why concepts should cohere. As fragmentary totalities, concepts are not even the pieces of a puzzle, for their irregular contours do not correspond to each other. They do form a wall, but it is a

dry-stone wall, and everything holds together only along diverging lines"
(Deleuze and Guattari 1994, 23).

The problem poses itself as a question which the concept, among other
things (Deleuze mentions also the percept in scientific formulations and affect in artistic production), attempts to answer or address, though in fact
the concept never answers or solves the problem; it transforms it. Problems are not simply enticements to solutions, but inducements to action and
thus to experimentation. Events are always problematic, they always address
problems, insofar as events are the disparate and unrepeatable alignment
of points, forces, planes, that come together provisionally yet effectively,
raising at the very least the question of their nature, their existence, their
provisionality, their force, and their speed.[7] Concepts are one mode of attempted "solution," a solution not of the problem but *in its vicinity.* Events
are themselves comprised of singularities, composites of unalike things; they
generate fields, within which problems are articulated and their concept-
tools generated. These concepts or concept-tools are themselves composites, not made of the same "things" as events, but somehow connected with
them. They are composites, events, with their own histories, generated by
their own singularities, which intersect, or attempt to, with the problem-
generating events: "We can speak of events only in the context of the problem whose conditions they determine. We can speak of events only as singularities deployed in a problematic field, in the vicinity of which the solutions
are organized" (Deleuze 1990, 56).

The problem, the question, is not solved or answered, that is, it is not
ended or annihilated by the concepts it raises and the solutions it devises.
The problem — whether the event inducing it is natural (the weather, geological forces, and so on), cultural (the emergence of new technologies, the
elaboration of new social relations), or political (a war, a struggle, a con-
tract) — is not to be solved so much as enacted, lived through, negotiated.
Events do not have "solutions," for at best they generate ways of living, the
realignment and transformation of habits and practices. The solution is a
practice, a mode of addressing these problems through concepts, which are
both generated by their own practices (in philosophy, the sciences, the arts)
and which in turn infiltrate and affect other practices. Indeed the event can
only become problematic, raise questions, insofar as it is ideal, insofar as it
is conceptualizable. The concept is generated through this appeal or resort
to ideas, the ideal. There is neither problem nor concept without ideas, or
thought. The concept or "solution" is that which enables the ideality of the
question to be localized, to become a "state of affairs" or a "fact":

There is always a space which condenses and precipitates singularities, just as there is always a time which progressively completes the event through fragments of future and past events. Thus, there is a spatio-temporal self-determination of the problem. . . . Solutions are engendered at precisely the same time that the problem determines *itself*. This is why people quite often believe that the solution does not allow the problem to subsist, and that it assigns to it retrospectively the status of subjective moment which is necessarily transcended as soon as the solution is found. The opposite, though, is the case. By means of an appropriate process, the problem is determined in space and time and, as it is determined, it determines the solutions in which it persists. (Deleuze 1990, 121)

In turn, it is thought that generates the problem out of the event, and produces thought itself as event. This may explain why one of Deleuze's most striking and consistent preoccupations is the separation of well-formed or legitimate questions or problems and how they can be distinguished from badly formed ones. A badly formulated question, a false problem, can generate only illusions as its "solutions." This may be why Deleuze seeks in Bergson his formulation of the badly posed question, and in Kant the notion of the false problem and illusion.[8] These misformulations of the problem preempt or foreclose the experiments, the inventions necessary for the development of a solution; they pose the question as already resolvable in given terms:

We are led to believe that problems are given ready-made, and that they disappear in the responses or the solution. Already, under this double aspect, they can be no more than phantoms. We are led to believe that the activity of thinking, along with truth and falsehood in relation to that activity, begins only with the search for solutions, that both of these concern only solutions. . . . Far from being concerned with solutions, truth and falsehood primarily affect problems. A solution always has the truth it deserves according to the problem to which it is a response, and the problem always has the solution it deserves in proportion to *its own* truth or falsity. (Deleuze 1994, 158–159)

To extract, then, some key points from a Deleuzian understanding of the connections between theory and practice:

1. All theory and practices are modes of heterogeneity, composites, provisionally and tenuously aligned: there is no pure interiority to either. They are neither systematic wholes nor are they the products of singular modes,

one purely conceptual and the other purely pragmatic, but interspersed, interleaved, interacting mixtures, weaving together disparate elements.

2. Theory is provoked by a problem or question, which is occasioned by an event, an eruption into and of the world. This event is a provocation to innovation, to the production of desire, that is, to the making of the real. This real also raises problems which generate knowledges, discourses, concepts as their mode of address. Concepts are one mode of response, just as percepts and affects are activities, productions that respond to the provocation of problems.

3. Theory is not a precondition of practice, nor is practice the material on which theory reflects. Rather, each runs into the other, forms a potential tool for use in the other's domain; concepts run into material practices, practices come to function as exemplars, as modes of incitement to theory. Each is a mode of the other's proliferation.

4. As composite or hybrid, concepts function not by unifying, cohering, systematizing, or explaining but by diversifying, proliferating, diverging, producing that which is different, that which is unlike, functioning as a virtual source for both the proliferation of other concepts and the diversification of new.

FEMINIST FUTURES

What does the future of thought, and thought of the future, have to offer feminist theory and practice? Do any of these Deleuzian concepts have use and effectivity for feminist concerns? And in turn, what does feminism itself have to offer the future of thought? Does feminism have a future in thought?

Here there are two quite distinct, even contradictory positions that mark current feminist theory. The first is that, at its best and most successful, feminist theory is a practice and a politics whose time is limited and whose function will cease to be necessary when certain political, social, and economic gains are achieved. Feminism itself is and always has been highly provisional and contextual: it arose only as a result of the growing awareness of the oppression of women and will cease when this oppression is overcome. Once women gain economic, legal, and political equality, once women have the right to live and function as equal to yet different from men, feminism will no longer be required. The future of feminism, on this understanding, is limited to the foreseeable and to contesting the recognized and the known. This limited temporality characterizes all feminist projects of equalization and inclusion[9] as well as a number of projects within postmodern feminism.[10]

This is not, however, a view shared by Irigaray, whose work on sexual difference has signaled the indeterminate, and possible interminable, necessity of feminist thought, a necessity which parallels or, in her terms, is isomorphic with, that of sexual difference, one of the incontestable and most inventive forms of biological and cultural existence. Irigaray is concerned with the ways in which philosophy has perpetrated its own masculinization and its self-interested phallocentric models of ontology and epistemology. Her work aims, in her earlier texts, to reveal the deep-rooted reliance on and repression of concepts of femininity in the major philosophy texts of the West; and in her later texts, to explore new modes of thought, new kinds of concepts, new relations between concepts and lived reality, new relations between the human, now understood in terms of (at least) two sexes, and the universe itself.

I don't want, for a moment, to suggest that there is an easy alignment between Deleuzian and Irigarayan philosophies: like those concept-atoms that constitute Deleuze's understanding of thought, they rub up again each other unevenly, and with jagged edges, and there is no possibility of a smooth or easy fit between them. Each functions as an agitating crystal for the other, creating an alignment that is always uneasy and uncomfortable. Nevertheless, they may offer each other relays, modes of access to other domains and to other modes of action that may be inaccessible without their conjunction or interaction, and without the potentially productive disjunctions they engender. The uneasiness that marks their juxtapositioning—Irigaray's accounts of subjectivity, identity, and desire sit uncomfortably with Deleuze's concern with intensities, planes, energies—may prove to be more productive, indeed more thought provoking, than any smooth and easy complementarity.[11]

Irigaray argues that sexual difference entails not only a reorganization of social and economic relations between the sexes but involves the entire restructuring of the symbolic order, of the social apparatuses, including language, forms of knowledge, and modes of representation. It entails rethinking thought itself by thoroughly understanding both the roots and forms of dominant knowledges, and their insufficiencies, points of excess or lack. And this is because, for her, feminism is not a project which seeks a definitive end or final solution to the problems that face women, but rather a renegotiation or reordering of the very concepts of order and solution. As an irreducible element of human existence, sexual difference pervades, in ways that are incapable of adequate recognition in the past and present, all of human creation: the advent of sexual difference too exists as a problem, a provocation to thinking and action, but a provocation that so far has resulted in the patriarchal fear and containment of women under men's economic and intellectual domination rather than in the development of modes of action, thought, and language appropriate to and developed by both of the sexes.[12]

She claims that sexual difference constitutes the singular question of the present, of our age: "Sexual difference is one of the major philosophical issues, if not the issue, of our age. According to Heidegger, each age has one issue to think through and one only. Sexual difference is probably the issue in our time" (1993, 5).

More than constituting the question of our age, for Irigaray, it is this question, and its provocations to practice and to innovation, that signal a mode of passage or transition to the future. The question of sexual difference signals the virtual framework of the future. What today is actual is sexual opposition or binarism, the defining of the two sexes in terms of the characteristics of one. Sexual difference is that which is virtual; it is the potential of this opposition to function otherwise, to function without negation, to function as full positivity. It is the future we may be able to make, but which has not yet come into existence: "Sexual difference would constitute the horizon of worlds more fecund than any known to date — at least in the West — and without reducing fecundity to the reproduction of bodies and flesh. For loving partners this would be a fecundity of birth and regeneration but also the production of a new age of thought, art, poetry and language: the creation of a new *poetics*" (1993, 5).

Sexual difference remains virtual because it has never had its day, it has never been able to appear as such, to become effective, to transform discourses, concepts, practices. Irigaray argues throughout her work that sexual difference is that which is elided, repressed, and covered over in phallocentric representations, that which is replaced by concepts and practices that are derived from only one broad perspective and set of interests rather than (at least) two. Which means not only that women and their interests remain neglected and undeveloped, but also that the domain of concepts itself remains impoverished, without the productive and surprising input of other interests and perspectives, other morphologies. In her claims for the opening up of knowledges, Irigaray also makes space, although she does not articulate this explicitly, for other morphologies, other differences, to have an effect on the production of knowledges and on various representations of the real. Sexual difference entails not only the political and economic transformation and self-reflection of women but also a revolution in thought, for without the transformation of concepts, the work of sexual difference cannot be accomplished: "A revolution in thought and ethics is needed if the work of sexual difference is to take place. We need to reinterpret everything concerning the relations between the subject and discourse, the subject and the world, the subject and the cosmic, the microcosmic and the macrocosmic. Everything, beginning with the way in which the subject has always been written in the masculine form, as *man*, even when it is claimed to be universal or neutral" (1993, 6).

This "revolution in thought" is not a revolution on any known model, for it cannot be the overthrow of all previous thought, the radical disconnection from the concepts and language of the past: a revolution in thought can only use the language and the concepts that presently exist or have already existed, and can only produce itself against the background and history of the present. Knowledges and discourses are no longer considered to be megalithic representations of power interests that exclude women: to suggest that they are simply male dominated is to deny women the resources of prevailing knowledges as a mode of critique of those knowledges. In short, these knowledges, whether patriarchal or not, empower as much as they disempower: they provide the resources for their own undoing in excess of their own conceptual frameworks or requirements. The kind of revolution Irigaray is proposing is one which takes historically given forms and materials of knowledges, of concepts and languages, and attempts to present and use them differently—a deflection and broadening, an opening up rather than a closing down and replacement of existing forms and structures. What Irigaray is suggesting is a certain kind of insinuation of sexual difference back into those places where it has been elided, the insistence on the necessity that every practice, method, and knowledge can be undertaken in another way. It is her claim that feminism is not about women, their suffering and oppression, but about the ways in which women have become associated with and conceptualized in terms of a vast array of qualities and attributes, which also require reconsideration. The position of women is intimately linked with the ways in which chemistry, physics, philosophy, and mathematics, as well as law and medicine, are conceptualized, and it will not be transformed until these disciplines, which have no apparent connection with women's oppression but nevertheless are associatively and more surreptitiously related and support each other, are transformed by the intervention of altogether different perspectives, interests, methods, and objectives.

What Irigaray makes clear throughout her writings, but most particularly in *An Ethics of Sexual Difference*, is that until existing knowledges, disciplines, concepts, and theoretical practices are regarded as fields for the interaction and expression of forces, relations of power, coercion, and constraint as well as relations of knowledge and utility, modes of selection and silencing as well as modes of production of truth, sexual difference cannot take place. Sexual difference implies that there are at least two ways of doing *anything*, without being able to specify in what ways they may develop or what form they may take. Which means that the production of concepts themselves must provide at least two paths of development, modes or processes, at least two (possibly incommensurable) modes of existence and practice: two modes not in competition with each other to find which is the best, not two modes which augment each other to provide a more complete picture, but two singularities that may either conflict or complement, that may be altogether incomparable or simply different. There is no way to judge in advance what forms and paths sexual difference, the perspectives of at least two sexes, may have to offer to concepts, thought, knowledges, except that sexual difference makes and marks a difference everywhere.

The encounter between these two modes of concept or thought, Irigaray's insistence on sexual difference as the (immanent rather than transcendental) horizon of thought, and Deleuze's understanding of concepts as the realm of force, like the encounter between two beings who recognize their sexual difference, always generates surprise, or wonder: wonder is both that which comes from the surprise of the unexpected encounter, the productivity of the encounter that defies expectation, as well as that which welcomes the future openly. Irigaray quotes Descartes's rich understanding of wonder as the first passion: "When the first encounter with some object surprises us, and we judge it to be new, or very different from what we formerly knew, or from what we supposed that it ought to be, that causes us to wonder and be surprised; and because that may happen before we in any way know whether this object is agreeable to us or is not so, it appears to me that wonder is the first of all the passions: and it has no opposite because if the object which presents itself has nothing in it that surprises us, we are in nowise moved regarding it, and we consider it without passion" (Descartes quoted in Irigaray 1993, 13).

Irigaray advocates a philosophy of wonder, a thought which involves wonder, the surprise of the unexpected, that which strikes us immediately with the awe of its newness, its difference. This wonder is not just what arises from our encounters with a sexual other, a being of the other sex whom we meet for the first time as other, as irreducibly different; it is also what emerges from our encounter with the new concept, the new idea, the new method or knowledge. To confront the idea of sexual difference is to open oneself up to be confounded by something incomprehensible in terms of existing frameworks and knowledges, to be open to the actualization of concepts and thoughts that have up to now existed only as virtual or latent.

FORCE

What does this mean for feminist theory and politics? How can a notion of the force of concepts and the power of sexual difference to generate new concepts be mobilized or used for thinking through key feminist strategies? Here, I can only be suggestive rather than elaborate, for these are concepts that might be regarded as germinal, potential, and yet to be accomplished.

1. Rather than seeing feminist politics as an active intervention into and struggle around the rights and needs of female subjects, considered both in their individuality and in terms of their membership in other minoritarian categories, that is, as subjugated subjects who require the recognition and respect of those subjects who oppress them (men, members of other religious, ethnic, national, or sexual groups) — a claim shared in common by quite diverse categories of feminist theory — feminism may be well served to position the subject not as aim or goal of struggles, but as a sieve or cipher through which dynamic forces struggle to emerge. Instead of understanding feminist political struggles as struggles around the constitution and maintenance of a recognized and respected female identity, it may be understood as the struggle around the right to act and to make according to one's own interests and perspectives, the mobilization and opening up of identity to an uncontained and unpredictable future. This makes feminism a struggle without end, a process of endless becoming-other rather than the attainment of recognizable positions and roles that are valued.

2. To the extent that identity is understood as a subjectively apprehended cohesion which requires personal and collective validation to take its place as real, as recognized, such an identity is always governed and regulated, in advance, by the image and value of the other, the socially dominant others who control the various processes of social validation. Rather than strive for a politics of recognition, where minoritarian groups seek affirmation in public life, it may be time for feminists to seek instead what I understand as a politics of the imperceptible, which has its effects through actions, but which actions can never be clearly identified with an individual, group, or organization. Such a politics does not seek visibility and recognition as its

goals; rather it seeks actions, effects, consequences, forces which generate transformation without directing that transformation to other subjects who acknowledge its force. The imperceptible harnesses the forces that make up subjects, not by confirming them but by making them larger and more effective than subjectivity, by linking them to the inhuman, to forces below and above the level of the subject's control, which generate the real. Political struggles on such a model are not directed to affirming categories or classes of subject, but categories or classes of action.

3. The encounter with the real that produces concepts is also that encounter with the political, with the exigent, that innovates and generates new problems and new experiments. Whether sexual difference—the impossibility of the representation of the two sexes in a singular "human" or "neutral" model—becomes and remains the problem, the real that generates new knowledges, I do not know; but it is clear, as Irigaray notes, that it has a place, or all places, staked out for it in advance. Sexual difference is that horizon, both spatial and temporal, that will always constitute a question, will always provoke a negotiation, a mode of practice, will always engender responses that resonate both materially and conceptually: materially, insofar as sexual difference is necessarily a factor in all human affairs and practices, whether it is recognized as such or not; and conceptually, insofar as sexual difference entails new modes of thought, new futures for knowledges. There is no culture, no moment of history that does not in some way address and attempt to deal with relations between the sexes as a problem of its constitution and regulation; and there is no "solution" to the force of sexual difference that is capable of forestalling or circumventing change.

4. Finally, this realm of the production of concepts is just as significant as that of concerted or directed political action, though its goals and methods are not as clear-cut. While the production of theory does not and should not direct or function as the judge of political practice already accomplished, or an anticipation of political practice yet to come—rather, it is a practice that functions alongside of other practices which also contribute to the production of concepts, percepts, and affects—nevertheless, political practice remains incomplete without an accompanying production of concepts that help welcome and generate political, conceptual, and artistic experimentation. This of course involves an intimate familiarity with the history of concepts and knowledges, but rather than a reverential relation to history, which keeps us contained within its already existing terms, the history of each disci-

pline can be regarded as the site of unactualized virtualities, of potentialities that never had their time to emerge. Sexual difference constitutes one, but certainly not the only, such insistence, one which has remained latent in the entire history of Western thought but which still requires its own time—the future of thought.

CHAPTER 11

The Force of Sexual Difference

Turning back to the unthought of human becoming is indispensable. But sometimes the task of discovering it will not be easy. Because what is inadequately thought paralyzes the spirit as well as the domain to which it is applied.
—Luce Irigaray, *The Way of Love*

It is time to rethink some of the key questions that have occupied feminist, queer, and postmodern theories of subjectivity, identity, and "gender." Indeed, I believe that it is time to move beyond the very language of identity and gender, to look at other issues left untouched, questions unasked, assumptions unelaborated, which feminist and queer politics need to address in order to revitalize themselves and to propel themselves into new conceptions of desire, power, and pleasure, and into the development of new practices. Among these underdeveloped and unasked questions are those deemed the most offensive and disputed within the last decades: *not* the body, which of course is now the most valorized and magical of conceptual terms within the social sciences and the humanities, but messy biology, matter, materiality, which have had to be organized and contained (as body) and dematerialized (through language); *not* ideology, which continues to be privileged as the object of intellectual analyses of power, but force, energy, affect, which are today rarely discussed but relegated to abjection and the outside position of the Real; and *not* gender, which is again the contained, represented, socialized ideal, but sexual difference, that untidy and ambiguous invocation of the prestructuring of being by irreducible difference. Mat-

ter, force, and difference remain elided in most forms of contemporary political discourse and theoretical analysis; they remain too destabilizing, too
difficult to direct into concerted political pathways to provide the basis of a
new politics. Yet matter, force, and difference, or matter *as* force and difference, remain the prerogatives of science and are either treated fearfully and
with distrust or ignored all together in the humanities and social sciences.

In this chapter, I want to look at that which both preconditions and
destabilizes gender and bodies, that which problematizes all identity, that
which discourse and representation cannot contain and politics cannot direct: sexual difference as force; and force itself as divided, differentiated,
sexualized. In this process I want to bring together again Irigaray and Deleuze, who, as we saw in the previous chapter, while they may share little else
in common, are nevertheless most directly linked through the preeminence
they grant to difference as force, to the force of difference, to the forces of
differentiation and the differentiation of forces. I want to present an impres-
sionistic overview of the ways in which an understanding of difference — difference not tied to opposition, difference not determined by identity, difference not subsumed by comparison, difference as an ontological force — can
disturb and displace the politics of identity on which most feminist, queer,
and minority politics are currently based, and can provide new research
questions and new political experiments by which these political programs
may revitalize themselves.

Instead of exploring the phenomenology of — the experiential, autobiographical, and subjective ingredients of — sexual difference, what it is like to
live as a woman or a man, a lesbian or a heterosexual, as black or as white
(which the feminist investment in psychoanalysis and phenomenology, in
autobiography and memoir has privileged for the last three decades or
more), it may be time to explore instead what such approaches leave out,
what we might understand as the *physics* or matter of sexual difference, its
materiality, its force, its ontological weight, and above all, its time. Lying
beyond and framing these primarily epistemological approaches is the pressing but forgotten question of ontology. Far from providing an alternative
to the positivistic approaches of contemporary analytic philosophy, structuralism and poststructuralism have shared uncritically in its reduction of
ontology to epistemology, and in its concomitant reduction of materiality to
representation. Through, for example, the Lacanian conception of the Real,
all that is beyond representation, beyond symbolization is equated with the
ineffable, with what cannot be represented, with what must be left unarticulated; and through Derrideanism, the outside, that which is beyond the text,

that which is incapable of being construed as writing or trace—force, un-configured matter, nature, the prediscursive—is inevitably returned back to the text and to writing, to images and representations, and thus reterritori-alized, blunted as surprise, excess, or immanence, robbed of its impact and understood only in terms of the human and its collective control. Psycho-analysis and deconstruction, today preeminent forms of interpretation and analysis within the humanities, restrict themselves to the inside of represen-tation, which provides its own vested "reading" of an outside or a real as always already codified, or only accessible through some kind of represen-tational codification.

It is for this reason, I believe, that Deleuze's work, which is not particu-larly feminist, may be of tremendous use for feminist politics: it is his con-centration on the ontological questions, on the problems raised by matter, by force, by power, by time for thought—by what he sometimes calls "the outside" (Deleuze 1988b)—that may provide a new direction for a more ab-stract approach to feminism, the kind of abstraction that is needed to bring about new frames of reference and new kinds of question. This return to on-tology is also, I believe, one of the major concerns of Irigaray, particularly in her middle period, in her analyses of Nietzsche (1991) and Heidegger (1999), in her work on the elemental, and especially in *An Ethics of Sexual Difference* (1993), on which I will concentrate here.

Irigaray makes it clear that feminism has just barely begun to fathom the intellectual depths of its project. To affirm in full positivity the existence and capacities of (at least) two sexes—the project of sexual difference—is to ac-knowledge two things: first, the failure of the past to provide a space and time for women as women, with the consequence that all forms of prevail-ing practices and of knowledge, including the most objective of the sciences and the most abstract forms of mathematics and cosmology, represent the interests and perspectives of only one sex. All forms of knowledge are open to the augmentation of their objects, fields, methods, and questions through an acknowledgment of their necessary limits, their perspectival emergence in specific rather than universal interests. Second, linked to this recognition, is the necessity, in the future, of providing other ways of knowing, other ontologies and epistemologies that enable the subject's relation to the world, to space and to time, to be conceptualized in different terms. Irigaray makes it clear that a transformation of ontology, our conceptions of what is, en-tails a transformation in our conceptions of epistemology, how we know, in the ways in which we understand space and time, which in turn transform our conceptions of matter, subjectivity, and politics. Space and time can no longer be understood as neutral or transparent media whose passivity enables the specificity of matter to reveal itself; rather they are active ingredients in the making of matter, and thus in the constitution of objects and subjects. A reconfiguration of the subject will, sooner or later, require that our understanding of space and time themselves undergo dramatic metamorphoses. Irigaray understands this as a becoming beyond the one, beyond the phallic, a becoming in which the all-too-human is understood as the all-too-patriarchal, and the future is beyond recognition, beyond the dualities of the sexes as we know them today and as they existed in the past.

Sexual difference, like the very notion of difference itself, can be understood in one of two ways. First, as a difference between two preexisting entities (such as the difference between oranges and apples); and second, as a constitutive difference, a difference that preexists the entities that it produces. This second notion, shared by both Derrida and Deleuze, is also a constitutive ingredient in Irigaray's understanding of sexual difference. Sexual difference is not the differences between the sexes as we know them today, or as we know them from the past. This is because, as Irigaray has argued, the differences between the sexes have never taken place.[1] Here she is not claiming unique experiences that one sex has which the other does not: rather, she is arguing that there has never been a space in culture for women *as* women. Women have only ever been represented as a lack, the opposite, the same as, or the complement of the one subject, the unique human subject.

In making the claim that sexual difference has yet to take place, she is arguing that there is no space in culture, in representation, exchange, ethics, politics, history, or writing, for the existence of *two* sexes, only the one sex and its counterpart. Insofar as women are conceived as the afterthought, the reflection, the augmentation, the supplement, the partner of men, they are contained within a phallocentrism that refuses alternative positions and spaces, that refuses the right of any autonomous representations, that eradicates sexual difference, that refuses to accord women the possibility of being otherwise than defined in some necessary relation to men.

Phallocentrism is explicitly *not* the refusal of an identity for women (on the contrary, there seems to be a proliferation of identities—wife, mother, teacher, nun, secretary, whore, etc.), but rather, the containment of that identity by other definitions and other identities. Thus Irigaray does not seek the "real" woman somehow beyond her patriarchal containment: instead she aims to challenge conceptual systems which refuse to acknowledge their own limitations, and their own specific interests. This is a challenge less to do with harnessing the lives, experiences, and energies of "real" women than with challenging and undermining the legitimacy of modes of their representation, models and systems which represent, theorize, and analyze the world and which help to produce them as such. Irigaray's questions are thus not questions about what to do, how to act, how to write in such a way as to be faithful to the lives and experiences of "real" women: her strategies instead are philosophical and methodological, even though they are no less activist for being so. The questions she asks focus on how to develop conceptual schemas, frameworks, systems that reveal what is at stake in dominant representational systems, and how to develop different ways of theorizing, based on the recognition of what has been left out of these dominant models. In other words, how to think, write, or read *not* as a woman but more complexly and less clearly, how to think, write, and read otherwise, whether one is a man or a woman, how to accommodate issues, qualities, concepts that have not had their time before.

It is this challenge that Irigaray issues to feminist thought — not simply to take women as the objects of intellectual investigation (though of course this is not to be very easily accomplished in some contexts), but rather to open up the position of knowing subject to the occupation of women. To enable women in the position of knower so that knowing itself may be done differently, different questions need to be asked, different criteria of evaluation need to be developed, and different intellectual standards and goals need to emerge. Irigaray cannot specify in advance how women, and men, might occupy positions of knowing when sexual difference finally takes place: that would be to preempt the specificities of other women's positions and their specific modes of occupation of those positions.

After Irigaray's work, a feminist future cannot be identified with the attainment of a sameness with men, of the same rights as men and the same access to their conceptual frameworks and systems of value: rather, it is now understood as a proliferation of alternative and different discourses, knowledges, frames of reference, political investments. The productivity of exchange across boundaries between disparate knowledges may be facilitated and developed on the same model as the interchange between the sexes themselves, the sexes as they *will have been* from the point of the view of the future, rather than the sexes as they are in the present or have been in the past.

Sexual difference is that which has yet to take place, and thus exists only in virtuality, in and through a future anterior, the only tense that openly addresses the question of the future without preempting it in concrete form or in present terms. Sexual difference does not yet exist, and it is possible that it has never existed. The sexes as we know them today have only one model, a singular and universal neutrality. At best, equal participation is conceptualized. But the idea that sexual difference entails the existence of *at least two* points of view, two sets of interests and perspectives, two types of ideal, two modes of knowledge has yet to be considered. The only time of sexual difference is that of the future. All the work of sexual difference, its labor of producing alternative knowledges, methods, and criteria, has yet to begin. Sexual difference is entirely of the order of the surprise, the encounter with the new, which is why Irigaray invokes the emotion of "wonder" as its most sensible attribute; it is an event yet to occur, an event strangely out of time, for it does not yet have a time and its time may never come, at least not without considerable risk and effort.

This is how Irigaray saves herself from the by-now tiresome charges of essentialism and utopianism: by refusing to speculate on what this sexual difference might consist in or how it might manifest itself, in refusing to posit a norm or a form for men or women in the present and the future, in seeing that the future for feminism is that which is to be made, invented, rather than foreseen or predicted: "To concern oneself in the present about the future certainly does not consist in programming it in advance but in trying to bring it into existence" (Irigaray, quoted in Whitford 1991, 14).

Sexual difference implies that there are at least two ways of doing *anything*, from the most abstract forms of thought to the most concrete forms of production to the most intense practices of pleasure, without being able to specify in what ways they may develop or what form they may take. Which means that the production of concepts themselves must provide at least two paths of development, at least two (possibly incommensurable) modes of existence, not in competition with each other to find which is the best, nor in augmentation of each other to provide a more complete picture, but as two singularities that may either conflict with or complement each other, that may be altogether incomparable or simply different. There is no way to judge in advance what forms and paths sexual difference, what the perspectives of at least two sexes, may have to offer to concepts, thought, knowledges, except that sexual difference makes and marks a difference everywhere and in everything. Sexual difference entails not only new epistemologies — new ways of knowing which recognize and affirm the existence of at least two different types of knower, two different ideals for knowledge, criteria of evaluation, methodologies, goals, and so on; it also entails the existence of an ontology, a world, being, which can no longer be understood as self-identical but must be conceptualized as bifurcated, composed of difference and engaged in becoming. Part of this self-division is the necessary difference central to all of ontology, a difference between space and time, which Irigaray places at the heart of a new ontology in *An Ethics of Sexual Difference* and which Deleuze also highlights in both his reading of Kant's critical philosophy (Deleuze 1984) and in his understanding of Foucault's concept of the outside (Deleuze 1988b).

Irigaray affirms that the question of time, and of conceptualizing women's closer alignment with temporality, is crucial to the struggles of sexual difference, insofar as the feminine has remained largely associated with space, place, containment, and habitation, while having its becoming—its interiority, its transformations in time, its alignments with the subjective and Godly apprehension of its possible perfection—curtailed and contained. In affirming the conceptual resonances of Kant's identification of time as the subject's mode of auto-affection, and of space as the subject's mode of engagement with things and others, Kant affirms the temporal interiority of the subject and its spatial exterior. For Irigaray, as for Deleuze, Kant in effect masculinizes time and feminizes space, aligning time with the mind's inner affect on itself, and space with the mind's outer dispersion, its being affected by what is outside.[2]

One of the most challenging issues facing any future feminism is precisely how to articulate a future in which futurity itself has a feminine form, in which the female subject can see itself projected beyond its present position as other to the one. Which may, ironically, mean that this future feminine may render itself obsolete or the object of profound and even inhuman (or imperceptible) becomings rather than rest itself on the forms of femininity as they have been represented and idealized within sexual indifference, within patriarchy as it has existed up to now. This conception of sexual difference as yet to come, as virtual within patriarchy, is not, I believe, a utopian conception, although it has often been understood as such: rather, Irigaray's claim is ontological. There are (at least) two types of sexual being, irreducibly different, and not adequately representable under a single model or image. There is no guarantee that this difference will adequately emerge from its present containment, but without considerable effort on the part of feminists, it may never take place. It is because sexual difference hides itself in other concepts and terms, other oppositional forms—in the distinctions between form and matter, between space and time, between mind and body, self and other, nature and culture, and so on, that it remains the latent condition of all knowledges and all social practices:

> In the beginning there was space and the creation of space, as is said in all theogonies . . . God would be time itself, lavishing or exteriorizing itself in its action in space, in places.
>
> Philosophy then affirms the genealogy of the task of the gods or God. Time becomes the *interiority* of the subject itself, and space, its *exteriority* (this problematic is developed by Kant in the *Critique of Pure Reason*). (Irigaray, 1993: 7)

Irigaray's understanding of sexuality entails conceptualizing an ontology of becoming, whose central concern is the re-elaboration of time and space, in which time is privileged as a repressed or feminized condition of the world, where temporality must be conceived, not in terms of the (perceptual and practical) privilege of the present, but rather in terms of the preeminence of an undeterminable future. This is a paradoxical conception of time modeled on an unknowable future; and a paradoxical conception of the relations of subjects and objects based on this paradoxical temporality. We are dealing with a subject that is never what it is, a subject that is always in the process of becoming something else, perhaps even a subject becoming beyond subjectivity, which necessarily produces as its correlate and complement an object that is more than an inert, given passivity, and also becomes something else than it was. Time, even more than space, needs to be thought in terms which liberate it from the constraints of the present, for time is the force of differing, whatever stability and order spatialization enables or entails.

Such an understanding of time as inherently dislocated, bifurcated, is of course not easy to come by. It is rare in the history of Western thought that there has been any consideration of a time beyond or outside of the strictures of counting, calculism, and ideally (as science desires), determinism, that is, outside the causal control that the past exerts over the present and future. From Plato to Einstein, from philosophy to physics, the reality of the experience of time, time as an irreversible pull toward the future, time marked by an arrow of directionality that always impels it forward and never backward, has been denied. Time is reduced to formalized representations, to counting, to space and spatialization, which leads many of the most respected physicists and cosmologists to regard the experience of time's irreversibility as mere subjective illusion, beneath which a timeless or unchanging calculability, measure, or ratio is discernible. Even fewer affirm the positivity of a future not controlled and directed by calculable forces in the present.[3]

Feminist discourses interested in the question of time and its openness to transformation may find themselves in strangely compromising relations with a number of theorists they may have hoped to otherwise avoid, theorists whose unhinging of time may also provide a mode of unhinging subjectivity while nevertheless affirming sexual difference. The strange allies would include, above all, Darwin, who, as I argued in chapter 2, brought the question of indeterminacy to the center of the study of life; Nietzsche, who rendered time the affirmative movement of force, a force that eternally returns to affirm its positive openness, which undermines and complicates every system and every order, as I claim in chapter 10; Bergson, who makes explicit the bodily and conceptual cost of the mathematization of time and its reduction to spatialization as required by the natural sciences, as discussed in chapter 6; and finally Deleuze, who, in recognizing all these as predecessors, affirms that time is a multiplicity that nevertheless expresses a fundamental unity, its multiplicity an affirmation of the singularity of the eternal return and of the irreducibility of life to prediction (the basis of Deleuze's opposition to Badiou's (2000) valorization of the mathematical, and particularly set theory).

This cluster of theorists may form an uneasy alliance, especially given the self-evident and possibly not misapplied apprehensiveness of feminist theorists to them and what they seem to represent, arguably some of the most misogynist thinkers of their generation. Such, however, are the most productive and complex engagements of contemporary feminist theory—the encounter with what is alien, the meeting with what is outside, with what might otherwise be an irritant, which forces feminism to expand itself to develop and accommodate the new, to actively "evolve," to transform or remake itself.[4] Such feminist theory would engage, not in critique or demolition, nor in the defensive hold on already acquired gains, nor in the abandonment but in the revitalization of discourses to which they might otherwise seem opposed. This is part of feminism's own self-overcoming, its movement from policing to production, its self-expansion into the terrain of knowledge production. Critique, ironically, affirms the privilege and priority of the position being critiqued. The more interesting questions of knowledge production are not bound up with the discovery of what is "wrong" with a discourse or position, what problems it exemplifies, what errors it commits. Rather, they are linked to how discourses and positions, whatever their problems might be, can be used differently, can be developed beyond themselves, can be utilized to highlight, analyze, or explain what they were not able to originally. No doubt, every discourse is problematic, makes assumptions it cannot justify, commits itself to claims that are beyond its scope, and omits frameworks and questions that may prove relevant to its concerns. Nevertheless, the question remains: how can it be of use? What can we do with it that we may be unable to do without it? What kind of concept-tools can it provide us with?

To adequately begin this feminist requestioning of the structures of futurity means taking on a two-pronged project: on the one side, to address discourses, knowledges, and practices undertaken under the auspices of the hard sciences, including the ways in which time and change are conceptualized in physics, chemistry, biology, astronomy, and so on, discourses that analyze the time of materiality; and, on the other, to explore the ways in which temporality and change are lived and experienced in cross-cultural and cross-historical terms, the psychic materiality of duration. Neither the material explorations of time undertaken in the natural sciences nor the psychological or phenomenological understanding of the lived experience of time provides us with a definitive truth, one which supersedes or overrules the truth or force of the other. As Bergson (1988) makes clear, each provides resources whose tension together needs to be explained rather than resolved. Together, they provide us with the parameters of the question of time and becoming: what kind of an understanding of time can be developed in feminism that is able to provide an explanation of the dynamism of the material world, and of the place of living beings within that world in the same language, using the same conceptual apparatuses and levels of explanation (Deleuze's requirement of the univocity of being, a multiplicity of beings which nonetheless speak in one voice, or with one language)? How can we use the concept of time to dynamize or revitalize the continuity between the human and the inhuman, in other words, to liberate a becoming-beyond the human? Which is directly linked to the feminist question: how to move beyond the sexes as we know them, and beyond sexuality as it is usually practiced? But also, how to understand this dynamism as always bifurcated and bifurcating, driven primarily by difference (Irigaray's requirement of a multiplicity irreducible to the logic of the one)?

Some brief characterization of time is required, although it must remain schematic here:

1. Time is an active force. It implies an irreversible and irresistible movement forward, which is also a movement of division, complication, and elaboration. It has only one direction or vector: ever-forward.

2. Time is not added to a separate space or objects but is the underlying principle that enables objects to come into existence, to transform or metamorphose themselves, and to cease existing. It is not outside of space or

objects but inheres in them and is their inner condition of existence and becoming.

3. Time itself, while it is the principle of emergence and transformation, never itself emerges or transforms but is the continuous and thus eternal force of variation, a force that directs the universe itself as a whole, as well as all of its components. Time is this variation, this difference. In this sense, it is not, as Einstein suggests, created with the eruption of the material universe, a variable or factor of matter, but is the ongoing condition of becoming that enables even the universe itself to become.

4. While the things that develop in time tend toward complexity and dispersion, toward evolutionary elaboration rather than simplification, time itself remains continuous, singular, smooth, a unity constituted out of the multiplicity of changing things, processes, movements; it underlies them all and enables them to be placed in relations of simultaneity or before and after.

5. Time is that outside in which other forces — whether material, such as gravitational or electrical forces, or cultural and political forces — play themselves out and impinge on each other as well as on subjects. As such, it is an ongoing regulative principle of both matter and life, and also the principle that ensures the ongoing movement of difference, change, and surprise.

6. Thus time is both an enduring past, a past that accumulates as the present unfolds, and a continuous present. It is fractured between the virtual past and the actual present. This past, a past created simultaneously with the present and always carried along with it, is the ongoing resource, the site of virtuality, that provides any possibility of disruption to the forces that dominate the present because the past is able to be revivified, actualized, in different ways according to the different possibilities the present affords it and the future opens up to it. The past is not inert, given, fixed, but is able to be illuminated, brought to life again, only through the active work of the present, which harnesses its hitherto unactualized resources.

Such an understanding of time as dynamic force, as activity rather than as passive wearing away, erosion, is, I believe, of vital importance for feminist theory: we need an account of time that enables us to have at least partial or mediated access to the resources of the past, those resources consecrated as history and retaining their traces or tracks in the present, which do not tie us to the past in any definitive way or with any particular orientation and which provide for us the very resources by which to supersede the past and the present — the very project of radical politics. It is only our immersion in temporal becoming that enables our access to the untimely, to that which in the past was not able to be contained there, to that which is out of time enough to jar the present and to adequately disrupt it, thereby bringing about a different temporal trajectory, different modes of becoming. The project of radical politics, and thus of a radical feminist politics, remains directed at how to envisage and engender a future unlike the present, without being able to specify in advance what such a future entails. It is thus an investment in the power of the leap, by which the actual emerges and produces itself from its virtual resources, that generates the new, in both politics and theory.

As we have seen, it is by no means clear that there can be an easy alignment between Deleuze and Irigaray, although there have been a number of attempts, particularly on the part of feminist philosophers, to utilize the resources of Deleuzianism for Irigarayan ends.[5] Their concepts are not readily integratable into a single cohesive position and they do not share a body of agreed upon concepts, methods, or principles. Rather, each provokes questions from the other, each directs the other, through their juxtapositioning, into dealing with questions they do not address, expanding and to some extent transforming them beyond themselves. They form an uneasy alliance largely through the productive tensions their relation provokes: Irigaray's insistence on subjectivity, identity, and their entwinement and complexity through sexual difference sits uneasily with Deleuze's concern with the impersonal, the outside, intensities and speeds, though they share a number of common intellectual resources and predecessors, most notably Nietzsche, whose orientation beyond the orbit of Hegelianism provides one of the most powerful alternatives to Hegel's emphasis on identity, recognition, and desire.

What these two (series) — Irigaray and Deleuze — have to offer each other is an expansion rather than a consolidation: Deleuze may enable the Irigarayan concern with the production of sexual difference to understand its need for a reconceptualization of the terms by which time is understood as the mode of actualization of the virtuality of the past. And Irigaray may enable the Deleuzian focus on becoming to understanding that the becoming-woman of all identity is not just the recognition of micro-sexualities within each subject, but is also the becoming-other of all knowledges and all practices, the becoming-more available to each of the sexes in their own ways.

Why then should feminism turn or perhaps return to concepts like matter, time, space, force, energy — that is to questions usually occupying either the natural sciences or metaphysics — which seem to deflect from its basic occupation with direct changes in the position of women (and men), or of homosexuals (and heterosexuals)? I am not suggesting that *all* feminists should turn to these rather obscure and abstract reflections on the broad conditions of being and its complication through becoming: clearly this is a project far removed from direct application and from concrete projects aimed at transforming women's everyday lives. Nevertheless, unless *some* feminist theorists take the philosophical and theoretical exploration of the implications of sexual difference, and of difference more generally, seriously, and follow these obscure lines where they might lead—however strange— we have no hope of something entirely other; we will remain tied to the recognized and the known, mired in the past and the present instead of able to address or at least face the undecidability of the future.

Feminism is no longer required to look only inward, at the conditions and effects of subjectivity, desire, pleasure, at the interpersonal networks and oppressive impingements of institutions on socially subordinated groups; it is now also urgent that it direct its gaze outward, not only at the social and historical conditions of patriarchy, but also to the larger material and natural forces at play in the social, the historical, and the sexual. Needless to say, such projects are already under way in a wide variety of feminist research agendas across different academic disciplines.[6] Ironically, it seems as if philosophy lags behind many other disciplines in generating feminist ontology as a research program.[7] It is, however, as Irigaray and Deleuze demonstrate, in a unique position to analyze and transform the underlying assumptions governing other disciplines, even if it is not in any position to supplant them. Without a more adequate recognition of the impersonal forces at work in social, cultural, and subjective relations and about their fundamental tendency to differentiation and diffusion (in the present) and realignment and evolution (in the future), the resources for thinking a feminist future, a future in which sexual difference, and the forces it harnesses and unleashes, will remain impoverished and its virtual force will remain untapped. A feminism without end, without definitive goal, without pregiven aims or objects, a feminism invested in processes, becomings, materialities, a feminism prepared to risk itself in its engagement with what is outside itself, will make a difference, will ensure that difference continues to be made, elaborated, proliferated, and celebrated.

CHAPTER 12

(Inhuman) Forces:
Power, Pleasure, and Desire

Our pleasures and pains exhaust themselves; our laughter and our tears die away; our blessing and our cursing are carried away into the enigmas of the future and the silences of the past. They are of themselves gratuitous outpourings of force, expenditures without return. Their glory is purely worldly; their force does not hold or redeem.
—Alphonso Lingis, *Foreign Bodies*

I am interested here in how to think two basic concepts, two of the most central concerns of feminists and political theorists for the last few decades—pleasure and power—without, however, seeing women as subjugated by an oppressive, dominating power, and without seeing power as a form of constraint and limitation on pleasure. Instead of the older, pre-Foucauldian question: "How does power limit pleasure, how does pleasure rebel against power?" we need to ask how to think pleasure and power in and as relations of internality with each other, how to see them as each other's condition of existence. This exploration of the pleasure of power and the power of pleasure is possible only because of major shifts in the ways in which feminism, power, resistance, struggle, and identity have been reconfigured, especially in the light of the Foucauldian complication of the opposition between power and pleasure proposed by the discourses of transgressive pleasure associated with many of the earlier writings in feminist and queer theory on sexuality. I will put forward some propositions here, in highly abbreviated but I hope suggestive form, that push even further the drive to antihumanism that has been central in some key post-Foucauldian developments in feminist theory; these propositions problematize and question the drive to identity, recognition, and self-affirmation that is so pervasive in contemporary feminist, queer, and minoritarian politics and theory.

What I propose here is a sketch or outline of an ontology, not of *subjects* and their *desires*, but of *forces* and *actions* which produce subjects and pleasures as their crystallized forms, which is, for me, part of a larger project of developing an ontology of becoming. It seems to me that we can push even further the impetus to antihumanism by acknowledging the formative, productive role of inhuman forces which constitute the human as such and provide the conditions and means by which it may overcome itself. At the same time, I hope to indicate that a viable and complex, nonreductive understanding of psychic and social structures can be developed without submitting to the exigencies of a theory of the subject.

In this sense, this project involves a detour away from the most pervasive movement within feminist and political theory in the United States, the United Kingdom, and in parts of Europe that uses psychoanalytic discourse as a mode of political analysis, either in the tradition initiated by the Freudo-Marxism of Althusser (Althusser 1972, 1996) or more recently in the work of Žižek (1989, 2004). This same tendency pervades much contemporary feminist thought, from Juliet Mitchell's pioneering writings on the relations between psychoanalytic theory and women's oppression (Mitchell 1974), through to Judith Butler's more recent attempts to link psychoanalytic discourse to feminist and gay politics through its connections to both Foucault and Austin (Butler 1990; 1994).

FORCES, NOT SUBJECTS

Force has been an underlying conception that has provided dynamical fuel for a series of philosophical models from at least the time of the British empiricists (Hobbes, Locke, Hume), if not long before, though the philosophy of force reached its culmination in the work of Friedrich Nietzsche. The historical ingredients are there for one to be able to write a philosophical history of force. But force, or forces, are rarely if ever conceptualized in feminist terms. Indeed there seems to be a general awkwardness with taking the concept into the intellectual orbit of feminist concerns, a suspicion that perhaps this may engage feminism in a complicity with its patriarchal "other." This may be because force is commonly associated with *will*, with the forcible enactment of one person's will on another (which of course is a classical definition of oppression) or on the world (a definition of exploitation); in other words, force is usually identified with coercion and authority, and thus with masculinities and masculine modes of power. But this maneuver of identifying force with the masculine is already to humanize force (which in effect is to masculinize it, in a phallocentric logos), to anthropomorphize it and to refuse to see its role not as the effect but as the condition of subjectivity and subjective will. It is one of Nietzsche's most profound insights that will, subjectivity, consciousness, the human are not causes, and that causation is indeed a habit or explanatory model that puts the subject's position as a being of habit at the center without adequate recognition of that which "causes," produces the very fiction that is the subject:

> That which gives the extraordinary firmness to our belief in causality is not the great habit of seeing one occurrence following another but our inability to interpret events otherwise than as events caused by intentions. It is belief in the living and thinking as the only effective force—in will, in intention—it is belief that every event is a deed, that every deed presupposes a doer, it is belief in the "subject." Is this belief in the concept of subject and attribute not a great stupidity?
>
> Question: is intention the cause of an event? Or is that also illusion?
> Is it not the event itself? (Nietzsche 1968, §550)

In place of conceptualizing the subject as an agent of causal effects or as a victim of another's agency, that is, as an intentionality, a will, a set of desires, especially as a "radical will" that acts and produces events or effects that can be seen to conflict with the forces of social regulation—that is, instead of seeing politics as the more or less violent negotiation between individuals, groups, and institutions, between individual and collective agents—Nietzsche may help provide a way of understanding politics, subjectivity, and the social as the consequence of the play of the multiplicity of active forces that have no agency, or are all that agency consists in. Which is to say, force needs to be understood in its full subhuman and superhuman resonances: as *the inhuman* which both makes the human possible and at the same time positions the human within a world where force works in spite of and around the human, within and as the human.[1] Rather than seeing subjectivity and the social, pleasure and power, libido and law as two sides of a divide that need to be somehow reconciled, force provides us with a way of thinking pleasure and power, the psychical and the social as terms leveled by that which runs through them, that which they share in common and depend upon for their existence. The psychical and the social can be understood as two different directions or orientations of impersonal or pre-personal forces, the same forces that regulate the natural world as well as cultural life.

Force has a number of attributes or activities in Nietzsche's understanding that I will broadly indicate rather than develop in detail:

1. Force is always both specific and a multiplicity: there are always and only for*ces* in the plural. These multiple, struggling, willing, competing forces share in common a force, a charge, that enables them to compete with each other, to exert and extend themselves and to thereby affect each other. Yet each force has its own characteristics, its own quantum, its own quality, circumstances, effectivity, its own will or goal. Force is that which both establishes and severs connections between (the forces that compose) things and relations. Force makes forces level, able to connect with and affect each other, able to compose higher unities or to detach themselves in a form of decomposition without ever making them the same or equal.

2. Force is always engaged in becoming. It is never stationary. It has a history and a duration. Force does not seek intentions, goals, purposes, but simply its own expansion and magnification—always more. Force seeks intensification, elaboration, celebration; it seeks to act. (This is why force is named "the will to power" in Nietzsche's work.)

3. Force is always a relation of intensity and thus of magnitude (a relation of more or less, never ceasing, never depleting itself). Force thus functions quantitatively,[2] though not through any absolute measure. Quantity is thus differential not absolute.[3]

4. If force is differentiated quantitatively, out of these quantitative differences come qualitative differences: it is differences in the quantity of forces that produces differences in quality[4] (to which Nietzsche gives the names "active" and "reactive," "noble" and "servile").

5. Force is always contestatory. Each force seeks its own expansion in its own way and time; but this inevitably places forces in relations of hostility and competition with each other, where forces seek to subdue each other, to subvert or convert each, where the stronger seeks to overcome the weaker: "All events, all motions, all becoming, [i]s a determination of degrees and relations of force . . . a struggle" (Nietzsche 1968, §552).

6. Force is not only that which produces competition and struggle between forces functioning in the same sphere and level, but it is also that which produces relations of alignment, cooperation, and tension between forces functioning at different levels. Force is thus also the condition of the assemblage (in Deleuzian terms), the complex, the molecular.

Rethinking the concept of subject and the subject/object relation in terms of force means profound transformations in all related concepts — of objects, of the social, of action and agency. It is no longer a subject that takes before it an object on which to enact its desire or will; rather, forces act through subjects, objects, material and social worlds without distinction, producing relations of inequality and differentiation, which in turn produce ever-realigning relations of intensity or force. They constitute an inhuman, subhuman field, a field of "particles" or elements of force which are only provisionally or temporarily grouped together in the form of entities and actions. This field is itself an individuality without individuals, a singularity without identity:[5]

> If we give up the effective subject, we also give up the object upon which the effects are produced. Duration, identity with itself, being are inherent neither in that which is called subject nor in that which is called object: they are complexes of events, apparently durable in comparison with other complexes — e.g., through the differences in tempo of the event. . . .
>
> If we give up the concept "subject" and "object," then also the concept "substance" — and as a consequence also the various modifications of it, e.g., "matter," "spirit," and other hypothetical entities, "the eternity and immutability of matter" etc. (1968, §552)

We have a theoretical choice. Either we can subscribe to a theory of the subject which strives to have its identity affirmed through relations, especially relations of desire but also relations of identification or recognition, with other subjects, a subject who seeks the mutual and reciprocal identification with and recognition of others and a place as a subject within culture. This, for example, is the basis of Butler's understanding of performativity: the subject performs its identity through acts of subject-constitution and consolidation. These performances in fact produce the identity that they reportedly express. What makes them performances, though, rather than simply acts, is that they entail and require a mode of address, an audience. It is this audience or witness — central to Austin's understanding of the performative and so carefully analyzed by Derrida as the site of iteration in *Limited Inc*, whether it is the heterosexual world that abjects the gay subject or the gay world that produces an identity for itself — that is crucial to Butler's understanding of identity.[6]

Alternatively, we can subscribe to a theory of the impersonal (and ultimately a "politics of imperceptibility," the opposite of identity politics: a politics of acts, not identities), in which inhuman forces, forces that are both living and nonliving, macroscopic and microscopic, above and below the level of the human are acknowledged and allowed to displace the centrality of both consciousness and the unconscious.[7] At the very least, this means that there are wills, forces, powers that can be ascribed no humanity, no life, but which have "their" perspectives and interests, their own trajectories, a "life" of their own. Forces have their own wishes, interests, or intentionalities — to win, to expand, to become more and other. The human, the subject, its innermost psychological recesses can equally, Nietzsche conjectures, be explained in terms of competing impersonal forces, forces that will, that struggle and strive, and that constitute the very interior of all psychological processes: "The *victorious* concept "force," by means of which our physicists have created God and the world, still needs to be *completed*; an *inner* will must be *ascribed* to it, which I designate as 'will to power'" (Nietzsche 1968, §619).

PLEASURE AND DESIRE AS FORCE

What is pleasure? How can it be refigured in terms of force, rather than in terms of the subject and its desires and satisfactions? Is not force itself, as affect and intensity, one of the crucial elements of pleasure and of desire, whatever conception one has of it? Pleasure, as much as and in the same ways as pain, is the corporeal or sensory registration of the differential of forces, whether these forces are muscular and neuronal, or psychical and representational, or perceptual and sensory.[8] It is the registration of the intensity of forces, subhuman, subcorporeal forces, forces which "compete" with each other, strive against each other, for oxygen, for nutrients, at the level of cells and organs, for activity and privilege at the level of individuals, for conceptual space and for geographical territory at the level of collectives, in each case for the capacity to function to their fullest. Pleasure and pain are the corporeal registrations of the forces of the world, the visceral impact of forces, what we use to struggle with and against, in order to become more and other. They are the most powerful aids to learning and the most direct and effective stimuli for action, and thus for the expansion of force. Pleasure and pain are not the object or goal of forces but rather their by-products, the epiphenomena that result from the drive to exertion and self-expansion of the will to power. How, then, do pleasure and pain connect with desire and power? How can they be thought in terms of force?

Deleuze suggests, in an intriguing and suggestive essay ("Desire and Power," 1997b), that what Foucault describes as pleasure, in his alignment of bodies with pleasures on the one side of a divide that separates them from desire and power on the other (in *The History of Sexuality*, vol. 1 [1978]), he, Deleuze, would call "desire."[9] And to the degree that he, Deleuze, has an aversion to the concept of pleasure (which for him, is always linked to an apparatus of subjectification, that is, to a theory of the subject), so too Foucault has an aversion to the notion of desire (which he wants to link to a fundamental negation or lack, to the negative conception of power as repression or suppression). This leads one to suspect that perhaps the ways in which Foucault uses the term *pleasure* (as a wedge to oppose psychoanalytic and psychiatric theory with a more primordial and potentially resistant body) may be linked and cross-fertilized with Deleuze's closely related notion of desire as production or assemblage. What then is pleasure, for Foucault, and desire for Deleuze? How may these concepts be understood in terms of force? And what might such an understanding offer to feminist theory?

In *The History of Sexuality* Foucault positions pleasure in close association with the body as a whole, and the body is understood as the locus of both the operations of power and the engendering of resistance. Pleasure is a crucial hinge, a bodily resource, that is of enormous strategic utility in the ongoing interplay and transformations of power and resistance. Pleasure is that which induces bodies to participate in power; pleasure is that which provides power with some of its techniques for the extraction of information or knowledge, and for imposing discipline through the subject's very complicity in speaking and acting according to requirements of disciplinary regimes. But if pleasure can function in the service of power, as a means and end of power's operations, so too pleasure is that wedge which serves and consolidates resistance. Foucault attributes to the normative, disciplinary power that characterizes the modern era the capacity to thoroughly entwine itself in pleasures, inducing new and more refined pleasures as it refines and complicates its own procedures, and the capacity to find in those pleasures, at least in some of them, the possibilities for a transformation of power through the generation of resistances.[10]

The current consequence of this alignment of power with the pleasurable forces of the body is the constitution of the complex "sexuality," which must be regarded as an amalgam of bodily pleasures, programs, desires, inclinations, fantasies, and so forth, a complex that has come to provide a unique and central key to the "identity" of a subject. Pleasure and power spiral inward on each other, pleasure inducing itself in its engagement with, or its resistance to, power, and power proliferating itself and enabling for itself a more microscopic access to bodies through the investment and intensification of the body's pleasurable forces. Pleasures are directly inscribed by the tactics and procedures of power. This directness is why Foucault seems to align pleasures with bodies and with resistance, and why he wants to more closely associate desire with power-sovereignty, and the rule of law.[11]

It is significant that in Deleuze's writings the relations between desire and pleasure seem reversed. Deleuze argues that because desire (in his works) is not a psychological concept at all, and because desire cannot be represented by the (Hegelian/psychoanalytic) model of lack—for desire is always and only productive—desire produces and makes the real by establishing connections or generating disjunctions; it is pleasure that must be understood to interrupt and transform desire. Deleuze notes his objections to the concept of pleasure: "I cannot give any positive value to pleasure because pleasure seems to me to interrupt the immanent process of desire; pleasure seems to me to be on the side of strata and organization; and it is in one and the same movement that desire is subject to the law from within and scanned by pleasure from without; in both cases, there is the negation of the field of immanence proper to desire" (Deleuze 1997b, 189–190).

He suggests that it may be the privileging of desire over pleasure that draws him to Sacher von Masoch,[12] while it may be the capacity of pleasure to outstrip and complexify the law, which is closely identified with desire in Foucault's writings that draws Foucault to Sade: "What interests me in Masoch are not the pains but the idea that pleasure interrupts the positivity of desire and the constitution of its field of immanence (just as, or rather in a different manner, in courtly love there is the constitution of a field of immanence or a body without organs in which desire lacks nothing and refrains as long as possible from the pleasures that would interrupt its processes" (1997b, 90). In short, pleasure is of significance for Deleuze only insofar as it forms part of an assemblage or machine, only insofar as it is able to interact with other objects, flows, and forces to form something new and unpredictable, rather than serve as a purpose, goal, object, or criterion for subjects or for power. If pleasure functions to slow down, speed up, direct, or organize desire, it can function as an obstacle to rather than an enhancement of the assemblage.

Foucauldian pleasure lines up on the side of resistance, as other to the law and to power, as a point beyond or perhaps before the impact and force of the law. Pleasure has the role of both force and counterforce, a mobile energy (actually remarkably like Freud's conception of the unbounded drive), capable of being bound into habituated, disciplined practices, particularly those constituting the docile body, but also, under the right circumstances, capable of unleashing the unpredictable forces of rebellion and transformation. *Deleuzian desire*, too, functions as a primarily mobile and mobilizing impetus, a force of connections: of those conjunctions and disjunctions that form provisional "entities" and groupings, not so much functioning "against" power as entwined in modes of stratification or territorialization and deterritorialization. Pleasure and desire, for both, are force, whether bodily (as in Foucault) or impersonal (for Deleuze), which can be mobilized in particular contexts (contexts that cannot be determined in advance). For both, it is forces, and not subjects, which act and produce, which proliferate and transform, which are subjected to becoming and self-overcoming.

What does this mean for feminist theory and politics? How can the notion of force be mobilized or used for thinking through key feminist strategies? Here, I can only be suggestive rather than elaborate, for these are concepts that might be regarded as germinal, potential, and yet to be accomplished.

1. Feminist theory needs to reconceptualize the terms by which it understands subjectivity. Instead of regarding feminist politics as a struggle around the rights and needs of female subjects, individually or as a category, subjugated by male subjects, who require a more adequate and respectful recognition by male subjects—the basic assumptions behind various non-aligned feminists: liberal feminism, identity politics, and the politics of performativity—feminist and other forms of political struggle may more ably function as a mode of rendering the subject the backdrop to a play of forces which are themselves what constitute the ever shifting and uncontrollable terrain of politics and identities. Feminist theory is not the struggle to liberate women, even though it has tended to conceive of itself in these terms (if this is its function, it has failed miserably!); it is the struggle to render more mobile, fluid, and transformable the means by which the female subject is produced and represented. It is the struggle to produce a future in which forces align in ways fundamentally different from the past and present. This struggle is not a struggle by subjects to be recognized and valued, to be and to be seen to be what they are, but a struggle to mobilize and transform the position of women, the alignment of forces that constitute that "identity" and "position," that stratification which stabilizes itself as a place and an identity. Politics can be seen as the struggle of imperceptible forces, forces in and around us, forces in continual conflict, forces including those mobilizing pleasure, pain, and desire. It is a useful fiction to imagine that we as subjects are masters or agents of these very forces that constitute us as subjects, but it is misleading, for it makes the struggle about *us*, about our

identities and individualities rather than about the world; it directs us to questions about being rather than doing; it gives identity and subjectivity a centrality and agency that they may not deserve, for they do not produce themselves but are accomplishments or effects of forces before and outside of identity and subjectivity.

2. From the vantage point of (micro-)forces, wills to power, if politics constitutes itself as the struggle for recognition, the struggle for identity to be affirmed by the others who occupy socially dominant positions and among peers for mutual respect, it is a politics that is fundamentally servile; if identity is a "useful fiction," a subjectively apprehended cohesion which required personal and collective validation to take its place as a subject, then this identity is always governed, in advance, by the image and value of this socially dominant other. Instead of a politics of recognition, in which sub-jugated groups and minorities strive for a validated and affirmed place in public life, feminist politics should, I believe, now consider the affirmation of a politics of *imperceptibility*, leaving its traces and effects everywhere but never being able to be identified with a person, group, or organization. It is not a politics of visibility, of recognition and of self-validation, but a pro-cess of self-marking that constitutes oneself in the very model of that which oppresses and opposes the subject. The imperceptible is that which the in-human musters, that which the human can sometimes liberate from its own orbit but not control or name as its own: it is that which is unleashed by the force of events, by unexpected impacts, surprising encounters.

3. Pleasures and desires are allowed to be pleasures and desires without necessarily being tied directly to a larger political framework or system of justification. Engaging in whatever sexual and other pleasures one chooses may produce political effects, but it is not primarily the political that is at stake in this relation. It is instead a relation of production or assemblage, which may have political effects at particular moments, but is primarily pro-ductive or creative rather than critical. It is the subject for whom pleasure functions as a disruptive or confirming process. (Much of contemporary queer theory defines itself in relation to the radicality of its sexual practices, their social transgressiveness and ability to break social taboos. Many claim to be political activists simply because of these sexual practices. While I have no doubt that many have suffered as a result of these sexual practices, the performance of them is a matter of pleasure and/ or production, and needs to be assessed in those terms, severing rather than consolidating the links between power and pleasure outlined by Foucault.)

4. Which is not to say that pleasure is entirely disconnected from power;

on the contrary, it is to say that it is not the same as power. They are each apparatuses, assemblages, each composed of forces (of differing quantities and qualities) which clearly interlock and struggle at certain volatile points of intensity, and which coexist at other more benign regions, and that are connected, not directly or in any one-to-one way, but through and as the forces which underlie them both and make them both productive and generative.

Deleuze's notion of desire as assemblage may prove to be a productive way of thinking about how these different regimes (sexuality, pleasure, power) become fragmented and the elements of one become operative and transforming vectors in the functioning of the others. It may explain why pleasure and desire today may function as sites of exacerbation and resistance, but also how they may be harnessed to forms of power and modes of discipline the subject may enjoy but does not control.

Feminist, queer, and other struggles around sexuality and pleasure may find their struggles are strengthened rather than weakened if, instead of focusing on the sexed subject and its unconscious and conscious aims and aspirations, they acknowledge the pre-personal forces at work in the activities of sexed bodies, institutions, and social practices. These forces, these micro-agencies, ensure that sexuality, and identity itself, are fundamentally mosaiclike fields composed of aligned but disparate elements, energies, goals, wills. These bodies do not so much require recognition and validation as activity and action: our sexualities and identities are not one thing, but a multiplicity of disparate yearnings, interests, orientations, unified at this historical moment through the identification of the object of sexual desire (heterosexual and homosexual, normal and perverse are today identified through the type of object they take as sexual partner, through the apparently recognizable coherence of the sexual object, though this object is as composed of a multiplicity of ambiguous and conflicted forces as the subject) but fundamentally disparate. This profusion of energies and forces functioning within and as subjects is not the denial of sexual difference but its increasing elaboration, for sexual difference, the systematically differing morphologies of (most) living bodies, operates not only at the level of the body-as-a-whole, but also within the body's microscopic functions and processes.

CHAPTER 13

The Future of Female Sexuality

Ownership and property are doubtless quite foreign to the feminine. At least sexually. But not *nearness*. Nearness so pronounced that it makes all discrimination of identity, and thus all forms of property, impossible. Woman derives pleasure from what is *so near that she cannot have it, nor have herself*. . . . This puts into question all prevailing economies: their calculations are irremediably stymied by woman's pleasure, as it increases indefinitely from its passage in and through the other.

— Luce Irigaray, *This Sex Which Is Not One*

The topic of human sexuality, and in particular female sexuality, has always generated and combined fascination and perplexity, knowledge and ignorance, immersion and distance, allure and revulsion, contradictory impulses and tendencies to nearness and distance. The relatively recent imperative to know sex, to understand it through the methodological ordering and discipline of rigorous science, an imperative that has been operative for less than 150 years according to Michel Foucault, has attempted, with quite mixed results, to understand and contain sexuality as a knowable, measurable, containable object of analysis, a thing, an organ, a series of distinguishable, recognizable processes. The turbulent, disturbing, erupting indeterminacy of sexual attraction and pleasure, which is so forceful an impulse in everyday life and yet so ambiguous, precarious, and unpredictable in its objects and expression, seemed to require more and more careful containment, not within moral strictures but through epistemic systems, discourses, knowledges, medical practices, and so on.

As one of the dynamic and unpredictable forces of life, a force connected to the increasing elaboration and evolution of life that ties life irremediably to and through sexual difference, sexuality requires greater management and regulation as populations become larger, denser, and more diverse; hence its increasing medicalization, the attempt at its regulation through medicalized techniques of supervision and normalization. Sexuality can be ever more commodified and rendered an attainable, transformable product through the processes of analysis and synthesis that medicalization entails. In this chapter, I focus on one of the major moments or events in the history of (mid-)twentieth-century sexology, Alfred Kinsey's publication of his study of female sexuality (Kinsey, Pomeroy, Martin, and Gebhard, 1953), *not* because Kinsey's work is a particularly egregious form of the impulse to know but because in his writings the tension between knowing and containment, between the epistemological and the ontological remains clear, not yet covered over. The stakes involved—the containment of a messy and irregular series of impulses, activities, and practices within a regularizing, comprehensible, ordered grid—in the battle between the epistemological impulse to render the real knowable and the ontological impulse of sexuality to function as an openness to a future not yet known are as clear and explicit in Kinsey's writings as anywhere in the discourses of sexology.

THE KINSEY-EVENT

Alfred Kinsey had hoped that not only would a wide range of scientists and empirical researchers of various kinds—psychologists, psychiatrists, physicians, physiologists, endocrinologists, anatomists, ethnologists, sociologists, and so on—contribute to and expand his project of developing a taxonomic analysis of human sexuality, but also that philosophers, artists, and ethicists would reconsider their everyday assumptions about human sexuality and would eventually contribute to the analysis of the data he and his research team had so carefully accumulated.[1] Nevertheless, it was only science, in its disinterested search for truth, that could rid us of our prejudices and assumptions regarding sexuality, prejudices that many in the humanities, he believed, shared and that had inhibited an honest and detailed exploration of the "facts" constituting the sexuality of entire populations. Scientific method, with its emphasis on disinterested observation, observation undertaken without preconception, was a necessary corrective to moral and religious presumptions, particularly those that identified sexuality only with reproduction. Kinsey's study aimed to objectively explore sexuality wherever it led in the true spirit of scientific discovering: "No theory, no philosophy, no body of theology, no political expediency, no wishful thinking, can provide a satisfactory substitute for the observation of material objects and of the way in which they behave. Whether the observations are made directly through one's telescope or a microscope, or whether the information is acquired, as in much of our present study, from the reports of participants who were the observers of their own sexual activity, observation provides the information which the scientist most respects when material phenomena are involved" (Kinsey et al. 1953, 9).

Kinsey undertook a mind-blowing project: it was not or not only, as is commonly understood, a vast statistical analysis of the rates of performance of various sexual activities in the United States during the first half of the twentieth century but rather a more sophisticated and contradictory project: a statistical analysis of the *phenomenology of sexuality*, an analysis of a vast number of case studies, studies of the self-representation and experience of sexuality as it appears to the interviewed subject. While he is interested in the central place of observation in scientific method, he seems unaware of the complications that self-observation, represented in his texts in the form of the case study, adds to science, and the ways in which science is itself transformed, and its statistical aspirations problematized, through the individualization of the processes of detailed interviewing.

My goal here is not to undertake a philosophical critique of Kinsey's science (to provide philosophy its revenge over Kinsey's association of it with superstition and conservatism!), or indeed to question or criticize his empirical findings, which prove endlessly fascinating, whatever their truth, and which in any case I am in no position to evaluate as empirical research. On the contrary, I would like to make clear what I see is positive and of value in Kinsey's work today, and what its implications are for an understanding of the radical future of female sexuality. There are, however, major limits to the desire—one of the conceptual preoccupations of modernism most clearly expressed in Kinsey's monumental project—to find a precise, scientifically accurate knowledge, a neutral and numerical knowledge, of sexuality, and especially of female sexuality, and it is that borderline between its insights and its limits I am concerned here to address.

I am not really interested in undertaking an epistemological analysis of his researches—assessing the suitability of his methodology, the statistics he proffers, the nature of his sources and so on; nor am I interested in psychobiography, in analyzing the man behind the numbers, as has been the more recent preoccupation with his work, especially among some religious zealots and sexual conservatives who have recently taken Kinsey as a target for vo-ciferous attack.[2] Instead, I want to direct myself more to an *ontological* approach: the desire to know everything about a mysterious and unknown object, sexuality, to understand it in its intricacies as experienced, as measurable, as recordable, which seems to belong to a particular moment in history, the immediate postwar period, the late 1940s and 1950s, when we could still imagine that one day we would know everything, we would know it objectively, that is, without perspective or framework, and we would know it as an egalitarian leveler, at least in the field of sexual relations.[3] I am less interested in Kinsey's researches as scientific contributions to knowledge or truth, or in its sociological and cultural implications, its role, for example, in the so-called sexual revolution of the 1960s and 1970s and the advent of feminism that many have attributed to him, though no doubt these are worthy histories; instead I want to focus on his writings as an event, as a (prolonged) moment in the history of knowledge that has consequences, direct and indirect, foreseeable and unpredictable, that remain with us into the present and future. This event, in the briefest possible terms, was the creation of an image, and a practice, of rigorous, dispassionate, disinterested rational tabulation of the sexual activities of an entire population, the vision of a science which, through direct and indirect observation, would record and position every type of sexual behavior, would know, in the long run, through the correlation of different disciplinary knowledges, the complete picture of human sexuality and in the process would open up sexuality to public examination.

That is, I will act here as philosopher, not scientist or historian: I want less to connect Kinsey's researches to the traditions of the science of sexuality laid out by Havelock Ellis (1936), Magnus Hirschfeld (1935; 1948), Richard von Krafft-Ebing (1922), Sigmund Freud (1905; 1940), and continued by Masters and Johnson (1966), Shere Hite (1976; 2003), and others—though this is also a significant project—than to *detach* his two texts on the human male and the human female from their assumed context in sexology in order to view them as a single cultural and conceptual event. To understand them as an event does not, I believe, detract from whatever accomplishments, scientific, cultural, legal, and moral, it achieves, but rather focuses on something else, its qualitative characteristics, its uniqueness, its ability to generate unexpected connections and disconnections, its capacity to shift many relations that do not appear directly or predictably connected to its conceptual goals. To see it as an event involves detaching it from a linear history and from a social network in which it is temporally and culturally embedded, disconnecting it from its place within processes or stages to instead regard it as a phenomenon, as what cannot without violence be assimilated into its history and context and has its effects elsewhere, perhaps everywhere, but subtly and without direct causal connections. Kinsey inadvertently opened up science to the undecidable and the indeterminable, to the centrality of continuity and fluidity, the nonenumerable, through his unique analysis of female sexuality.

FIVE GREAT THINGS ABOUT KINSEY

In what does the event I here called "Kinsey" consist? What are some of the qualitative contributions he developed? Here I would like to briefly list what I see to be among the salient and unique contributions to knowledge of the Kinsey-event, some of the deflections and detours his event produced for the terrain of knowledge. These are five great ideas, concepts, Kinsey utilized—and no doubt, there are more.

1. Kinsey understood that a sweeping analysis of a surprisingly wide range of sexual activities and behaviors undertaken by large populations could not be adequately described or analyzed without first-person reports that involve introspection, recollection, and the qualitative assessment of experiences. With all his concern for producing rigorous scientific techniques for the questionnaire he and his associates developed, for transcribing answers into coded notation and crunching the statistics using carefully constructed computer programs, his project is irreducibly tied to the subjective, the intersubjective, the experiential, the phenomenological. Kinsey understood that sexual surveys and questionnaires were easily manipulable without quite detailed conversations between interviewer and interviewee, conversations which clearly varied immensely even while dealing with the same or similar questions, conversations primarily open to the specificities of the individual's experience, both relative to their own social, geographical, religious, and class identifications, and to their own intensities of sexual activity. This complicates his research projects, creating what seem productive tensions in his aspiration to a numerical knowledge of sex.

2. Kinsey recognized that there could be no generalized sexual survey of the American population; instead of producing a generic model of sexuality, he sought out highly specific groups—he sought out difference—in order to understanding the specificity of sexual response. What is true for white men is not necessarily true for black men; what is true for Christians is not necessarily true for Jews; what characterizes rural populations may not charac-

terize urban populations; what may hold for men does not necessarily hold for women; what occurs in prison populations may not occur to those same populations outside of the prison. The two published studies on male and female sexuality were explicitly directed to white Americans, though he had gathered data on black Americans as well—though not enough for a statistically significant analysis. He dreamed of future research that would fill in the gaps with specific, and often quite idiosyncratic groups. In short, Kinsey seemed prescient to the claims of sexual, racial, class, and religious differences that seem to dominate much of contemporary politics. The study of female sexual behavior is neither symmetrical with nor complementary to the study of male sexual behavior: they are neither radically incommensurable (although there are incommensurable elements) nor capable of being framed in the same terms (though they clearly share many sexual activities), for the two sexes are understood as systematically different from each other, even as they serve as the categorical locus for analyzing all sorts of other differences (racial, class, geographic, educational, religious, etc.).

3. Understanding that there were many religious, moral, legal, and cultural implications to the scientific analysis of sexual behavior, Kinsey also understood that religious, moral, legal, and cultural customs and values had no place in the selection of relevant subjects to function as research interviewees. Although it has become, not altogether surprisingly, the object of much moral condemnation by the cultural right and neoconservatives for this very reason, one of Kinsey's great strengths, one of the strengths of his research vision, was his refusal to exclude any group or individual from analysis, his willingness to seek out subcultures, prison groups, underground groups, cults, cultural and social groups, formal and informal alliances and networks, rather than what are considered average, representative, or respectable populations. In tabulating and analyzing sexual behavior, he needed access to the full range of sexual activities, which is possible only if there is no censorship of either relevant interviewees or of relevant activities. In other words, not only is difference central to his analysis, his work remains committed to the full range of differences, to all differences without privileging one or making it central.

4. Kinsey understood, at least by the time of the publication of the volume on female sexuality, that not only is human sexuality (and no doubt animal sexuality as well) a union of various psychological, physiological, natural, and cultural functions, activities, processes, beliefs, and affects—and thus its study involves a necessarily interdisciplinary and multidisciplinary approach[4]—but it is also capable of dislocating some or many factors com-

monly aligned together in union. In other words, rather than, as Freud did, understanding sexuality as a single libidinal drive that expressed itself in a variety of forms (Freud 1905), or as the behaviorists did, seeing sexuality as a cohesive series of disparate responses to various external triggers, Kinsey understood sexuality as an amalgam, a compound or multiplicity, neither organically unified nor culturally manifold, but a provisional alignment of disparate elements capable of any number of permutations and linkages.

5. Kinsey saw, through his research findings, that there is a disparity, even a misalignment of the operations of male and female sexual behavior: he recognized, for example, that the time when male sexual responsiveness is at its highest, in the teen years, occurs when many or most women are at their least sexually responsive, and that when women are more sexually active, in their thirties and forties, male sexual activity has significantly declined from its peak; that the activities men prefer for arousal are not necessarily or always the activities women prefer; that the rates of promiscuity for men and women vary quite widely; that there is and must be a tremendous effort of accommodation in establishing and maintaining marital relations (Kinsey calls it "marital adjustment") or ongoing sexual relations between the two sexes. There are even points at which it seems clear that homosexual activities may prove more satisfying because the two partners are more synchronized and have a greater understanding of their own and each other's sexual needs.[5] Moreover, he claims that the criticisms female homosexuals address to male homosexuals (e.g., their fixation on genitalia) and that male homosexuals address to female homosexuals (that they "do nothing") exactly parallels the complaints that each sex makes about the other in heterosexual relations (1953, 659). The two sexes need to be studied separately rather than as a couple; they require separate physiologies and psychologies; they have different morphologies, different sexual interests and orientations that need to be understood before they are assumed to be adequate for each other.

Kinsey effected a new understanding of sexuality, both mundane, as common as every other element of everyday life, as natural yet variable as eating (and thus capable of sociological and material analysis); and exotic, unexpected in its range, scope, and ingenuity, the subterranean secrets of individuals and culture, a kind of miraculous wonder of complexity within an otherwise ordered world, a complexity with its own character and order that cannot be understood except on the sweeping scale of entire populations. What remains fascinating about Kinsey's research, above and beyond the concrete results, the various frequencies, the categories of sexual activity, is his unshakeable belief that this complexity can, eventually, finally, be known.

Sexuality becomes an enormously complex but ultimately knowable phenomenon, no different in complexity from the material universe itself, one which, with patient research skills and huge numbers, could provide us with its truth. The Kinsey-event (with its natural science twin the space program), was the moment of the highest expectation of what a social or natural science could accomplish, a pinnacle of liberal enlightenment where, if the veil of prejudice and superstition was lifted, a genuine, rational freedom must be attained. Never again, after the 1950s would our belief in the social effects of science be so optimistic; never again would it be possible to believe that if the truth of sexuality were presented to all, the legal, moral, political, and religious restrictions to its free expression would be overcome.

THE SCIENCE OF SEX

Kinsey profoundly shook up the way we understand sexuality—especially its frequency and range. He partly facilitated the ever growing fascination with not only our own sexuality but that of our fellow subjects, a fascination that is strikingly more culturally visible with each year and has not yet reached saturation point. Yet he did so through the credibility of science; he wrapped this subterranean, private activity in the cloak of a disinvested knowledge, through a pure neutral search for truth. He was arguably the last and greatest contributor to the impulse to generate a *scientia sexualis*, a science of sexuality, an impulse that erupted in the mid-nineteenth century and flourished for almost exactly a century.[6] There is no doubt that Kinsey is one of the leading innovators in what Foucault understood as our newest sexual activity: the activity of finding pleasure in putting truth into sex, the pleasure of talking about and listening to the discourses of sexuality: "We have at least invented a different kind of pleasure: pleasure in the truth of pleasure, the pleasure of knowing that truth, of discovering and exposing it, the fascination of seeing it and telling it, of captivating and capturing others by it, of confiding it in secret, of luring it out into the open—the specific pleasure of the true discourse on pleasure" (Foucault 1978, 71).

Kinsey was as invested as anyone in the proliferation of the (inter- or trans-disciplinary) truth of sex. The imperative to categorize, to calculate, to divide and analyze, that is, what he understood as rigorous scientific technique, guarantees that there is something about sexual practices and experiences that his method, or anything resembling its scientific aspirations, can never capture or understand—the continuity of sexuality with the body's activities, the transformation of sexuality in its later reports and representations, its affective intensity — in short, all its qualitative characteristics — which are lost in its quantitative calculation. Kinsey makes it clear, without knowing it, that the cost of calculation, of quantification, is a spatialization, a rendering as extensive what is lived or experienced as intensive.

Kinsey is dazzled by numbers, and the larger they are, the closer they come to providing, for him, a truthful detailed picture of sexual activity in the United States in the first half of the twentieth century. The female volume is dedicated to "the nearly 8000 females who contributed the data"; we rapidly learn that 5,940 case histories of white females make up the statistical content of his study; and that there are an additional 1,849 case studies that could not be included because, one presumes, the subjects were not white, were prisoners whose sexual behavior differed markedly from the nonprison population, or whose education ended at grade school. Rather than being excluded from relevance, they were to await the accumulation of further numbers for inclusion in future volumes Kinsey had hoped to compile. Kinsey rejected the notion of random sampling of interviewees in favor of the accumulation of large numbers of interviews, ideally 100 percent of various groups (1953, 93). He had hoped through further interviews to vastly increase information about smaller groups and communities and to eventually publish further researches about the sexual activities of these different groups — nonwhites, prisoners, and religious, rural, and uneducated groups. A quarter of each of the two volumes is devoted to explaining and justifying the use of numerical calculation.

Statistics provide Kinsey with the cover of objectivity, with the protection of scientific rigor. Yet there are many points in the two volumes at which the question of the incalculable or the nonnumerable problematizes his research goals, where there is an inherent undecidability that renders statistical analysis problematic: it becomes less and less clear what is being measured and whether the measurement is not an effect of the analysis rather than of the phenomenon itself. I will elaborate only a few examples, though they seem central to Kinsey's analysis. These are sites where Kinsey himself seems to discern that the numerical may have overstepped its boundaries.

First, Kinsey admits the problem of using orgasm as a unit of statistical measurement in the case of the female, as it has functioned unambiguously in the case of the male: "Although the male is frequently aroused without completing his response, he rarely engages in such activities as masturbation or coitus without proceeding to the point of orgasm. On the other hand, a considerable portion of the female's activity does not result in orgasm" (1953, 45). Arousal and orgasm function as clear-cut indicators of sexual activities in males; Kinsey makes it clear that orgasm cannot be directly equated with sexual activity in women: what then functions as a clear-cut and calculable sign of sexual excitation? If orgasm is not a direct index of sexuality, is arousal itself so clear and unambiguous in the case of women that it could serve as a measurable quantity? Kinsey nevertheless persists in using orgasm as the object of measurement in his survey of female sexuality in spite of his recognition that it may not serve as a marker of sexual excitation in women in the same ways it does for men: "There seems no better unit for measuring the incidences and frequencies of sexual activity" (46); "the procedure may have overemphasized the importance of orgasm, but it would have been impossible in any large-scale survey to have secured as precise records on some other, less certainly identifiable aspects of sexual behavior" (510).

Kinsey also admits there is a problem in using recorded, that is, nonverbal or pre-interview sources (calendars, diaries, correspondence, drawings, etc.) in which distortion, wish-fulfillment, and other psychological factors may intrude on the information provided. "Even though it has been difficult to quantify and statistically treat most of this recorded material, it has been invaluable in its portrayal of the attitudes of the subjects in the study, the social, moral and other factors which had influenced the development of their patterns of sexual behavior" (83).

In addition, Kinsey admits that there is a problem in dividing, as he has and in some version must, the psychological from the physiological, form from function, material from conceptual; that is, he is aware that he continually risks falling into the problem of dualism: "It is important to understand how nebulous the distinctions are between the psychologic and the physiologic aspects of behavior" (642). In place of a rigid division between mind and body, the psychological and the physiological, Kinsey proposes a notion of "coordinate qualities" (642), by which he means that the psychological and the physiological are separable but must eventually be coordinated with each other through a kind of complementarity. They *can* be studied separately (this is precisely why Kinsey offers separate chapters for the psychology, neurology, and endocrinology of sexuality [chapters 16, 17, and 18 respectively]), as long as they are integrated back together, correlated in some way. Yet the problem of dualism reasserts itself in the very language and methods that distinguish psychological from physiological factors. Once they are studied in different ways, as different types of subjects, it is almost impossible to find a language and conceptual framework through which they may be integrated.

Finally, Kinsey acknowledges that the distinction between the sexual and the nonsexual is decidedly porous, especially in the case of women. How one distinguishes, say, affection from sexuality, is not clear: "It is often impossible to secure frequency data on the incidence of such experience [sexual activities that do not lead to orgasm] because of the difficulty of distinguishing between non-erotic social activities—a simple kiss, for instance—and similar activities which do bring erotic arousal" (45). "It has been difficult, for instance, to secure exact data on the incidences and frequencies of self-stimulation which was non-genital, on the frequency of sexual dreams which did not lead to orgasm, and on the incidences and frequencies of the non-genital socio-sexual contacts" (510). In other words, it is not entirely clear what the scope and limits of female sexuality are or what unambiguously counts as sexual excitation.

It is not as if Kinsey is unaware of the limitations of the statistical methods he utilizes: it seems quite clear that he recognizes that there are experiences and activities that either cannot be quantified, or if they are quantified are transformed in their qualitative characteristics. The point of a numerical or statistical analysis is that *anything* can be calculated, but the calculation is not a neutral activity: it transforms what is a continuity into comparable units, it imposes the form of the unit onto all particulars, it is transformational of quality into quantity.

When we say "six sheep" or "six thousand women," what we articulate is a commonality, real or imposed, between "sheep" as a category or "women" as a category. We reduce what is particular about the sheep or the women in order to enable that number "six" or "six thousand" to apply equally to all of them. And this is equally true even when these "six thousand women" are further divided into what Kinsey considers the relevant subcategories (women are divided in terms of age, location, education, occupation, parental occupations, religion, marital status: the category "young rural working-class grade-school-educated female" is still a generalization, still the amalgam of many ignored differences, which are blurred into a singularity). There is, of course, nothing wrong with such a reduction, as long as it is clear that there is a neutralization of what is being counted in the process of making particulars countable. To make things countable, they must be rendered identical, at least in one term or element; their individuality or particularity neglected or bracketed off, they become part of a set, a category of resemblance.

Every number is a kind of paradox, for it is both a unit and something composed of or decomposable into other units (this is true even for the number one). The number six is indivisible as a number, although it is the equivalent of many other numbers: we grasp it as a whole through a kind of intuition, just as we grasp five, four, and three as equally integrated and whole, though capable of further, indeed infinite, decomposition.[7] Bergson, the philosopher of continuity and critic of the misapplication of the numerical to the nonnumerical (whose clearest expression is the representation of the temporal by the spatial),[8] argues that the numerical, that is, the field of extensive magnitudes, is the proper approach only to the domain of objects and of space; it is incapable of explaining intensive magnitudes or qualities. Numbering is a process of abstraction that transforms quality into quantity. This is its strength and pragmatic usefulness. Since individual differences are ignored when terms are numbered or counted, space becomes the means of separating units, as well as of constituting them as a whole, as a set. As each term is considered identical for the purposes of counting, there must nevertheless still be some means of differentiating them, and this can only be their location. Bergson follows Aristotle in claiming that number is a potential quality of the numbered which is actualized only in thought. Number is the virtuality of any object, which can give itself to be counted or numbered, but only by losing some of its actual qualities.

In the case of material objects, nonliving forms, this outlines for us the possibilities of control and prediction, part of the process of rendering the material world amenable to our needs and interests. But when numbering is addressed to the field of the intensive, the qualitative — Bergson identifies the intensive primarily with the domain of lived experience, experience not simply exemplified by the human, but which extends to all life, which contains no units, and which flows in time — we get the illusion of science, the illusion of objectivity and of countability. We come up against the central dilemma of knowledges that aspire to the status of social science. Their objects of analysis are social, cultural, economic, and living — they function qualitatively, even if we develop boundaries, divisions, and categories to render the social as what can be utilized by living beings. Where the various social sciences seek out the qualitative characteristics of culture (which occurs in the best of biological research),[9] we have an attunement to the particular and the specific. But where social sciences strive to emulate the natural sciences, and especially physics, in its reliance on numerical calculation, formulae, the statistical analysis of large populations, the manipulation and control of variables, and so on, we produce a "science" that is often well-funded and has the aura of objectivity but which loses contact with what is most central in its objects: their continuity, their mutual embeddedness, their intensity, their dynamism and force.

Kinsey produced a *scientia sexualis* through the submission of the information of the case studies and their various recorded materials to the process of statistical analysis. In the process he lost what is sexual about sexual behavior, while providing us with a great deal of information about the purported operations of orgasm, an extracted and constructed unit within some sexual behavior which he used as its marker. In the following section, I argue that instead of inventing more detailed categories, interviewing more subjects, adding to the populations sampled (Kinsey's hope for the radical future of sexology), we may need to develop something more akin to what Foucault describes as an *ars erotica*, or what Bergson understands as intuition, the qualitative immersion in and attunement to sexuality, if we are to more adequately understand female sexuality.

THE RADICAL FUTURE OF FEMALE SEXUALITY

The concept of number may be alien to female sexuality. Not to female sexuality as it has been transcribed and analyzed in the history of sexology, which has, until very recently, been developed only by men who seemed to have a limited or self-interested understanding of female sexuality. But to female sexuality as most women experience it. Number may also prove alien to male sexuality, depending on how it is reconfigured, but in the present forms male sexuality takes, there is something countable, perhaps even the very origin of number itself, in the clear-cut and unambiguous, thoroughly decidable nature of male sexual response and activity. Here I want to explore what I listed as some of the problems Kinsey noted about his researches into female sexual behavior, and to see if they may suggest alternative forms of knowledge, other modes of knowing by which female sexuality may be conceptualized. It may be, as Irigaray suggests, that the specificity of female bodies and pleasures are the invisible and repressed foundation of knowledges, which makes them fundamentally unknowable according to the methods of "rational" science, especially social science parading as natural science.[10]

Is female sexuality countable? And what is it that is being counted in Kinsey's survey of sexual behavior? What is left uncounted? Irigaray has long suggested—perhaps even as a delayed and philosophically mediated response to Kinsey and statistical researches on sexuality more generally—that although female sexuality and pleasure can be submitted to the imperative of identification and neutralization that is inherent in numbers, there is something about female sexuality—its morphology, its anatomy, its phenomenology—that defies precision, clarity, form, identity. Wryly describing female sexuality as "not one"—as that which is neither one nor none—Irigaray argues female sexuality has only been understood in the social and natural sciences as that which can be measured, known, only through some correlate provided either by a male subject or a masculinized category.[11]

If woman's morphology and experience "is never simply one" (1985, 31), if woman's anatomy, physiology, psychology resist the imperative of self-identity which is the condition of numerical survey, Irigaray hypothesizes that women's resistance to, and their commonly enigmatic status for, scientific speculation relates to the notion of *proximity* or *nearness*. The distance required by scientific observation, the stasis necessary, even if momentarily, for identification, and the capacity to remain at least nominally the same over time are the conditions of statistical analysis that female organs, pleasures, and practices cannot achieve except through the imposition of an external grid or set of categories. Proximity, the overwhelming immersion in one's own activities, the nearness of that which is in and as oneself and cannot be articulated or represented directly or in everyday discourse, the contiguity of one process, activity, and pleasure with another, the impossibility of distinguishing between the sexual and nonsexual, which Irigaray describes as the "auto-affection" of what has no center (1985, 79)—these generate for female sexuality, and female subjectivity, either a paradoxical or an unknowable position within knowledges that seek definite categories, identities, and boundaries: paradoxical insofar as it is an object that isn't one, an organ that isn't one, an orgasm that isn't one but that isn't none either; and unknowable, insofar as that which falls outside the grid or categories counts as nonexistent rather than as unrepresented or awaiting a different form of representation.

Kinsey was aware that there were other characteristics and representations of female sexuality than those calibrated and calculated through his questionnaire. They are what he discovered in women's art, fiction, letters, diaries, and correspondences and which he acknowledges are not readily quantifiable. But what if female sexuality has a self-proximity, a contiguity or fluidity that renders these fragments the *only* representations of the quality or experience of female sexuality? What if Kinsey was counting something other than female sexuality: that is, what is it in female sexuality that is recognizable by men and for men as sexual, that in some ways paralleled or complemented what men saw as sexual activity?

This question may be inverted: can it be that male sexuality, or at least its self-representation, is the origin of number itself? Is the imperative to know through counting, through analysis and synthesis, through decomposition and recomposition, through subtraction and the control of variables, through the constitution of terms and processes within closed systems, an expression of (male) sexuality? Is mathematics itself the result of a certain sexualization? If sex is capable of enumeration, is it conversely true that enumeration is the expression of (a certain kind of) sex? Kinsey clung to the sciences of knowing—the natural sciences and the social sciences—as his way of objectively understanding the sexual practices of a culture. While he knew that there was much he could not quantify or reduce to the terms of a statistical survey, he did not understand that what is most proximate, what is nearest, most central to that sexuality that has no center, is what he cannot count, what cannot be counted, what is continuous, inter-enveloped, explicable only through its own terms, elaborating and developing in time rather than locatable, and countable, in space.

To take one central example: while acknowledging that female orgasm is no certain indicator of sexual activity, Kinsey nevertheless provides a detailed and elaborate analysis of the average rates of heterosexual, homosexual, penetrative, masturbatory, and solitary orgasms, in women of various ages, locations, and economic categories, in the same terms and categories as used in his analysis of men. And while he acknowledges that women may achieve multiple orgasms in a number of different ways (as he claims, teen boys are sometimes wont to do), he does not provide any principle of identity that would distinguish one orgasm from another (how many is a difficult question to answer, not simply because the more one is absorbed in sexual activity the less one is able to count, but also because it is difficult to tell where one temporal process ends and another begins, where one region, location, or sensation ends and what is contiguous with it begins, a difficulty arbitrarily overcome through the imposition of or correlation with some form of spatialized representation). Where female orgasm is anatomically located remains an enigma even with today's rapidly advancing biomedical industries—whether it is clitoral, vaginal, located in a "g-spot," or labial—and how one distinguishes this biological continuity into its separable parts, and harnesses those parts for orgasm, remain unclear and of considerable debate (within women's magazines, in the discipline of sexology, and in the manufacture of marketable sexual enhancements). The comparative straightforwardness of male excitation and orgasm, its amenability to counting relative to the obscurity and ambiguity of female excitation and orgasm is not, I believe, a function of the impossibly complex physiology, psychology, or phenomenology of women, but of the masculinization of knowledges, or what Irigaray describes as their phallocentrism. It is only when knowledges are adequately attuned to the particularity of their objects of investigation, when they function through what Bergson understood as intuition rather than a form of scientific intelligence, that a different kind of science of female sexuality, and a different kind of female sexuality itself, can emerge.

Irigaray suggests, only fleetingly and with some provocation, that perhaps the science of far-from-equilibrium systems undertaken by Ilya Prigogine and others (Prigogine and Stengers [1984]) may provide a more appropriate scientific metaphor for female sexuality than the prevailing hydraulic or thermodynamic metaphors which underlie both psychoanalytic theory and Kinsey's understanding of orgasm as a reliable marker of sexuality:

> [Female sexuality] is less subject to the alterations of tension-release, to the required conservation of energy, to the maintenance of a state of equilibrium, to operating in a circuit closed and reopened by saturation, to the reversibility of time, etc. Feminine sexuality could perhaps better be brought into harmony — if one must evoke a scientific model — with what Prigogine calls "dissipating" [dissipative] structures that operate via an exchange with the external world, structures that proceed through levels of energy. The organizational principle of these structures has nothing to do with the search for equilibrium but rather with the crossing of thresholds. This would correspond to a surpassing of disorder or entropy without discharge. (Irigaray 1985b, 81)

Kinsey understood the value of first-person reports of sexuality across a range of sexual activities, sexual partners, sexual objects and fantasies: he collected them almost obsessively. Yet he submitted them to the form of the questionnaire, standardizing individual answers through submitting them to the leveling and neutralization of statistical analysis: he understood this information as data, rather than as experiment itself (data is what is extracted from experiments; it is the collation of relevant information from the continuity of a myriad of factors that experiment entails). I am not suggesting that his subjects undertook scientific experiments in their sexual activities, but rather that they undertook various forms of *ars erotica*, from which others, scientists, could extract information awaiting processing and transformation as data in order to produce a *scientia sexualis*. This transformation or translation converts the experiment in affect into an understanding through concepts; it transforms an intuitive process into an activity of intelligence.

What is the radical future of female sexuality? This is in part generated by its resistance to knowledge, its fluid continuity, its indeterminacy and openness. What Kinsey and others who were committed to the scientific study of sexuality accomplished was a tabulation of the past and present of female sexuality. What they could not address is its future. Sexuality is an open system: its future is not necessarily contained in and constrained by its past and present. One's sexuality is contained in the *next* sexual encounter, rather than in the synthesis of all one's past sexual activities. One is what one has done, but also what one can do, what is actualized but also what is virtual. This is partly why sexual and other forms of identity politics remain limited: they tend to understand identity as the synthesis of one's past (one is where one was born, what class, race, and sex one was born into, the events or history that constitute one's life) rather than a synthesis oriented to an open or indeterminable goal, a trajectory or direction.

Female sexuality resists knowledges that seek clear-cut, definitive borders, boundaries, organs, pleasures: it thus resists the imperative to speak its own truth directly. It also resists the scientific impulse to render it a transparent, predictable object, one capable of being known in its breadth and depth so as to eventually become amenable to precise causal analysis, to make it function in a more or less guaranteed fashion. This is its radical quality: not that it is unknowable, but that it is unknowable through any particular discourse or method, which at best sheds light on only some of its elements and leaves the continuity of the rest unknown. No one form of knowledge, whether in the form of a *scientia sexualis* or in the form of an *ars erotica*, is capable of knowing its objects from both a close enough perspective to understand its detailed continuity and from a far enough distance to understand its integration as a whole.

Female sexuality does not resist as a form of inertia or defiance; instead, it resists the impulse to know precisely by giving itself up to all sorts of knowledges, forming the unspoken or direct object of analysis, without apparent or registered residue. It resists insofar as it transforms itself into precisely what the researcher is looking for — a camouflage of apparent passivity — like time itself, or like any continuity. But in the process of imposing categories, forms, organs, what is sexual about female sexuality, and what is female about it, are lost. What we can say about female sexuality — its fluidity, its contiguity with the nonsexual, its indeterminacy of organs and sensations, its tactility, formlessness, open-endedness — means that any attempt to know the sexuality of all women will lose the specificity of each particular woman rather than indicate in probabilistic terms her general features.

All continuous, analogue processes exhibit this facility: they are available to infinite types of possible division and analysis, they lend themselves to the imposition of discrete categories, they allow infinite numerical orderings, but what is invariably lost is their contiguity, their cohesion and unity, their reality as concrete, diverse, moving and changing phenomena. They are rendered minutely complex, because they are reduced to component parts which must be then resynthesized, instead of being understood as a specificity. Female sexuality awaits future knowledges that respect specificity and particularity, that are attuned to the uniqueness of their objects, to what is left out in the reduction of objects to generalization. It awaits adequate intuition, which may not be able to formalize and neutrally symbolize its object, but remains nevertheless in touch with it, operating in its own domain and in its own terms. We await, no longer a science of sexuality, its formalization and abstraction, but an art of sexuality, not its analysis but its celebration as diverse becoming, not knowing and thereby containing it, but elaborating and extending it.

The Kinsey-event was the moment at which it became desirable to know sexuality through its standardized, egalitarian formalization, the moment science devised ways of objectifying sexuality according to countable rates, dividing it into its knowable, measurable elements. I have suggested that this event had its positive and negative effects, its liberatory and its limiting consequences. It came close to providing a survey of the measurable elements of the sexuality of certain sectors of the American population, but by its very nature it misunderstood the integration of sexuality into the body and behavior of individuals, its open-ended immersion in and transformation through the life of individuals and cultures. What was misunderstood, unrepresented, was the surprise of sexuality, its liability to unpredictability, to openness, formlessness, boundlessness. The future of female sexuality is precisely the social acknowledgment and celebration of this openness.

INTRODUCTION

1 One of the central arguments of this book is the claim that temporality is elided, forgotten, or unrepresented in the discourses and practices of philosophy and social, cultural, and political theory. This is not simply the consequence of a correctable elision, but is a function, in part, of language systems themselves. The language by which we represent temporality, at least in the West from at least the time of Ancient Greece, is a language of spatiality, in which spatial terms and relations come to represent temporal movements. This text is no more able to resist these spatializing tendencies than any other: it is ironic that the metaphor of time travels I have used as a theme to bind together this collection enacts this very spatialization! Indeed, it may be that the very concept of metaphor (along with its rhetorical twin, metonymy) function primarily through spatialization.

2 Deleuze 1989, 81.

3 Nevertheless, there has been an immense effort invested in the management of time and its "rational" regulation, which has been construed primarily in attempts to measure time, to synchronize different locations according to the same modes of measurement, and to structure the behavior of individuals and groups according to the interests of such management. See, for example, Waugh (1999) for further details. See also Galison (2003).

4 I have discussed in considerable detail the phallocentric structure of binarized terms in *Sexual Subversions* (1989).

5 Derrida, *Positions* (1981b).

1. DARWIN AND FEMINISM

1   There is of course no unanimity in any feminist endeavor. There are certainly
a number of feminists who have actively lauded the virtues of women's connections with nature. These have been variously described as cultural feminists,
radical feminists, and eco-feminists. This project must be carefully differentiated
from the interests of eco-feminism and its cognates on several grounds: (1) this
project is directed primarily at ontological and epistemological claims, while
eco-feminism seems largely oriented to ethical, moral, and economic issues;
(2) this project disputes the a priori commitment to wholism, the presumption
that the interconnectedness of ecological orders forms a systematic whole, which
lies at the basis of much ecological and eco-feminist thought. It argues that Darwin's work stresses difference, divergence, bifurcation, and division, the fractur-
ing of a social and biological field, rather than interconnectedness and whole-
ness. It is the *asystematicity* of the Darwinian system that is of interest to me here;
and (3) this project is not concerned with placing women in a different position
from men in their relations to nature; women have no more, or any less, connection to the natural (or the social) order. The question here is not to explore
women's particular connection to nature, but rather the role that different, criti-
cally revitalized conceptions of nature may play in our understandings of the
becomings open to each sex.

2   There is, of course considerable feminist scholarship involved in science itself
(e.g., Keller, Fausto-Sterling, Oyama), but it is only recently that feminist theorists in the humanities and social sciences have exhibited an openness to the
relevance of biological research in the analysis of the social relations between
the sexes. See, for example, the work of Elizabeth A. Wilson (1998, 1999, 2004);
Margrit Shildrick and Janet Pryce, eds. (1999), Griet Vandermassen (2004), and
Catherine Waldby (1996, 1999, 2000).

3   It is not entirely clear whether there are three or two principles governing the
movement of evolution. Most scientists regard evolution as governed by two
broad principles—individual variation and natural selection—and they sub-
sume under the category of individual variation the idea of the heritability of
variation. I prefer here, in a nonscientific, philosophical context to make as explicit as I can the conceptual nuances involved in his account. The heritability of
individual variation is not conceptually contained in an understanding of individual variation (as Lamarckianism attests) so I will consider it a separate principle and deal with it separately.

4   "A high degree of variability is obviously favourable, as freely giving the materials for selection to work on; not that mere individual differences are not amply
sufficient, with extreme care, to allow of the accumulation of a large amount of
modification. . . . When the individuals of any species are scanty, all the indi-

viduals, whatever their quality may be, will generally be allowed to breed, and this will effectively prevent selection" (Darwin 1996, 35).

5 Stephen Jay Gould (1989) makes it clear from his analysis of the Burgess Shale — a discovery of ancient fossils with bodily forms of a type never seen before or since — that there is the possibility (indeed the actuality) of almost unimaginable morphological variations, of creatures so unlike those usually discovered in fossil records or living today, that they appear otherworldly.

6 While the teratological influence on mutation and genetic transformation is commonly noted, there is currently a body of research on epigenetic markers that indicates a more direct relation between the forces of natural selection, or at least environmental effects, and the heritability of genetic variations they produce: "Over the course of evolutionary time, a variety of mechanisms, mediated by epigenetic factors, have emerged to generate new variation with the potential of 'bailing out' organisms that have become dysfunctional under conditions of stress. Selection — intracellular, cell lineage, or organismic — provides the conditions under which adaptive variants can become fixed. For many organisms that normally reproduce asexually, a switch to sexual reproduction can provide this diversity" (Keller 1998, 116).

7 See Rosser 1992, 57:

> Aside from noting its statement in terms of upper-class Victorian values and decrying the misuse of his theory of natural selection by social Darwinists, feminist scientists by and large have not critiqued the theory of natural selection. As scientists, they have recognized the significance of the theory for the foundations of modern biology. Given the strong attacks on natural selection by creationists and other groups not known for their profeminist stances, most feminist scientists who might have critiqued some minor points have been reluctant to provide creationists with evidence they might misuse.
>
> In contrast to accepting his theory of natural selection, many feminist scientists have critiqued Darwin's theory of sexual selection for its androcentric bias. The theory of sexual selection reflected and reinforced Victorian social norms regarding the sexes.

8 See Darwin 1981, 2:135, 157–158.

9 There has been a tremendous amount of literature on the question of the biology of race, and it is significant that a good deal of it devoted to the critique of Eurocentrism has suggested that racial categories are social constructs. I have no doubt that the various distinctions and categories that mark race today and in the past are historically variable, politically motivated, and highly volatile in their operations. But it is also clear that there are systematic, visible and invisible differences between groups of individuals that we can mark in various, perhaps arbitrary, ways. Darwin's understanding of race in no way preempts the study of the

history and politics of racialized categories. Nor does it preempt further analysis
of bodily differences, including genetic differences. What these differences are
remains unclear. Darwin's work does, however, imply that what we understand
as racial differences are primarily, or in the first instance bodily, variations, variations that in themselves may have no particular or a priori social significance and
that come to acquire their significance and value only in social contexts. These
bodily variations do not in themselves form racial categories, which imply conceptual discontinuities from other races, for they constitute individual variations,
variations in a continuum of bodies and body types.

10 The rate by which the ever-changing status of natural selection functions is quite
variable and specific: Darwin's position is closely tied to the presumption that
many of these changes are imperceptible over generations, and only come to acquire significance when measured in geological or cosmological time.

11 See Dennett 1996, 51: "What Darwin discovered was not really *one* algorithm, but
rather, a large class of related algorithms that he had no clear way to distinguish.
We can now reformulate his fundamental idea as follows: 'Life on earth has been
generated over billions of years in a single branching tree—the Tree of Life—by
one algorithmic process.'" That there is something fundamentally mindless and
automatic about the Darwinian system is certainly one of its explanatory advantages. And Dennett is quite correct to recognize that the mindlessness of these
processes renders no category, including the most hallowed of philosophy, untouched. All reason, conscience, nobility, all the human virtues and inventions,
are the long-term effects of the same kind of automatism that regulates the existence of the most humble bacteria. What is dangerous about Darwinism is that
it sets the whole of cosmology into a framework of forces that are incapable of
being controlled by its participants.

12 In some of the recent literature, there has been an argument that there is a non-
random variation induced by natural selection—an epigenetic inheritance; that
natural selection may have a more direct impact on selectable and heritable variations: "One of our major themes is that the variation on which evolutionary
change is based is affected by instructive processes that have themselves evolved.
In addition to random genetic change, natural selection has produced systems
that alter the base sequence of DNA by responding to special external stimuli.
Other sources of heritable variation that have clearly been molded by natural
selection are the epigenetic inheritance system, which transmits information between individuals through social learning. The adaptability that these additional
inheritance systems allow can be the basis of long-term genetic adaptations" (Jablonka and Lamb 1998, 120–121).

13 While Dennett provides one of the more rigorous philosophical readings of Darwinism, and has, further, acknowledged and explored the "danger" (his term) of
Darwin's idea, the threat it poses, not only to received religions but also to those
humanists who wish to attribute a post- or non-evolutionary status to the prod-

ucts of mind or reason—this, after all, was the limit of Alfred Russel Wallace's version of evolution: he exempted mind from the operations of evolution—Dennett himself submits to the same exigency when he distinguishes the biological evolution of species from what he describes, following Richard Dawkins's (1976) usage, as the "memetic" evolution of cultural and mental concepts. Dennett effectively reproduces precisely the mind/body split that he so convincingly criticizes in Wallace, Stephen Gould, and a series of other evolutionary thinkers. He argues that the evolution of concepts is subject to the same principles of evolution as the evolution of biological entities. With this claim, I have no disagreement. However, he presents the evolution of ideas in a separate landscape than the evolution of biological beings, when the evolution of concepts and cultural activities can be regarded simply as the latest spiral or torsion in the function of one and the same biological evolution. For Dennett, as for Dawkins, memes are "analogues" of genes, rather than, as Darwin himself would imply, the ramifying products of genes. (See Dennett 1996, 345, 347.) Memes are to mind what genes are to bodies! I have further developed my criticisms of Dennett's understanding of evolution in *The Nick of Time*.

14 I am not suggesting, to put it bluntly, that the violent persecution of various individuals or minorities is a good thing; rather, I am suggesting that, given that oppressions, damages, and injustices have occurred and cannot be undone, the political task is not simply to mourn or lament them, but to use them, their memory, precisely as a spur to transformation, to difference. It is this violence, this memory of injustice and pain, that is the ballast that may serve to produce a different future.

15 See *The History of Sexuality*, vol. 1 (1978), particularly the section called "Method."

16 As Irigaray claims, in *I Love to You: Sketch of a Possible Felicity in History* (1996, 47),

> Without doubt, the most appropriate content for the universal is sexual difference. . . . Sexual difference is an immediate natural given and it is a real and irreducible component of the universal. The whole of human kind is composed of women and men and of nothing else. The problem of race is, in fact, a secondary problem—except from a geographical point of view— . . . . and the same goes for other cultural diversities—religious, economic, and political ones. .
>
> Sexual difference probably represents the most universal question we can address. Our era is faced with the task of dealing with this issue, because, across the whole world, there are, there are only, men and women.

I do not believe that Irigaray here denies the centrality of other differences, other modes of oppression. Racial relations and oppressions based on sexual preference or religious affiliation clearly have a relative autonomy from the question of sexual difference. Where Darwinism confirms Irigaray's position is in claiming that the structures of racial, religious, and sexual orientation are open to potentially infinite historical transformation, given a long enough period of time, in ways that may or may not be true for sexual difference. This in no way places sexual difference outside historical or biological transformation, nor does it render it any more significant than other forms of oppression in explaining the complexities of social and cultural evolution; it simply insists that whatever other factors are at work, sexual difference must be a consideration, a relevant factor.

2. DARWIN AND THE ONTOLOGY OF LIFE

1 "It is clear that scientific propositions and their correlates are just as signed or created as philosophical concepts: we speak of Pythagoras's theorem, Cartesian coordinates, Hamiltonian number, and Lagrangian function just as we speak of the Platonic Idea or Descartes' cogito and the like. But however much the use of proper names clarifies and confirms the historical nature of their link to these enunciations, these proper names are masks for other becomings and serve only as pseudonyms for more secret singular entities" (Deleuze and Guattari 1994, 23–24). These proper names mark the advent of a concept, a method, a technique, a map: an invention within knowledge-production.

2 The conception that there is something biologically invariant was first developed by August Weismann (1893) and has more or less become orthodoxy in genetics, which focuses on the eternal line of genetic terms rather than the infinite variability of phenotypes in analyzing biological development.

3 As Dennett (1996) has recognized. For my disagreement with Dennett's overall argument, in which I claim that Dennett can only understand steps or stages retrospectively, after a species has emerged or a goal has been accomplished, see Grosz 2004.

4 See Nietzsche's *Thus Spoke Zarathustra* (1965).

3. THE NATURE OF CULTURE

1 In the manner, for example, of the most well known sociobiologists, such as E. O. Wilson (1980), Dawkins (1976), and Dennett (1996), who reduce individual, social, and collective practices to genetic strategies for self-propagation.

2 See, for an example of one of the more questionable uses of sociobiology, Randy Thornhill and Craig T. Palmer (2000). For a feminist response to and critique of this surprisingly popular and influential text, see Cheryl Brown Travis, ed. (2003).

3 To take a recent example, see Paul H. Rubin (2002).

4 I resist an ecological understanding of the natural order primarily because most

ecological models restore the notion of system to the natural order. Nature itself is now regarded as a system, a cohesive and totalized structure, which is unified and all-encompassing, and which thus contains a normative force of unification and balance. My interests lie largely in what is outside systems, what disrupts them and makes them undergo change, a change that may or may not be coordinated with a transformation in global organization. If an ecology that values not only the living—the present—but also the future could be possible, it would be very close to the (non)moral ontology of Darwinism, which mourns no particular extinction and which waits, with surprise, to see what takes the place of the extinct.

5 Clearly in the natural sciences—as well as those social sciences that aspire to its methods—it is culture (or history or the social) that is the subordinated or excluded term, the term more commonly reduced to or explained by the natural.

6 See in particular, Deleuze's *Foucault* (1988b) for an elaboration of this conception of the force of the outside.

7 For an example of feminist readings of a more productive understanding of biology, see Elizabeth A. Wilson (1999, 2004).

8 See Henri Bergson, *Matter and Memory* (1988). See also part III of this volume for further elaboration of Bergson's account of perception as a silhouetting of objects and relations.

9 As I have argued in *The Nick of Time*, chapter 4, Nietzsche is perhaps more Darwinian than he would be happy to accept: the overman is to a large extent the child of a Darwinian or evolutionary overcoming of man.

10 See part IV of this volume, where I argue that concepts of subjectivity, sexuality, and politics can be refigured in terms of Nietzschean impersonal forces.

11 Darwin understands this outside precisely as natural selection, which erupts into and transforms individual variation from beyond its operations. As Deleuze has it, "the outside concerns force: if force is always in relation with other forces, forces necessarily refer to an irreducible outside which no longer even has any form and is made up of distances that cannot be broken down through which one force acts on another or is acted upon by another. It is always from the outside that a force confers on others or receives from others the variable position to be found only at a particular distance or in a particular relation. . . . It is *an outside which is farther away* than any external world and even any form of exteriority, which henceforth becomes infinitely closer" (Deleuze 1988b, 86; emphasis in the original).

12 "Thinking is not the innate exercise of a faculty, but must become thought. Thinking does not depend on a beautiful interiority that would reunite the visible and the articulable elements, but is carried under the intrusion of an outside that eats into the interval or dismembers the internal" (Deleuze 1988b, 87).

13 "According to Kant, time was the form in which the mind affected itself, just as space was the form in which the mind was affected by something else: time was

therefore 'auto-affection' and made up the essential structure of subjectivity. But time as subject, or rather subjectivation, is called memory. Not that brief memory that comes afterwards and is the opposite of forgetting, but the 'absolute memory' which doubles the present and the outside and is one with forgetting, since it is itself forgotten and reconstituted" (1988b, 107).

14 See Butler (1990; 1994) and Derrida (1988).

4. THE TIME OF VIOLENCE

1 This is the position adopted by Seyla Benhabib (1995), Nancy Fraser (1984; 1996; 1997), and Linda Nicholson (1990), among many feminist theorists, as well as Habermas and the followers of the Frankfurt school, or post-Althusserian Marxists. It must also be noted, however, that there are clearly a number of other feminists and postcolonial theorists for whom deconstruction has proved to be a timely, even indispensable political tool. See, for example, Judith Butler (1990; 1994); Drucilla Cornell (1991; 1992; 1993); Pheng Cheah (1996; 2003); and Gayatri Chakravorty Spivak (1982; 1984–85; 1987).

2 Fraser argues that Derrida's "negative transcendental reflection" (159), his espousal of a recognition of that which is unchanging, which she identifies as that which is outside of social and institutional arrangements, is the more serious political problem with deconstruction: "[Derrida presents an account of] the so-called violence in law that is constitutive and inescapable. This is a 'violence' that can in no meaningful sense be called 'political,' as it is independent of any specific institutional or social arrangements, and as it is not subject, even in principle, to change. Thus, 'the force of law' in Derrida's account is essentially metaphysical" (Fraser 1997, 160). Fraser assumes that politics relies on and cannot function without specific, changing institutional and social arrangements: what is inescapable or constitutive is, for her, outside the political and moral arena, which can neatly separate itself off into a mode of administration of these institutional and social arrangements without the contamination of inescapable problems and complications. Fraser views politics as that which we can pragmatically recognize and understand in the present, not as a mode of addressing futures we cannot know with resources we are not sure will be adequate. She believes that a well-structured critique will reveal political problems and help us to "correct" them, as if they were conceptual oversights instead of forms of power. She is committed to the solution, where Derrida's work, along with Deleuze's, addresses questions, problems, and how to live with them.

3 McCarthy in effect accuses Derrida because Derrida's questions are not McCarthy's, or the critical tradition he represents. Yet this is already the refusal to engage with Derridean questions, a mode of refusal of the possibility of a Derridean politics: "Although he explicitly eschews any idea of a radical break, the

politics of friendship gestures toward a transformation so radical that we can
say nothing (positive) about what lies beyond it. I have found nothing in Derrida's writings to persuade me that his quasi-apocalyptic, near-prophetic mode
of discourse about politics should displace the more prosaic modes available or
constructible in our tradition" (McCarthy 1989–90, 162).

4 On this question, see Bennington (1994); and Bennington and Derrida (1993).

5 For another angle of Derrida's understanding of violence, which connects his
   work directly to Girard, see McKenna (1992).

6 As Derrida makes clear: "For me, it is always a question of differential force,
   of difference as difference of force, of forces as *différance, différance* is a force
   (*différée-différante*), of the relation between force and form, force and signification, performative force, illocutionary or perlocutionary force, of persuasive
   or rhetorical force, of affirmation by signature, but also and especially of all
   the paradoxical situations in which the greatest force and the greatest weakness strangely enough exchange places. And that is the whole history" (1991,
   929).

7 Derrida locates violence, law, transgression as the field of deconstructive play:
   "Deconstruction is justice. It is perhaps because law (which I will consistently
   try to distinguish from justice) is constructible, in a sense that goes beyond the
   opposition between convention and nature, it is perhaps insofar as it goes beyond this opposition that it is constructible and so deconstructible" (1990, 929).
   Derrida, though, is even stronger in his claim: for law, force, and violence are the
   "proper place" of deconstruction, if this phrase has any meaning: "It was normal, foreseeable, desirable that studies of deconstructive style should culminate
   in the problematic of law (*droit*), of law and justice. (I have elsewhere tried to
   show that the essence of law is not prohibitive but affirmative.) It is even the most
   proper place for them, if such a thing exists" (929).

8 See LaCapra (1990), "Violence, Justice, and the Force of Law."

9 As outlined in "Violence and Metaphysics," Derrida wants to suggest that the
   encounter with the other is somehow outside an economy of the logos—or at
   the least, that Levinas's understanding of the ethical relation sets up a "logic"
   or "structure" other than the Greek conception of the relation between self and
   other: "What, then, is the encounter with the absolutely-other? Neither representation nor limitation, nor conceptual relation to the same. The ego and the other
   do not permit themselves to be dominated or made into totalities by the concept of relationship . . . there is no way to conceptualize the encounter; it is made
   possible by the other, the unforeseeable and 'resistant to all categories.' Concepts
   suppose an anticipation, a horizon within which alterity is amortized as soon as
   it is annulled precisely because it has let itself be foreseen. The infinitely-other
   cannot be bound by a concept, cannot be thought on the basis of a horizon; for
   a horizon is always a horizon of the same" (1978, 95).

10 Cf. Derrida's footnote in "Plato's Pharmacy": "We are asked why we do not examine the etymology of *gift*, translation of the Latin *dosis*, itself a transcription
of the Greek *dosis*, dose, dose of poison" (1981, 131).

11

One must — *il faut* — opt *for* the gift, for generosity, for noble expenditure, for
a practice and a morality of the gift ["il faut donner," one must give]. One
cannot be content to speak of the gift and to describe the gift without giving
and without saying *one must* give, without giving by saying one must give . . .
to do more than call upon one to give in the proper sense of the word, but to
give beyond the call, beyond the mere word.

But — because with the gift there is always a "but" — the contrary is also
necessary: It is necessary [*il faut*] to limit the excess of the gift and also generosity, to limit them by economy, profitability, work, exchange. And first of
all by reason or by the principle of reason: it is *also* necessary to render an
account, it is also necessary to give consciously and conscientiously. It is necessary to *answer for* [*répondre*] the gift, the given, and the call to giving. It is
necessary to answer to it and answer for it. One must be *responsible* for what
one gives and what one receives. (1992, 63)

12 For further discussion of feminism's relation to gift, hospitality, and generosity,
and particularly the links between Derrida, Levinas, and Irigaray, see Chanter
(1994), Feder, Rawlinson, and Zakin, eds. (1997), and Diprose (2002).

5. DRUCILLA CORNELL, IDENTITY, AND POLITICS

1 I have attempted to address the problems of utopian visions for feminists, and
for theorists of space, in a chapter, "Embodied Utopias," in my book *Architecture
from the Outside: Essays on Virtual and Real Space* (2001).
2 See Irigaray's *An Ethics of Sexual Difference* (1993) for her discussion of Cartesian
wonder.
3 Especially, for example, Drucilla Cornell and Sara Murphy's "Anti-Racism, Multiculturalism, and the Ethics of Identification" (2002).
4 Cornell's relations with Irigaray seem more complex and ambivalent than her
earlier writings attest. For a more explicit and recent representation of her ambivalent relation to Irigaray, see the interview Butler and Cornell (1998) gave on
Irigaray's relevance to their writings. There are other feminist theorists, however,
who, since the early 1990s, have taken up Irigaray's understanding of the interminable and indeterminable struggles of sexual difference, most notably Whitford (1991), Oliver (1994), Mortensen (1994), Colebrook (1997), Lorraine (1999),
Olkowski (2000), and Deutscher (2002).
5 Derrida is quite explicit about the future directedness of dissemination, of differ-

ence, and of deconstruction: "An interval must separate the present from what it is not in order for the present to be itself, but this interval that constitutes it as present must, by the same token, divide the present in and of itself, thereby also dividing, along with the present, everything that is thought on the basis of the present, that is, in our metaphysical language, every being, and singularly substance or the subject. In constituting itself, in dividing itself dynamically, this interval is what might be called *spacing*, the becoming-space of time or the becoming-time of space (*temporization*). And it is this constitution of the present, as an "originary" and irreducibly nonsimple . . . synthesis of marks, or traces of retentions and protentions . . . , that I propose to call archi-writing, archi-trace, or *différance*. Which (is) (simultaneously) spacing (and) temporization" (Derrida 1982, 13). See my discussion of Derrida in the previous chapter.

6 This argument is very convincingly developed by Pheng Cheah in his analysis of Butler's *Bodies That Matter* and the concept of materiality underlying her conception of materialization, in his paper "Mattering" (1996).

7 This, in brief, is the argument I developed in chapter 3 of this volume.

8 It is significant that, while we are free to identify ourselves with any social category we may choose, for the limits of identification are as broad as our imaginations, nevertheless we are not free to undertake any type of identification whatsoever: our identificatory relations depend not only on who we are and how we see ourselves (our self-definition), but as significantly, who others are and how they see us (their self-identification). To undertake imaginative identifications within a solipsistic vacuum, where I alone dictate who and what I will identify with, without the symbolic confirmation of collective inclusion, is to risk the very notion of identity itself in its psychotic self-elaboration.

9 Judith Butler, whose Hegelianism is most explicit in her earliest writings (1987), while certainly not a representative of identity politics, nevertheless remains today probably Hegelianism's most active feminist proponent. Her understanding of performative production of identity, and the centrality of recognition — or the withholding of recognition — by dominant social groups in the constitution of subject-positions (1990; 1994) is among the most current and powerful reenvisionings of Hegelian dialectics.

10 There are also many feminist and queer theorists who work outside and beyond the problematic of recognition. See, for example, the writings of Eve Sedgwick, Irigaray, or Sarah Kofman.

11 This tradition of subject-interpellation dates from Althusser's earliest musings on the subject of ideology (1972) to Žižek's more recent attempts to revitalize the same problematic (1989); and the use of Althusserian and Lacanian concepts of subject-constitution for explaining raced, sexed, and class or ethnic identifications.

12 As pervasive as the Hegelian tradition has been in feminist theory, the Nietz-

schean tradition has also had its feminist proponents, among them Luce Irigaray (1991; 1993), Claire Colebrook (2001), Ellen Mortensen (1994), and Kelly
Oliver (1994).

13   The model of lordship and bondage has been the object of feminist investigation for several decades, ever since it was recognized that Hegel's schema of two
"equal" self-consciousnesses could be read in terms of a kind of mythic pre-
history of the relations between man and woman, or even between mother and
child, that is, a relation between two different subjects that transforms into a relation of unequal subjects, a hypothesis that was certainly not part of Hegel's own
understanding. See Angela Davis (1998) for an early feminist and antiracist reading of Hegel's master/slave dialectic; and Patricia Mills (ed. 1996) for an overview
of more recent feminist writings.

14   Outlining such a model of politics is the task of part IV of this text.

6. DELEUZE, BERGSON, AND THE VIRTUAL

1   There are some exceptions: see in particular Douglass (1992), Hardt (1993), Boundas (1993), Bogue (2003), Pearson (2002), and Massumi (1992, 2002).

2   As Deleuze suggests: "I have been criticized for going back to Bergson's analyses.
To distinguish as Bergson did, though, between perception, affection and action
as three kinds of movement is a very novel approach. It remains novel, and I don't
think it's ever been quite absorbed; it's one of the most difficult and finest bits
of Bergson's thought. . . . Bergson presents one of the first cases of self-moving
thought" (Deleuze 1993, 282).

3   "My way of getting out of [the philosophical tradition] at that time was, I really
think, to conceive of the history of philosophy as a kind of buggery or, what
comes to the same thing, immaculate conception. I imagined myself getting onto
the back of an author, and giving him a child, which would be his and which
would at the same time be a monster. It is very important that it should be his
child, because the author actually had to say everything that I made him say.
But it also had to be a monster because it was necessary to go through all kinds
of decenterings, slips, break-ins, secret emissions, which I really enjoyed. My
book on Bergson seems to me a classic case of this" (Deleuze quoted in Douglass
1992, 369).

4   I will explore the connections between Bergson, James, and the pragmatist tradition in more detail in chapter 8.

5   As Bergson himself remarks, the images that constitute my perception and those
that constitute the universe are the same images with a different orientation.
Those organizing the universe subsist in their own indifference to each other,
while those organizing the body condition and cohere the others: "Here is a system of images which I term my perception of the universe, and which may be
entirely altered by a very slight change in a certain privileged image — *my body*.

This image occupies the center; by it all the others are conditioned; at each of its movements everything changes, as though by a turn of the kaleidoscope. Here on the other hand, are the same images, but referred each one to itself, influencing each other no doubt, but in such a manner that the effect is always in proportion to the cause: this is what I term *the universe*. The question is: how can these two systems coexist, and why are the same images relatively invariable in the universe and infinitely variable in perception" (1988, 25).

6 Bergson's claim seems to be that the more complex the form of life, the more unpredictable the response, the more interposing and disconnecting the delay or gap: "In a word, the more immediate the reaction is compelled to be, the more must perception resemble a mere contact; and the complete process of perception and of reaction can then hardly be distinguished from a mechanical impulsion followed by a necessary movement. But in the measure that the reaction becomes more uncertain, and allows more room for suspense, does the distance increase at which the animal is sensible of the action of that which interests it. By sight, by hearing, it enters into relation with an ever greater number of things, and is subject to more and more distant influences; and, whether these objects promise an advantage or threaten a danger, both promises and threats defer the date of their fulfilment. The degree of independence of which a living being is master, or, as we shall say, the zone of indetermination which surrounds its activity, allows, then, of an a priori estimate of the number and distance of the things with which it is in relation" (1988, 32).

7 By way of confirmation, Bergson claims that this principle of action indicates that perception is not primarily epistemic in its orientation, aimed at providing or securing knowledge, but pragmatic, aimed at movement and action: "But, if the nervous system is thus constructed, from one end of the animal series to the other, in view of an action which is less and less necessary, must we not think that perception, of which the progress is regulated by that of the nervous system, is also entirely directed toward action, and not toward pure knowledge?" (Bergson 1988: 31).

8 "In other words, personal recollections, exactly localized, the series of which represents the course of our past existence, make up, all together, the last and largest enclosure of our memory. Essentially fugitive, they become materialized only by chance.... But this outermost envelope contracts and repeats itself in inner and concentric circles, which in their narrower range enclose the same recollections grown smaller, more and more removed from their personal and original form, and more and more capable, from their lack of distinguishing features.... There comes a moment when the recollection thus brought down is capable of blending so well with the present perception that we cannot say where perception ends or memory begins" (Bergson 1988, 106).

9 This is already an indication of the strangely postmodernism, indeed, surprisingly posthuman character of Bergson's writings, even those characterized as the

most committed to humanism: "Bergson is not one of those philosophers who ascribes a properly human wisdom and equilibrium to philosophy. To open us up to the inhuman and the superhuman (*durations* which are inferior or superior to our own), to go beyond the human condition: This is the meaning of philosophy, in so far as our condition condemns us to live among badly analyzed composites, and to be badly analyzed composites ourselves" (Deleuze 1988, 28).

10 "This time-image extends naturally into a language-image, and a thought-image. What the past is to time, sense is to language and idea to thought. Sense as past of language is the form of its pre-existence, that which we place ourselves in at once in order to understand images of sentences, to distinguish the images of words and even phonemes that we hear. It is therefore organized in coexisting circles, sheets or regions, between which we choose according to actual auditory signs which are grasped in a confused way. Similarly, we place ourselves initially in the idea; we jump into one of its circles in order to form images which correspond to the actual quest" (Deleuze 1989, 99–100).

11 In Deleuze's reading, Bergson systematically develops a series of paradoxes regarding the past and present which run counter to a more common, everyday understanding. They are: "(1) we place ourselves at once, in a leap, in the ontological element of the past (paradox of the leap); (2) there is a difference in kind between the present and the past (paradox of Being); (3) the past does not follow the present that it has been, but coexists with it (paradox of coexistence); (4) what coexists with each present is the whole of the past, integrally, on various levels of contraction and relaxation (*détente*) (paradox of psychic repetition)."

These Bergsonian paradoxes, which are only paradoxical if duration is represented on the model of space, are all, Deleuze claims, a critique of more ordinary theories of memory, whose propositions include: "(1) we can reconstitute the past with the present; (2) we pass gradually from the one to the other; (3) that they are distinguished by a before and an after; and (4) that the work of the mind is carried out by the addition of elements (rather than by changes of level, genuine jumps, the reworking of systems)" (Deleuze 1988, 61–62).

12 It is important to understand that these conceptual pairs are not binary terms—that is, their relation is not characterized by negation and contradiction. Instead they are contrasting terms which indicate a movement between them and the possibility of the one emerging from the other. The one term—possibility, virtuality—is the condition from which the other—real, actual—distinguishes itself.

13 "In fact it is not the real that resembles the possible, it is the possible that resembles the real, because it has been abstracted from the real once made, arbitrarily extracted from the real like a sterile double" (Deleuze 1988, 98).

14 See here Deleuze, *Difference and Repetition* (1994, 209); *Bergsonism* (1988, 96).

15 Cf. Bergson: "One might as well claim that the man in flesh and blood comes from the materialization of his image seen in the mirror, because in that real is everything to be found in this virtual image with, in addition, the solidity which

makes it possible to touch it. But the truth is that more is needed here to obtain the virtual than is necessary for the real, more of the image of the man than for the man himself, for the image of the man will not be portrayed if the man is not first produced, and in addition one has to have the mirror" (Bergson 1992, 102).

16 "While the real is in the image and likeness of the possible that it realizes, the actual, on the other hand, does *not* resemble the virtual from which we begin and the actuals at which we arrive, and also the difference between the complementary lines according to which actualization takes place. In short, the characteristic of virtuality is to exist in such a way that it is actualized by being differentiated and is forced to differentiate itself, to create its lines of differentiation in order to be actualized" (Deleuze 1988, 97).

17 Deleuze wants to make this moment of convergence central to his understanding of what he calls the "crystal structure" of the time image in cinema. The crystal image is the coalescence of an actual image with "its" virtual image, a two-sided image, with one face in perception, and thus directed toward the present, the actual, while the other is seeped in recollection, in the past, the virtual: "What constitutes the crystal-image is the most fundamental operation of time: since the past is constituted not after the present that it was but at the same time, time has to split itself in two at each moment as present and past which differ from each other in nature, or, what amounts to the same thing, it has to split the present in two heterogeneous directions, one of which is launched towards the future while the other falls into the past. . . . In fact the crystal constantly exchanges the two distinct images which constitute the actual image of the present which passes and the virtual image of the past which is preserved: distinct and yet indiscernible, and all the more indiscernible because distinct, because we do not know which is one and which is the other" (Deleuze 1989, 81).

The crystal image, a central mechanism in modernist cinema, is of the very essence of time: it is duration itself which splits every image into a duality of actual and real. It is this duality of the image, the fact that as it is created each image is placed simultaneously in time (duration) and space (the present), that is the very mark of its temporal existence. The past can in this sense be seen as a dilated present, while the present can be regarded as an extremely contracted form of memory. The actual contracts virtual states within itself, and similarly, the virtual dilates. See Massumi 2002, 63–64.

7. THE QUESTION OF ONTOLOGY

1 This is not to say that feminists have altogether ignored Merleau-Ponty. Rather, his writings have become increasingly scrutinized, especially within feminist philosophy and philosophies of the body. While I am indebted to much feminist research in this area (see, for example, Iris Marion Young [1990], Gail Weiss [1999], and Rosalyn Diprose [2002]), I am more interested here in the ontological di-

mension of his argument than in his contributions to refiguring corporeality (as I did in an earlier article, Grosz [1993]).

2 In reasserting the centrality of ontological questions to feminist theory, and especially feminist philosophy, I am following the footsteps of some recent feminist texts, among them Mortensen (2002), Olkowski (1999), Colebrook (1997), all to some extent inspired by and developed through Irigaray's transfiguration of ontology as the domain of sexual difference (Irigaray 1993).

3 Bergson had long been out of fashion and discredited as a metaphysician by the generation before Merleau-Ponty. The works of Bergson alongside of the pragmatism of William James and the process philosophy of Alfred North Whitehead were one strand of influence on Merleau-Ponty but were largely overpowered by the influence of Husserl, coupled with Kojève's reading of Hegel, at least in his earlier writings. Perhaps there had not yet been enough time between them for Merleau-Ponty to accept their evolutionary relation, Merleau-Ponty's inheritance of a Bergsonism in spite of himself, the line of descent with modification that weaves itself through his work as well.

4 Ed Casey has suggested that "Bergson is often the most effective escort into Merleau-Pontian reflection on many subjects" (1984, 283); see also André Clair (1996) and John C. Mullarkey (1994) on the connections between Bergson and Merleau-Ponty.

5 "It is inconceivable — this is the mechanist argument — that an existing physical or chemical action not have its real conditions in other physical or chemical actions. But — this is the vitalist argument — since each constant chemical reaction in the organism (for example, the fixation of oxygen on the hemoglobin of the blood) presupposes a stable context, which itself presupposes another one, the physico-chemical explanation always seems deferred" (Merleau-Ponty 1983, 158).

6 "This special image which persists in the midst of others, and which I call my body, constitutes at every moment . . . a selection of the universal becoming. It is then *the place of passage* of the movements received and thrown back, a hyphen, a connecting link between the things which act upon one and things upon which one acts" (Bergson 1988, 151).

7 *The Structure of Behavior* (1983), *Phenomenology of Perception* (1962), and *Primacy of Perception* (1963).

8 "If it [the body] touches and sees, this is not because it would have the visibles before itself as objects; they are about it, they even enter into its enclosure, they are within it, they line its looks and its hands inside and outside. If it touches them and sees them, this is only because, being of their family, itself visible and tangible, it uses its own being as a means to participate in theirs, because each of the two beings is an archetype for the other, because the body belongs to the order of the things as the world is universal flesh" (Merleau-Ponty 1968, 137).

9 In *The Phenomenology of Perception*, the senses interact, form a union, and yield

access to a singular world. Sight and touch are able to communicate with each other because they are the senses of one and the same subject, operating simultaneously in a single world. The senses not only communicate with each other, adding to and enriching each other, they are transposable, at least within certain limits, onto each other's domains, although they remain irreducible in their differences. Sight, touching, hearing, smell function contemporaneously and are cumulative in their effects. The senses are transposable only because each lays claim to a total world, a world defining the subject's sensory relations, each of which is able to mesh with, be gridded in terms of, other "sensory worlds":

> The senses communicate with each other. Music is not in visible space, but it besieges, undermines and displaces that space. . . . The two spaces are distinguishable only against the background of a common world and can compete with each other only because they both lay claim to total being.
>
> The sight of sounds and the hearing of colors comes about in the same way as the unity of the gaze through the two eyes: in so far as my body is not a collection of adjacent organs, but a synergic system, all the functions of which are exercised and linked together in the general action of being in the world, in so far as it is the congealed face of existence. . . . When I say that I see a sound, I mean that I echo the vibration of the sound with my whole sensory being, and particularly with the sector of myself which is susceptible to colors. (1962, 232–234)

10 "We must habituate ourselves to think that every visible is cut out in the tangible, every tactile being in some manner promised to visibility, and that there is encroachment, infringement, not only between the tangible and the visible, which is encrusted in it, as, conversely, the tangible in itself is not a nothingness of visibility, is not without visual existence. Since the same body sees and touches, visible and tangible belong to the same world. . . . Every vision takes place somewhere in the tactile space. There is a double and crossed situating of the visible; the two maps are complete and yet they do not merge into one. The two parts are total parts and yet are not superposable" (1968, 134).

11 "One can say that we perceive the things themselves, that we are the world that thinks itself—or that the world is at the heart of our flesh. In any case, once a body-world relationship is recognized, there is a ramification of my body and a ramification of the world and a correspondence between its inside and my outside, between my inside and its outside" (1968, 136 n 2).

12 "What we are calling flesh, this interiorly worked-over mass, has no name in philosophy. As the formative medium of the object and the subject, it is not an atom of being, the hard in itself that resides in a unique place and moment: one can indeed say of my body that it is not *elsewhere*; but one cannot say that it is *here* or *now* in the sense that objects are; and yet my vision does not soar over them, it is not the being that is wholly knowing, for it has its own inertia, its ties. We must

not think the flesh starting out from the substances, from body and spirit—for then it would be the union of contradictories—but we must think it . . . as an element, as the concrete emblem of a general manner of being" (1968, 147).

13 It is interesting to note that while there are literally dozens of texts on feminist epistemology, dating from the pioneering writings of, among others, Sandra Harding (1986; 1991), Nancy Tuana (1989), and Linda Alcoff and Elizabeth Potter (1993), there is remarkably little published in the area of feminist ontology, and virtually nothing that described itself as feminist metaphysics.

8. THE THING

1 As William James implies in his discussion of the thing, or object, the object is that which has effects, directly or indirectly, on our perceptual responses and motor behavior. The object is the ongoing possibility of perception and action, the virtual trigger for responsiveness: "To attain perfect clearness in our thoughts of an object, then, we need only consider what conceivable effects of a practical kind the object may involve—what sensations we are to expect from it, and what reactions we must prepare. Our conception of these effects, whether immediate or remote, is then for us the whole of our conception of the object, so far as that conception has positive significance at all" (James 1970, 43).

2 As Kant demonstrated in *The Critique of Pure Reason*, time is given to neither inner apprehension nor to external sense: it is neither subjective nor objective but the a priori condition of the presentation of objects and subjects, the precedence or precession of pure temporality (and pure spatiality). For Kant, time cannot be subordinated to movement—whether the movement of objects or the movement of ideas—without changing its nature, without converting its intensive features into an extensive form. Movement does not inscribe time; rather time inheres or subsists in movement, movement presupposes time and comes to be understood, not as a determination of an object, but as the outline of space itself. The tangibility, the reality and materiality of movement, make sense, can be regarded as spatial and/or temporal, only insofar as time and space inhere in and are presupposed by movement. In this sense, the world of matter, of bodies, is itself the materialization or actualization of incorporeals, virtuals, forces which precede and surpass them: matter itself can be construed as the uncanny double, the ordered phantasm or simulacra of these intangibles. In Kant, time is no longer equivalent to the succession of moments which mark the object's transition from one position in space to another, the movements by which cosmological bodies travel in circular motion for the Greeks, or the movements by which atomic particles oscillate for the Pre-Socratics. Rather, it becomes, in Kant's formulation, the empty pure form, the retroactive imposition of the succession of determination on every possible movement, in other words, the synthesis by which movement is understood as unified, singular, movements "of" or attributable to a

thing or object, the success by which a thing gains its identity (for identity itself can only be conceived, even in its most minimal sense, as a relative cohesion over time and within a delimited and continuous space). Time is no longer adequately defined by the relations of the movements it measures; rather movement must be defined in relation to the time which conditions it. Succession is now construed as an effect rather than the essential characteristic of time. Everything that moves or changes moves or changes in time, but time itself does not move or change, nor does it measure or accompany movement and change. It must be understood to *inhere in* movement, underlying and explaining its possibility, without being identified with it.

3 Indeed, Bergson's discussion of William James's pragmatism in *Creative Mind* (in the chapter entitled "On the Pragmatism of William James") indicates that James's notion of truth is itself an acknowledgment of the limit of knowledge rather than its pervasiveness: "The definition that James gives to truth therefore, is an integral part of his conception of reality. If reality is not that economic and systematic universe our logic likes to imagine, if it is not sustained by a framework of intellectuality, intellectual truth is a human invention whose effect is to utilize reality rather than to enable us to penetrate it. And if reality does not form a single whole, if it is multiple and mobile, made up of cross-currents, truth which arises from contact with one of these currents, — truth felt before being conceived, — is more capable of seizing and storing up reality than truth merely thought" (1992, 259).

4 "We shall never explain by means of particles, whatever these may be, the simple properties of matter. . . . This is precisely the object of chemistry. It studies *bodies* rather than *matter*; and so we understand why it stops at the atom, which is still endowed with the general properties of matter. But the materiality of the atom dissolves more and more under the eyes of the physicist. We have no reason, for instance, for representing the atom to ourselves as a solid, rather than as a liquid or gaseous, nor for picturing the reciprocal action of atoms as shocks rather than in any other way. Why do we think of a solid atom, and why do we think of shocks? Because solids, being the bodies on which we clearly have the most hold, are those which interest us most in our relations with the external world, and because contact is the only means which appears at our disposal in order to make our body act upon other bodies. But very simple experiments show that there is never true contact between two neighboring bodies, and besides, solidity is far from being an absolutely defined state of matter. Solidity and shock borrow, then, their apparent clearness from the habits and necessities of practical life" (Bergson 1988, 199).

5 On the distinction between the analogue and the digital, see an early piece by Anthony Wilden, "Analog and Digital Communication: On Negation, Signification, and Meaning" in *System and Structure: Essays on Communication and Exchange* (1972).

6   Although it is commonly assumed that intuition is some vague feeling or sensibility, for Bergson it is a quite precise mode which refuses or precedes symbolization and representation: "We call intuition here the sympathy by which one is transported into the interior of an object in order to coincide with what there is unique and consequently inexpressible in it" (1944, 190). Instead of a mere sympathy or identification, which is nothing but a psychologization or subjectivization of knowledge, Bergson wants to link intuition to an understanding of the absolute. What the intellect provides is a relative knowledge, a knowledge of things from a distance and thus from a perspective mediated by symbols, representations, measurements, while intuition is what can provide an absolute analysis, which means one that is both internal and simple. This absolute is not understood in terms of an eternal or unchanging essence, but is rather, from the outside, a complex interplay of multiple forces and factors, which from the inside resolves itself into a simple unity: "Seen from within, an absolute is then a simple thing; but considered from without, that is to say relative to something else, it becomes, with relation to those signs which express it, the piece of gold for which one can never make up the change" (190).

9. PROSTHETIC OBJECTS

1   The question of the body's capacity to internalize prosthetic objects into its schematized image occupied my interests in chapter 3 of *Volatile Bodies*. There, however, I was primarily interested in the body's psychical capacity to incorporate the object into its own body-image; here, I am more interested in the ways in which prosthetic augmentation reveals the natural or biological plasticity of the body. These two interests are not, I believe, incompatible; they simply survey the same phenomenon from different vantage points.

2   These have been the object of much contemporary speculation in cyberculture, theorizations of the cyborg, and performance theory, as well as queer and feminist theory.

3   Do birds feel unattractive without appropriate adornment for their bodies or nests?

4   For further details regarding Bergson's and Deleuze's conceptions of the relations between the virtual and the actual, the possible and the real, see chapter 6.

5   "The most marvelous instincts of the insect do nothing but develop its special structures into movements: indeed, where social life divides the labor among different individuals, and thus allots them different instincts, a corresponding difference of structure is observed; the polymorphism of ants, bees, wasps and certain pseudoneuroptera is well known" (Bergson 1944, 140).

6   Deborah Gordon in her pioneering research on ant colonies, *Ants at Work*, has suggested that the nest, along with its growing population of ants, is the unit of

variation and natural selection more than individual ants or various categories of ant. Individual ants are not, usually, slaves of the colony as a whole, insofar as they seem to choose to be lazy or frenetically active, yet they are not entirely free either, insofar as their roles as patrolers, foragers, nest repair ants, queens, or reproductives seems to be structured entirely by their interactions with other ants and their place in the nest.

7 For Deleuze and Guattari, art, paradoxically, is an extension of the architectural imperative to organize the space of the earth. Art is developed alongside of the territory-house system, and that system is what enables the emergence of pure sensory qualities, the data or material of art. This roots art, not in the creativity of mankind but rather in a superfluousness of nature itself, in the capacity of the earth to render the sensory superabundant, in the bird's courtship song and dance, in the field of lilies swaying in the breeze under a blue sky ("art is continually haunted by the animal" (Deleuze and Guattari 1994, 184). I have explored Deleuze and Guattari's conception of the origins of art and architecture in Grosz (2003).

10. THE TIME OF THOUGHT

1 Although this emphasis on boldness and novelty has some resemblance to Karl Popper's understanding of the ideal development of the sciences (in *Conjectures and Refutations*), I am less interested in the generation of scientific knowledge derived from the verification and the potential falsification of scientific hypotheses through controlled experimentation—his major concern—than with the generation of discourses, methods, models, questions that cannot be directly verified or falsified. I am not here calling for a new feminist *science* so much as for new feminist epistemologies and ontologies.

2 See, for example, the careful analysis by Michele Le Doeuff of the historically constitutive exclusion of women from the institution of philosophy (1987; 1989).

3 As Irigaray has demonstrated. See Irigaray (1985; 1993).

4 Foucault has articulated a notion of texts as objects that do things (as opposed to representations that signify), which closely approximates this understanding of theory as an activity. See "The Discourse on Language" (1977). However, Deleuze and Guattari, in their understanding of rhizomatics, especially as developed in *A Thousand Plateaus* (1987) and in *What Is Philosophy?* (1994), are more directly the source for these questions.

5 See, for example, Deleuze and Foucault (1977).

6 In Deleuze and Guattari's terms: "The concept is not a proposition at all. . . . Propositions are defined by their reference, which concerns not the Event but rather a relationship with a state of affairs or body and with the conditions of this relationship" (Deleuze and Guattari 1994, 22).

7 "The mode of the event is the problematic. One must not say that there are problematic events but that events bear exclusively upon problems and define their
   conditions. . . . The event by itself is problematic and problematizing. A problem is determined by singular points which express its condition. We do not say
   that the problem is thereby resolved; on the contrary, it is determined as a problem. . . . It seems, therefore, that a problem always finds the solution it merits,
   according to the conditions which determine it as a problem. In fact, the singularities preside over the genesis of solutions of the equation" (Deleuze 1990, 55).
8 See *Bergsonism* 1988; and Kant's *Critical Philosophy: The Doctrine of the Faculties* (1984).
9 See, for example, Nancy Fraser, who chastises deconstruction and postmodernism, and disputes their relevance to feminism in terms of their transcendental
   qualities. Feminist theory, and other political discourses spawned by activism,
   remain for her primarily critical in their function. Their aim is to provide the
   critique of dominant positions and beliefs, with the aim of equalizing "real" social relations that these positions cover over. Derrida's primarily "metaphysical"
   concerns, and indeed all transcendental questions, questions without answers,
   questions that are ambiguous and indeterminable, are a kind of distraction from
   the primarily critical role of feminist theory, whose function, it seems, is to conceptually prepare for social equalization. (Fraser 1996; 1997).
10 For example, it characterizes the position of Julia Kristeva in her landmark essay
   "Women's Time" (1981), which represents a threshold moment in the advent of
   postmodern feminism. Here too, in accordance with some elements of de Beauvoir's position, Kristeva sees feminism as necessary to ameliorate women's unequal social status but as self-eradicating, to the degree that it accomplishes its
   goal of equalization.
11 As Claire Colebrook has argued, Irigaray's primary preoccupation is with the
   thinking subject, the ways in which the subject represents *him*self as a thinking
   being, and what this subject must leave out or cannot understand. By contrast,
   Deleuze has little interest in the theory of the subject, and is concerned more with
   the question of thought itself. The two cannot be collapsed into a single understanding of the relations between the (Irigarayan) sexed subject and (Deleuzian)
   concepts. Nevertheless, what their conjunction or juxtaposition may accomplish
   is a revitalization of metaphysics, no longer a metaphysics of presence, for feminist ethical and political concerns: "Given that the question of sexual difference
   has been, for the past decade at least, a *metaphysical* question, and that this metaphysics has been one of the conditions of the possibility of thought, feminist
   theory might now question its understanding of the ostensibly necessary connection between feminist ethics and metaphysics. If metaphysics remains the
   inevitable horizon for feminist questions, it may at least be worth asking *how*
   we are to understand what metaphysics is. Is feminism a critical inhabitation of

metaphysical closure, or the task of thinking a new metaphysics?" (Colebrook 2000, 112).

12 Irigaray should not be understood, as is common (in, for example, Butler and Cornell 1998), as advocating *only* two sexes, a rigid or essential divide, but, as she makes clear, *at least* two sexes. With the increasing fascination with intersexuality, with bodies that are difficult to define in a clear-cut and unambiguous way, the question of whether there are two sexes, or more, has been raised with increasing urgency in feminist texts (e.g., Fausto-Sterling 2000). I do not believe that Irigaray precludes the existence of a multiplicity of bodies and thus a far broader range of sexual difference than that between one (male) term and its (female) negation; but for her, the issue of phallocentrism still remains. To recognize a multiplicity of bodies, it is first necessary to go beyond the conception of a singular, idealized norm for bodies, the norm provided until recently without question by the male body and its sexual, political, and intellectual products. To have more than two sexes is to have at least two sexes.

11. THE FORCE OF SEXUAL DIFFERENCE

1 Irigaray, *This Sex Which Is Not One* (1985); *An Ethics of Sexual Difference* (1993).

2 See Irigaray's chapter "An Ethics of Sexual Difference" in her book of the same name (1993); see also Deleuze's chapter "Foldings, or the Inside of Thought" in Deleuze 1988b.

3 There have been of course a number of exceptions within the natural sciences to this understanding, especially over the last few decades. But those working with probabilities, and those working on far-from-equilibrium systems, and on complexity theory, have largely committed themselves to a temporality that is irreversible. See, in particular, Prigogine and Stengers (1984).

4 The relations between these theorists is the object of analysis in my book *The Nick of Time* (2004).

5 See Lorraine (1999), Olkowski (1999), Braidotti ((1994; 2002), Buchanan and Colebrook, eds. (2000), and Colebrook (2000; 2001) in particular for an overview of Deleuze's possible relevance to feminist thought.

6 In the natural sciences and in the field of science studies, there are now a number of major writers whose feminism has produced some of the key questions and methods of assessment of scientific research. See, for example, Fausto-Sterling (2000); Oyama (2000; 2000b); Wilson (2004); Hayles (1991); Keller (1984; 1996); Stengers (1997), among others.

7 Even here, there are some examples of the earliest explorations of feminist ontology in the writings of Colebrook (1996; 2000), Mortensen (2002), Weiss (1999), and Whitford (1991).

12. (INHUMAN) FORCES

1   See Keith Ansell Pearson, *Viroid Life* (1997).

2   "Our knowledge has become scientific to the extent that it is able to employ a number and measure. The attempt should be made to see whether a scientific order of values could be constructed simply on a numerical and mensural scale of force—All other "values" are prejudices, naiveties, misunderstandings.—They are everywhere *reducible* to this numerical and mensural scale of force" (Nietzsche 1968, §710).

3   " 'Mechanistic interpretation': desires nothing but quantities; but force is to be found in quality. Mechanistic theory can therefore only *describe* processes, not explain them" (Nietzsche 1968, §660).

4   "Might all quantities not be signs of qualities? A greater power implies a different consciousness, feeling, desiring, a different perspective; growth itself is a desire to be more; the desire for an increase in quantum grows from a *quale*; in a purely quantitative world everything would be dead, stiff, motionless.—The reduction of all qualities to quantities is nonsense; what appears is that the one accompanies the other, an analogy" (Nietzsche 1968, §564).

5   The concept of individuation, which becomes increasingly central in Deleuze's work, is derived from the researches of Gilbert Simondon, who is interested in analyzing the inhuman conditions for the elaboration of individuality. See Simondon 1993.

6   See Butler 1990 and 1994; see also my discussion of the problem of recognition in chapter 5 in this volume.

7   The position I espouse here is more in agreement with the kind of exploratory or "nomadic" feminism articulated by Braidotti (2002) and Colebrook (2001) than with more typical—deconstructive or psychoanalytic—forms of postmodern feminism that develop according to a theory of the (sexed) subject, developed by Butler, Cornell, and others.

8   "Man does not seek pleasure and does not avoid displeasure: one will realize which famous prejudice I am contradicting. Pleasure and displeasure are mere consequences, mere epiphenomena—what man wants, what every smallest part of a living organism wants, is an increase of power. Pleasure or displeasure follow from the striving after that; driven by that will it seeks resistance, it needs something that opposes it—Displeasure, as an obstacle to its will to power, is therefore a normal fact, the normal ingredient of every organic event; man does not avoid it, he is rather in continual need of it; every victory, every feeling of pleasure, every event, presupposes a resistance overcome" (Nietzsche 1968, §702).

9   "The last time we saw each other, Michel told me, with much kindness and affection, something like, I cannot bear the word *desire*; even if you use if differently, I cannot keep myself from thinking or living that desire = lack, or that desire is

repressed. . . . [F]or my part I can scarcely tolerate the word *pleasure*" (Deleuze 1997b, 189).

10 In a well-known passage, Foucault talks about the mutual intensification of power and pleasure: "The power which thus took charge of sexuality set about contacting bodies, caressing them with its eyes, intensifying areas, electrifying surfaces, dramatizing troubled moments. It wrapped the sexual body in its embrace. There was undoubtedly an increase in effectiveness and an extension of the domain controlled; but also a sensualization of power and a gain of pleasure. . . . Pleasure spread to the power that harried it; power anchored the pleasure it uncovered" (Foucault 1978, 44–45).

11 Cf.: "The problem is not to know whether desire is alien to power, whether it is prior to the law as is often thought to be the case, when it is not rather the law that is perceived as constituting it. This question is beside the point. Whether desire is this or that, in any case one continues to conceive of it in relation to a power that is always juridical and discursive, a power that has its central point in the enunciation of the law" (Foucault 1978, 89–90).

12 See in particular, Deleuze, *Masochism: Coldness and Cruelty* (1989b).

13. THE FUTURE OF FEMALE SEXUALITY

1 In this chapter I focus on the two major texts on sexuality now associated with Kinsey's name: *Sexual Behavior in the Human Male* (1948) and *Sexual Behavior in the Human Female* (1953).

2 See, for example, Judith Reisman (1998) and Judith Reisman et al. (1990).

3 Kinsey understood that if calm, rational reflection could proceed, then social, moral, and legal problems surrounding sexuality could be solved: "There cannot be sound clinical practice, or sound planning of sex laws, until we understand more adequately the mammalian origins of human sexual behavior, cultures outside our own, and the factors which shape the behavioral patterns of children and of adolescent youth. We cannot reach ultimate solutions for our problems until legislators and public opinion allow the investigator sufficient time to discover the bases of those problems" (1953, 8).

4 Kinsey added a section to the female volume in which he discusses not only the anatomical, physiological, and psychological but also the neurological and hormonal factors in play during sexual activity. See part 3 of Kinsey, Pomeroy, Martin, and Gebhard 1953.

5 "It is not generally understood, either by males or by females who have not had homosexual experience, that the techniques of sexual relations between two females may be as effective or even more effective than the petting or coital techniques ordinarily utilized in heterosexual contacts. . . . Females in their heterosexual relationships are actually more likely to prefer techniques which are closer

to those which are commonly utilized in homosexual relationships. . . . Heterosexual relationships could . . . become more satisfactory if they more often utilized the sort of knowledge which most homosexual females have of female sexual anatomy and female psychology" (1953, 467–468).

6   See Michel Foucault (1978), part 3, "Scientia Sexualis." The will to the truth of sex, to which Foucault attributes a long history, erupts as a scientific force in the mid-nineteenth century with a two-pronged goal: "We demand that sex speak the truth (but, since it is the secret and is oblivious to its own nature, we reserve for ourselves the function of telling the truth of its truth, revealed and deciphered at last), and we demand that it tell us our truth, or rather, the deeply buried truth of that truth about ourselves which we think we possess in our immediate consciousness. We tell it its truth by deciphering what it tells us about the truth; it tells us our own by delivering up that part of it that escapes us" (69–70).

7   As Bergson claims, "When we assert that number is a unit, we understand by this that we master the whole of it by a simple and indivisible intuition of the mind; this unity thus includes a multiplicity, since it is the unity of the whole" (1960, 80).

8   See *Time and Free Will* (1960) and *Matter and Memory* (1988); see also Ansell Pearson 2002, 18–21; and Adamson 2002, 26–35.

9   See, for example, Gordon (1999); and of course Darwin's own (1996) understanding of a biology largely outside and beyond a numerical frame. See also Keller's characterization of Barbara McClintock's scientific research (1984).

10   See Irigaray (1985b).

11   As Irigaray puts it in an often-quoted passage: "Whence the mystery that woman represents in a culture claiming to count everything, to number everything by units, to inventory everything as individualities. *She is neither one nor two.* Rigorously speaking, she cannot be identified either as one person, or as two. And her sexual organ, which is not *one* organ, is counted as *none*" (Irigaray 1985, 26).

Adamson, Gregory Dale. 2002. *Philosophy in the Age of Science and Capitalism*. London: Continuum Books.

Agamben, Giorgio. 1993. *The Coming Community*. Trans. Michael Hardt. Minneapolis: University of Minnesota Press.

Alcoff, Linda, and Elizabeth Potter, eds. 1993. *Feminist Epistemologies*. New York: Routledge.

Althusser, Louis. 1972. *Lenin and Philosophy and Other Essays*. Trans. Ben Brewster. London: Monthly Review Press.

———. 1996. *Writings on Psychoanalysis*. Trans. Jeffrey Mehlman. New York: Columbia University Press.

Badiou, Alain. 2000. *The Clamour of Being*. Trans. Louise Burchell. Minneapolis: University of Minnesota Press.

Beauvoir, Simone de. 1953. *The Second Sex*. Trans. H. M. Parshley. Harmondsworth: Penguin.

Benhabib, Seyla. 1995. "Feminism and Postmodernism." In *Feminist Contentions: A Philosophical Exchange*, ed. Seyla Benhabib, Judith Butler, Drucilla Cornell, and Nancy Fraser, 17–34. New York: Routledge.

Benhabib, Seyla, and Drucilla Cornell, eds. 1987. *Feminism as Critique: Essays on the Politics of Gender in Late-Capitalist Societies*. Cambridge: Polity Press.

Benjamin, Walter. 1978. "The Critique of Violence." In *Reflections: Essays, Aphorisms, Autobiographical Writings*, ed. Peter Dements, trans. Edmund Jephcott, 277–300. New York: Harcourt Brace Jovanovich.

Bennington, Geoffrey. 1994. *Legislations: The Politics of Deconstruction*. London: Verso.

Bennington, Geoffrey, and Jacques Derrida. 1993. *Jacques Derrida*. Trans. Geoffrey Bennington. Chicago: University of Chicago Press.

Bergson, Henri. 1921. *Mind-Energy*. Trans. H. Wildon Carr. London: Macmillan.

———. 1944. *Creative Evolution*. Trans. Arthur Mitchell. New York: Random House.

———. 1960. *Time and Free Will*. Trans. F. L. Pogson. Harper and Row: New York.

———. 1965. *Duration and Simultaneity with Reference to Einstein's Theory*. Trans. Leon Jacobson. Indianapolis: Bobbs-Merrill.

———. 1977. *The Two Sources of Morality and Religion*. Trans. R. Ashley Audra and Cloudesley Brereton. Notre Dame, Ind.: Notre Dame Press.

———. 1988. *Matter and Memory*. Trans. N. M. Paul and W. S. Palmer. New York: Zone Books.

———. 1992. *The Creative Mind: An Introduction to Metaphysics*. Trans. Mabelle L. Andison. New York: Citadel Press.

Bogue, Ronald. 1989. *Deleuze and Guattari*. Routledge: New York.

———. 2003. *Deleuze on Cinema*. Routledge: New York.

Boundas, Constantin. 1993. "Editor's Introduction." In *The Deleuze Reader*. New York: Columbia University Press.

Braidotti, Rosi. 1994. *Nomadic Subjects*. London: Routledge.

———. 2002. *Metamorphoses: Towards a Materialist Theory of Becoming*. Cambridge: Polity Press.

Brown, Wendy. 1995. *States of Injury: Power and Freedom in Late Modernity*. Princeton: Princeton University Press.

Buchanan, Ian, and Claire Colebrook, eds. 2000. *Deleuze and Feminist Theory*. Edinburgh: University of Edinburgh Press.

Butler, Judith. 1987. *Subjects of Desire: Hegelian Reflections in Twentieth Century France*. New York: Columbia University Press.

———. 1990. *Gender Trouble: Feminism and the Subversion of Identity*. New York: Routledge.

———. 1994. *Bodies That Matter: On the Discursive Limits of "Sex."* New York: Routledge.

Butler, Judith, and Drucilla Cornell. 1998. "The Future of Sexual Difference: An Interview with Judith Butler and Drucilla Cornell." *Diacritics* 28.1: 19–42.

Čapek, Milič. 1992. "Microphysical Indeterminacy and Freedom; Bergson and Peirce." In *The Crisis in Modernism: Bergson and the Vitalist Controversy*, ed. Frederick Burwick and Paul Douglass, 171–189. Cambridge: Cambridge University Press.

Casey, Edward S. 1984. "Habitual Body and Memory in Merleau-Ponty." *Man and World*, 17, 279–297.

Chanter, Tina. 1994. *Ethics of Eros: Irigaray's Rewriting of the Philosophers*. New York: Routledge.

Cheah, Pheng. 1996. "Mattering." *Diacritics* 26.1: 108–139.

———. 2002. "'Affordance,' or Vulnerable Freedom: A Response to Cornell and

Murphy's 'Anti-Racism, Multiculturalism, and the Ethics of Identification.' " *Philosophy and Social Criticism* 28.4: 451–462.

———. 2003. *Spectral Nationality: Passages of Freedom from Kant to Postcolonial Literatures of Liberation*. New York: Columbia University Press.

Clair, André. 1996. "Merleau-Ponty Lecteur et Critique de Bergson. Le Statut Bergsonien de l'Intuition." *Archives de Philosophie* 59: 203–218.

Colebrook, Claire. 1997. "Feminist Philosophy and the Philosophy of Feminism: Irigaray and the History of Western Metaphysics." *Hypatia* 12.1 (winter): 79–98.

———. 2000. "Is Sexual Difference a Problem?" In *Deleuze and Feminist Theory*, ed. Ian Buchanan and Claire Colebrook. Edinburgh: University of Edinburgh Press.

———. 2001. *Gilles Deleuze*. London: Routledge.

Cornell, Drucilla. 1991. *Beyond Accommodation: Ethical Feminism, Deconstruction, and the Law*. New York: Routledge.

———. 1992. *The Philosophy of the Limit*. New York: Routledge.

———. 1993. *Transformations: Recollective Imagination and Sexual Difference*. New York: Routledge.

———. 1995. *The Imaginary Domain: Abortion, Pornography, and Sexual Harassment*. New York: Routledge.

Cornell, Drucilla, and Sara Murphy. 2002. "Anti-Racism, Multiculturalism, and the Ethics of Identification." *Philosophy and Social Criticism* 28.4: 419–450.

Cornell, Drucilla, Michel Rosenfeld, and David Gray Carlson, eds. 1992. *Deconstruction and the Possibility of Justice*. New York: Routledge.

Darwin, Charles. 1981. *The Descent of Man, and Selection in Relation to Sex*. 2 vols. in one, each vol. separately paginated. Princeton: Princeton University Press.

———. 1996. *The Origin of Species*. Oxford: Oxford University Press.

Davis, Angela. 1998. "Unfinished Lecture on Liberation—II." In *The Angela Y. Davis Reader*, ed. Joy James. Oxford: Blackwell.

Dawkins, Richard. 1976. *The Selfish Gene*. Oxford: Oxford University Press.

Deleuze, Gilles. 1983. *Nietzsche and Philosophy*. Trans. Hugh Tomlinson. London: Athlone.

———. 1984. *Kant's Critical Philosophy: The Doctrine of the Faculties*. Trans. Hugh Tomlinson and Barbara Habberjam. London: Athlone.

———. 1986. *Cinema 1: The Movement-Image*. Trans. Hugh Tomlinson and Robert Galeta. Minneapolis: University of Minnesota Press.

———. 1988. *Bergsonism*. Trans. Hugh Tomlinson and Barbara Habberjam. New York: Zone Books.

———. 1988b. *Foucault*. Trans. Seán Hand. Minneapolis: University of Minnesota Press.

———. 1988c. *Spinoza: Practical Philosophy*. Trans. Robert Hurley. San Francisco: City Lights Books.

———. 1989. *Cinema 2: The Time-Image*. Trans. Hugh Tomlinson and Robert Galeta. Minneapolis: University of Minnesota Press.

———. 1989b. *Masochism: Coldness and Cruelty*. Trans. Jean McNeil. New York: Zone Books.

———. 1990. *The Logic of Sense*. Trans. Mark Lester. New York: Columbia University Press.

———. 1990b. *Expressionism in Philosophy: Spinoza*. Trans. Martin Joughin. New York: Zone Books.

———. 1993. "Mediators." Trans. Martin Joughin. In *Incorporations*, ed. Jonathan Crary and Sanford Kwinter, 281–294. New York: Zone Books.

———. 1994. *Difference and Repetition*. Trans. Paul Patton. New York: Columbia University Press.

———. 1997. *Essays Critical and Clinical*. Trans. Daniel W. Smith and Michael A. Greco. Minneapolis: University of Minnesota Press.

———. 1997b. "Desire and Pleasure." In *Foucault and His Interlocutors*, ed. Arnold I. Davidson. Chicago: University of Chicago Press.

———. 2004. *Desert Islands and Other Texts, 1953–1974*. Los Angeles: Semiotexte.

Deleuze, Gilles, and Michel Foucault. 1977. "Intellectuals and Power." In *Language, Counter-Memory, Practice: Selected Essays and Interviews by Michel Foucault*, ed. D. Bouchard. Oxford: Basil Blackwell.

Deleuze, Gilles, and Félix Guattari. 1987. *A Thousand Plateaus: Capitalism and Schizophrenia*. Vol. 2. Trans. Brian Massumi. Minneapolis: University of Minnesota Press.

———. 1994. *What Is Philosophy?* Trans. Hugh Tomlinson and Graham Burchell. New York: Columbia University Press.

Deleuze, Gilles, and Claire Parnet. 1987. *Dialogues*. Trans. Hugh Tomlinson and Barbara Habberjam. London: Athlone.

Dennett, Daniel. 1996. *Darwin's Dangerous Idea: Evolution and the Meaning of Life*. New York: Touchstone.

Derrida, Jacques. 1974. "The Violence of the Letter: From Lévi-Strauss to Rousseau." In *Of Grammatology*. Trans. Gayatri Chakravorty Spivak, 101–140. Baltimore: Johns Hopkins University Press.

———. 1978. "Violence and Metaphysics." In *Writing and Difference*. Trans. Alan Bass, 79–153. London: Routledge and Kegan-Paul.

———. 1978b. "Freud and the Scene of Writing." In *Writing and Difference*. Trans. Alan Bass, 196–231. London: Routledge and Kegan-Paul.

———. 1979. *Spurs. Éperons*. Trans. Barbara Harlow. Chicago: University of Chicago Press.

———. 1981. "Plato's Pharmacy." *Dissemination*. Trans. Barbara Johnson, 61–171. Chicago: University of Chicago Press.

———. 1981b. *Positions*. Trans. Alan Bass. London: Athlone.

———. 1982. "Différance." In *Margins of Philosophy*. Trans. Alan Bass, 1–28. Chicago: University of Chicago Press.

———. 1982b. "Choreographies." Trans. Christie V. McDonald. *Diacritics* 12.2: 66–76.

———. 1983. "Geschlecht: Sexual Difference, Ontological Difference." Trans. R. Berezdivin. *Research in Phenomenology* 13: 65–83.

———. 1985. "Racism's Last Word." In *"Race," Writing, and Difference,* ed. Henry Louis Gates Jr., 329–338. Chicago: University of Chicago Press.

———. 1985b. "But, Beyond: Open Letter to Anne McClintock and Rob Nixon." In *"Race," Writing, and Difference,* ed. Henry Louis Gates Jr., 351–368. Chicago: University of Chicago Press.

———. 1986. *Glas.* Trans. John P. Leavey Jr. and Richard Rand. Lincoln: University of Nebraska Press.

———. 1987. *The Post Card: From Socrates to Freud and Beyond.* Trans. Alan Bass. Chicago: University of Chicago Press.

———. 1988. *Limited Inc.* Trans. Samuel Weber. Evanston: Northwestern University Press.

———. 1989. "Psyché: Invention of the Other." Trans. Catherine Porter and Philip Lewis. In *Reading de Man Reading,* ed. Vlad Godzich and Lindsay Waters. Minneapolis: University of Minnesota Press.

———. 1990. "Force of Law: The 'Mystical Foundations of Authority.'" *Cardoza Law Review* 11.5–6: 920–1045.

———. 1991. " 'Eating Well,' or the Calculation of the Subject: An Interview with Jacques Derrida." In *Who Comes after the Subject?,* ed. Eduardo Cadava, Peter Connor, and Jean-Luc Nancy, 96–119. New York: Routledge.

———. 1992. *Given Time: 1. Counterfeit Money.* Trans. Peggy Kamuf. Chicago: University of Chicago Press.

———. 1993. "The Rhetoric of Drugs." Trans. Michael Israel. *differences: A Journal of Feminist Cultural Studies* 5.1: 1–24.

———. 1994. "The Deconstruction of Actuality: An Interview with Derrida, Jacques." *Radical Philosophy* 68 (autumn): 28–41.

———. 1995. *The Gift of Death.* Trans. David Wills. Chicago: University of Chicago Press.

———. 1997. *Of Hospitality.* Trans. George Collins. London: Verso.

———. 1999. *Adieu: To Emmanuel Levinas.* Trans. Pascale-Anne Brault and Michael Naas. Stanford: Stanford University Press.

———. 2000. *Of Hospitality: Anne Dufourmantelle Invites Jacques Derrida to Respond.* Trans. Rachel Bowlby. Stanford: Stanford University Press.

Deutscher, Penelope. 2002. *A Politics of Impossible Difference: The Later Work of Irigaray.* Ithaca: Cornell University Press.

Diprose, Rosalyn. 2002. *Corporeal Generosity: On Giving with Nietzsche, Merleau-Ponty, and Levinas.* Albany: State University of New York Press.

Douglass, Paul. 1992. "Bergson's Deleuze: Bergson Redux." In *The Crisis in Modern-*

ism: Bergson and the Vitalist Controversy*, ed. Frederick Burwick and Paul Douglass, 368–388. Cambridge: Cambridge University Press.

Ellis, Havelock. 1936. *Studies in the Psychology of Sex*. New York: Random House.

Fanon, Frantz. 1991. *Black Skin, White Masks*. Trans. Charles Markmann. New York: Grove Press.

Fausto-Sterling, Anne. 2000. *Sexing the Body: Gender Politics and the Construction of Sexuality*. New York: Basic Books.

Feder, Ellen K., Mary C. Rawlinson, and Emily Zakin, eds. 1997. *Derrida and Feminism: Recasting the Question of Woman*. New York: Routledge.

Foucault, Michel. 1977. *Discipline and Punish: The Birth of the Prison*. Trans. Alan Sheridan. London: Allen Lane.

———. 1977b. "The Discourse on Language." In *Language, Counter-Memory, Practice: Selected Essays and Interviews by Michel Foucault*, ed. D. Bouchard. Oxford: Basil Blackwell.

———. 1978. *The History of Sexuality*. Vol. 1. *An Introduction*. Trans. Robert Hurley. London: Allen Lane.

Fraser, Nancy. 1984. "The French Derrideans: Politicizing Deconstruction or Deconstructing Politics." *New German Critique* 23: 127–154.

———. 1996. *Justice Interruptus: Reflections on the "Postsocialist" Condition*. New York: Routledge.

———. 1997. "The Force of Law." In *Feminist Interpretations of Jacques Derrida*, ed. Nancy J. Holland. University Park: Pennsylvania State University Press.

Freud, Sigmund. 1905. "The Three Essays on the Theory of Sexuality." *Standard Edition of the Complete Psychological Works of Sigmund Freud* (hereafter *S.E.*). Vol. 7, 125–248. Oxford: Hogarth Press.

———. 1929. "Civilization and Its Discontents." *S.E.*, vol. 21, 59–148.

———. 1940. "An Outline of Psychoanalysis, *S.E.*, vol. 23, 141–208.

Galison, Peter. 2003. *Einstein's Clocks and Poincaré's Maps: Empires of Time*. New York: Norton.

Gordon, Deborah. 1999. *Ants at Work: How an Insect Society Is Organized*. New York: Free Press.

Gould, Stephen Jay. 1989. *Wonderful Life: The Burgess Shale and the Nature of History*. New York: Norton.

Gowaty, Patricia Adair, ed. 1997. *Feminism and Evolutionary Biology: Boundaries, Intersections, and Frontiers*. New York: Chapman and Hall.

Grosz, Elizabeth. 1989. *Sexual Subversions: Three French Feminists*. Sydney: Allen and Unwin.

———. 1993. "Merleau-Ponty and Irigaray in the Flesh." *Thesis Eleven* 36: 37–60.

———. 1994. *Volatile Bodies: Toward a Corporeal Feminism*. Sydney: Allen and Unwin.

———. 2001. *Architecture from the Outside: Essays on Virtual and Real Space*. Cambridge, Mass.: MIT Press.

———. 2003. "Deleuze, Theory, and Space." *Log* 1 (fall): 77–86.

———. 2004. *The Nick of Time: Politics, Evolution, and the Untimely*. Durham, N.C.: Duke University Press.

Harding, Sandra. 1986. *The Science Question in Feminism*. Ithaca: Cornell University Press.

———. 1991. *Whose Science? Whose Knowledge?* Ithaca: Cornell University Press.

Hardt, Michael. 1993. *Gilles Deleuze: An Apprenticeship in Philosophy*. Minneapolis: University of Minnesota Press.

Hayles, N. Katherine. 1991. *Chaos and Order: Complex Dynamic Systems in Literature and Science*. Chicago: University of Chicago Press.

Hegel, Georg W. F. 1969. *The Phenomenology of Mind*. Trans. J. B. Baillie. New York: Harper and Row.

Hirschfeld, Magnus. 1935. *Sex in Human Relationships*. London: John Lane.

———. 1948. *Sexual Anomalies: The Origins, Nature, and Treatment of Sexual Disorders*. New York: Emerson Books.

Hite, Shere. 1976. *The Hite Report: A National Study of Female Sexuality*. New York: Seven Stories Press.

———. 2003. *The Hite Report on Male Sexuality*. 2nd edition. New York: Seven Stories Press.

Irigaray, Luce. 1985. *This Sex Which Is Not One*. Trans. Catherine Porter with Carolyn Burke. Ithaca: Cornell University Press.

———. 1985b. "Is the Subject of Science Sexed?" *Cultural Critique* 1.1: 73–88.

———. 1991. *Marine Lover: Of Friedrich Nietzsche*. Trans. Gillian Gill. New York: Columbia University Press.

———. 1993. *An Ethics of Sexual Difference*. Trans. Carolyn Burke and Gillian C. Gill. Ithaca: Cornell University Press.

———. 1996. *I Love to You: Sketch of a Possible Felicity in History*. Trans. Alison Martin. New York: Routledge.

———. 1999. *The Forgetting of Air in Martin Heidegger*. Trans. Mary Beth Mader. Austin: University of Texas Press.

———. 2002. *The Way of Love*. Trans. Heidi Bostic and Stephen Pluhácek. London: Continuum Books.

Jablonka, Eva, and Marion J. Lamb. 1998. "Bridges between Development and Evolution." *Biology and Philosophy* 13: 119–124.

James, William. 1970. *Pragmatism and Four Essays from The Meaning of Truth*. Cleveland: Meridian Books.

———. 1996. *A Pluralistic Universe: Hibbert Lectures at Manchester College on the Present Situation of Philosophy*. Lincoln: University of Nebraska Press.

Kant, Immanuel. 1970. *The Critique of Pure Reason*. Trans. Norman Kemp Smith. London: Macmillan.

Keller, Evelyn Fox. 1984. *Feeling for the Organism: The Life and Work of Barbara McClintock*. New York: Henry Holt.

————. 1996. *Reflections on Gender and Science*. New Haven: Yale University Press.

————. 1998. "Structures of Heredity." *Biology and Philosophy* 13: 113–118.

Kinsey, Alfred C., Wardell B. Pomeroy, and Clyde E. Martin. 1948. *Sexual Behavior in the Human Male*. Philadelphia: W. B. Saunders.

Kinsey, Alfred C., Wardell B. Pomeroy, Clyde E. Martin, and Paul H. Gebhard. 1953. *Sexual Behavior in the Human Female*. Philadelphia: W. B. Saunders.

Kofman, Sarah. 1994. *Nietzsche and Metaphor*. Trans. Duncan Large. Stanford: Stanford University Press.

————. 1997. *The Enigma of Woman: Woman in Freud's Writings*. Trans. Catherine Porter. Ithaca: Cornell University Press.

Krafft-Ebing, Richard von. 1922. *Psychopathia Sexualis*. Brooklyn: Physicians and Surgeons Book Co.

Kristeva, Julia. 1981. "Women's Time." *Signs* 7:1.

LaCapra, Dominick. 1990. "Violence, Justice, and the Force of Law." *Cardoza Law Review* 11: 5–6.

Laplanche, Jean. 1985. *Life and Death in Psychoanalysis*. Trans. Jeffrey Mehlman. Baltimore: Johns Hopkins University Press.

Le Doeuff, Michele. 1987. "Women and Philosophy." In *French Feminist Thought: A Reader*, ed. Toril Moi, 181–209. Oxford: Basil Blackwell.

————. 1989. *The Philosophical Imaginary*. Trans. Colin Gordon. London: Athlone.

Leroi-Gourhan, André. 1993. *Gesture and Speech*. Trans. Anna Bostock Berger. Cambridge, Mass.: MIT Press.

Lestienne, Rémy. 1998. *The Creative Power of Chance*. Urbana: University of Illinois Press.

Lingis, Alphonso. 1994. *Foreign Bodies*. New York: Routledge.

Lorraine, Tamsin. 1999. *Irigaray and Deleuze: Experiments in Visceral Philosophy*. Ithaca: Cornell University Press.

Lyotard, Jean-François. 1991. *The Inhuman*. Trans. Geoffrey Bennington and Rachel Bowlby. Stanford: Stanford University Press.

Massumi, Brian. 1992. *A User's Guide to Capitalism and Schizophrenia: Deviations from Deleuze and Guattari*. Cambridge, Mass.: MIT Press.

————. 2002. *Parables of the Virtual: Movement, Affect, Sensation*. Durham, N.C.: Duke University Press.

Masters, William H., and Virginia E. Johnson. 1966. *Human Sexual Response*. Hagerstown: Lippincott Williams and Wilkins.

McCarthy, Thomas. 1989–90. "The Politics of the Ineffable: Derrida's Deconstructionism." *Philosophical Forum* 21.1–2: 146–167.

McClintock, Anne, and Rob Nixon. 1985. "No Names Apart: The Separation of Word and History in Derrida's 'Le Dernier Mot du Racisme.'" In *"Race," Writing, and Difference*, ed. Henry Louis Gates Jr., 339–350. Chicago: University of Chicago Press.

McKenna, Andrew J. 1992. *Violence and Difference: Girard, Derrida, and Deconstruction*. Urbana: University of Illinois Press.

Merleau-Ponty, Maurice. 1962. *The Phenomenology of Perception*. Trans. C. Smith. London: Routledge and Kegan-Paul.

———. 1963. *The Primacy of Perception*. Trans. James M. Edie. Evanston: Northwestern University Press.

———. 1964. *Signs*. Trans. R. C. McCleary. Chicago: Northwestern University Press.

———. 1968. "The Intertwining—the Chiasm." In *The Visible and The Invisible*, trans. Alphonso Lingis. Chicago: Northwestern University Press.

———. 1970. *In Praise of Philosophy and Other Essays*. Trans. J. Wild, J. Edie, and J. O'Neill. Chicago: Northwestern University Press.

———. 1983. *The Structure of Behavior*. Trans. A. L. Fisher. Pittsburgh: Duquesne University Press.

Mills, Patricia Jagentowicz. 1996. *Feminist Interpretations of G. W. F. Hegel*. University Park: Pennsylvania State University Press.

Mitchell, Juliet. 1974. *Psychoanalysis and Feminism*. London: Allen Lane.

Mortensen, Ellen. 1994. *The Feminine and Nihilism: Luce Irigaray with Nietzsche and Heidegger*. Oslo: Scandinavian University Press.

———. 2002. *Touching Thought: Ontology and Sexual Difference*. Oxford: Lexington Books.

Mullarkey, John C. 1994. "Duplicity in the Flesh: Bergson and Current Philosophy of the Body." *Philosophy Today* 38 (winter): 339–355.

Nancy, Jean-Luc. 1993. "In Statu Nascendi." In *The Birth to Presence*. Trans. Brian Holmes, 211–233. Stanford: Stanford University Press.

Nicholson, Linda J., ed. 1990. *Feminism/ Postmodernism*. New York: Routledge.

Nietzsche, Friedrich. 1965. *Thus Spoke Zarathustra: A Book for All and None*. Trans. Walter Kaufmann. Harmondsworth: Penguin.

———. 1968. *The Will to Power*. Trans. Walter Kaufmann. New York: Random House.

———. 1969. *On the Genealogy of Morals*. Trans. Walter Kaufmann. New York: Vintage Books.

———. 1974. *The Gay Science*. Trans. Walter Kaufmann. New York: Random House.

Nussbaum, Martha. 2001. *Women and Human Development*. Cambridge: Cambridge University Press.

Oliver, Kelly. 1994. *Womanising Nietzsche: Philosophy's Relation to the "Feminine."* New York: Routledge.

Olkowski, Dorothea. 1999. *Gilles Deleuze and the Ruin of Representation*. Berkeley: University of California Press.

———. 2000. "The End of Phenomenology: Bergson's Interval in Irigaray." *Hypatia* 15.3.

Oyama, Susan. 2000a. *The Ontogeny of Information: Developmental Systems and Evolution*. Durham, N.C.: Duke University Press.

————. 2000b. *Evolution's Eye: A Systems View of the Biology-Culture Divide*. Durham, N.C.: Duke University Press.

Pearson, Keith Ansell. 1997. *Viroid Life: Perspectives on Nietzsche and the Transhuman Condition*. London: Routledge.

————. 2002. *Philosophy and the Adventure of the Virtual: Bergson and the Time of Life*. London: Routledge.

Pitkin, Hanna Fenichel. 1998. *The Attack of the Blob: Hannah Arendt's Concept of the Social*. Chicago: University of Chicago Press.

Popper, Karl. 2002. *Conjectures and Refutations: The Growth of Scientific Knowledge*. New York: Routledge.

Prigogine, Ilya, and Isabelle Stengers. 1984. *Order Out of Chaos: Man's New Dialogue with Nature*. London: HarperCollins.

Reisman, Judith. 1998. *Kinsey, Crimes, and Consequences*. Crestwood, Ky.: Institute for Media Education.

Reisman, Judith, et al. 1990. *Kinsey, Sex, and Fraud*. Lafayette, La.: Huntington House.

Rorty, Richard. 1982. *Consequences of Pragmatism*. Brighton: Harvester.

Rosser, Sue V. 1992. *Biology and Feminism: A Dynamic Interaction*. New York: Twayne.

Rubin, Paul H. 2002. *Darwinian Politics: The Evolutionary Origin of Freedom*. New Brunswick: Rutgers University Press.

Russell, Bertrand. 1912. "The Philosophy of Bergson." *The Monist* 22.3: 321–347.

Saussure, Ferdinand de. 1974. *The Course in General Linguistics*. Trans. Charles Bally and Albert Secherhaye. New York: Fontana/Collins.

Sayers, Janet. 1982. *Biological Politics: Feminist and Anti-Feminist Perspectives*. London: Tavistock.

Sedgwick, Eve. 1992. *Epistemology of the Closet*. Durham, N.C.: Duke University Press.

Shildrick, Margrit, and Janet Pryce, eds. 1999. *Vital Signs: Feminist Reconfigurations of the Bio/logical Body*. Edinburgh: University of Edinburgh Press.

Simondon, Gilbert. 1993. "The Genesis of the Individual." Trans. Mark Cohen and Sanford Kwinter. In *Incorporations*, ed. Jonathan Crary and Sanford Kwinter, 297–319. New York: Zone Books.

Spivak, Gayatri Chakravorty. 1982. "Displacement and the Discourse of Woman." In *Displacement: Derrida and After*, ed. Mark Krupnick, 169–193. Bloomington: Indiana University Press.

————. 1984/85. "Criticism, Feminism, and the Institution." *Thesis Eleven* 10/11: 175–189.

————. 1987. *In Other Worlds*. Routledge: New York.

Stengers, Isabelle. 1997. *Power and Invention: Situating Science*. Minneapolis: University of Minnesota Press.

Thornhill, Randy, and Craig T. Palmer. 2000. *A Natural History of Rape: Biological Bases of Sexual Coercion*. Cambridge, Mass.: MIT Press.

Travis, Cheryl Brown, ed. 2003. *Evolution, Gender, and Rape*. Cambridge, Mass: MIT Press.

Tuana, Nancy. 1989. *Feminism and Science*. Bloomington: Indiana University Press.

Vandermassen, Griet. 2004. "Sexual Selection: A Tale of Male Violence and Feminist Denial." *European Journal of Women's Studies* 11.1: 9–26.

Waldby, Catherine. 1996. *AIDS and the Body Politic: Biomedicine and Sexual Difference*. London: Routledge.

———. 1999. "IatroGenesis: The Visible Human Project and the Reproduction of Life." *Australian Feminist Studies* 14.29: 77–90.

———. 2000. *The Visible Human Project: Informatic Bodies and Posthuman Medicine*. London: Routledge.

Waugh, Alexander. 1999. *Time: Its Origin, Its Enigma, Its History*. New York: Carroll and Graf.

Weismann, August. 1893. *The Theory of Heredity*. Trans. W. Newton Parker and H. Ronnfeldt. London: Walter Scott.

Weiss, Gail. 1999. *Bodies Images: Embodiment as Intercorporeality*. New York: Routledge.

Whitford, Margaret. 1991. *Luce Irigaray: Philosophy in the Feminine*. London: Routledge.

Wilden, Anthony. 1972. *System and Structure: Essays on Communication and Exchange*. London: Tavistock.

Wilson, Edward O. 1980. *Sociobiology: The Abridged Edition*. Cambridge, Mass.: Harvard University Press.

Wilson, Elizabeth A. 1998. *Neural Geographies: Feminism and the Microstructure of Cognition*. New York: Routledge.

———. 1999. "Introduction: Somatic Compliance—Feminism, Biology and Science." *Australian Feminist Studies* 14.29: 7–18.

———. 2004. *Psychosomatic: Feminism and the Neurological Body*. Durham, N.C.: Duke University Press.

Young, Iris Marion. 1990. *Throwing Like a Girl and Other Essays in Feminist Philosophy and Social Theory*. Bloomington: Indiana University Press.

———. 2002. *Inclusion and Democracy*. Oxford: Oxford University Press.

Žižek, Slavoj. 1989. *The Sublime Object of Ideology*. London: Verso.

256   *Index*

Many of the essays published here were originally published elsewhere. They have all been modified and revised for their current version. I would like to acknowledge their original publication details and to add my gratitude for being able to reprint them here. "Darwin and Feminism: Preliminary Investigations into a Possible Alliance" was first published in *Australian Feminist Studies* 14, no. 29 (1999), special issue on "Feminism and Science"; "Darwin and the Ontology of Life" was published in *Public* 26 (2002), special issue on "Nature"; "The Time of Violence: Derrida, Deconstruction, and Value" originally appeared in *Cultural Values* 2 (1998). A version of "Deleuze, Bergson, and the Virtual" was originally published as "Deleuze's Bergson: Duration, the Virtual and a Politics of the Future" in *Deleuze and Feminist Theory*, ed. Ian Buchanan and Claire Colebrook (Edinburgh: University of Edinburgh Press, 2000); "The Thing" was published in *ANYThing*, ed. Cynthia Davidson (Cambridge, Mass.: MIT Press, 2001); "Prosthetic Objects" was published in *The State of Architecture at the Beginning of the Twenty-First Century*, ed. Bernard Tschumi and Irene Cheng (New York: Monacelli Press, 2004); and "(Inhuman) Forces" was originally published in Russian under the title "Forces" (translator Zaven Bablojan) in *Gender Studies* 6 (2001), published by the ZKharkov Center for Gender Studies.

All the other essays were originally drafted as conference or seminar presentations. I would like to thank the various conference organizers for provoking me from my slumbers to think and write. "The Nature of Culture" was presented first at the Media, Communications and Cultural Studies Association Annual Conference, University of Sussex, UK, 2003; a portion of "Drucilla Cornell, Identity, and the 'Evolution' of Politics" was presented at the Society for Phenomenology and Existential Philosophy Conference, Lexington, Kentucky, in 1997, while another portion was originally published as "A Politics of Imperceptibility: A Response to 'Anti-Racism, Multiculturalism and the Ethics of Identification" (by Drucilla Cornell and Sara Murphy) in *Philosophy and Social Criticism* 28, no. 4 (2002): 463–472; "Merleau-Ponty, Bergson, and the Question of Ontology" was presented to the Merleau-Ponty Circle, Washington, D.C., 2001; "The Future of Female Sexuality" was written for the Women's Sexualities: Historical, Interdisciplinary, and International Perspectives Conference, Indiana University, 2003. "The Time of Thought" was originally presented to the Humanities at the Millennium Lecture Series, Central Michigan University, 2000; and "The Force of Sexual Difference" was first presented to the Beyond Parity? Sexual Difference Revisited Conference, University of Bergen, Norway, 2001.

ELIZABETH GROSZ is a professor of women's
and gender studies at Rutgers University.
She is the author of *The Nick of Time: Politics,
Evolution, and the Untimely*; *Architecture
from the Outside: Essays on Virtual and Real
Space*; *Space, Time, and Perversion: Essays
on the Politics of Bodies*; and *Volatile Bodies:
Toward a Corporeal Feminism*.

Library of Congress Cataloging-in-
Publication Data
Grosz, E. A. (Elizabeth A.)
Time travels : feminism, nature, power /
Elizabeth Grosz.
p. cm. — (Next wave)
Includes bibliographical references and index.
ISBN 0-8223-3553-0 (alk. paper) —
ISBN 0-8223-3566-2 (pbk. : alk. paper)
1. Time. 2. Feminism. I. Title. II.Series.
BD638.G745 2005
115 — dc22   2005000323